CANADIAN MILITARY HERITAGE

Volume III
1872 – 2000

Previously published volumes by
RENÉ CHARTRAND

Canadian Military Heritage
Volume I
1000 – 1774
Volume II
1775 – 1871

SERGE BERNIER

CANADIAN
MILITARY HERITAGE

Volume III

1872 – 2000

ART GLOBAL

Canadian Cataloguing in Publication Data

Chartrand, René

    Canadian military heritage
    Issued also in French under title: le patrimoine militaire canadien
    Includes bibliographical references and indexes.
    contents: v.1. 1000-1754 - v.2. 1755-1871 - v.3. 1872-2000 / Serge Bernier.

    ISBN 2-920718-49-5 (v.1) - ISBN 2-920718-45-2 (v.2) - ISBN 2-920718-51-7 (v.3)

    1.Canada - History, Military. 2. New France - History, Military.
    3. Armies - Canada - History. 4. Soldiers - Canada - History. I. Bernier, Serge. II. Title

    FC226.C4513 1993   355'.00971   C93-096790-9
    F1028-C4513 1993

This work was published at the initiative and under the auspices
of Communications M.C. Stratégiques
and the Directorate of History and Heritage,
Department of National Defence of Canada

Project director: Ara Kermoyan

Picture Research and Captions: René Chartrand

© Art Global Inc., 2000
384 Laurier Avenue W.
Montreal, Quebec H2V 2K7
Canada

ISBN 2-920718-51-7
1st quarter 2000
Printed and bound in Canada

Art Global aknowledges the financial support of the Government of Canada,
through the Book Publishing Industry Development Program, for its publishing activities.

Cet ouvrage a été publié simultanément en français sous le titre :
PATRIMOINE MILITAIRE CANADIEN – d'hier à aujourd'hui
Tome III
1872-2000
ISBN 2-920718-47-9

TABLE OF CONTENTS

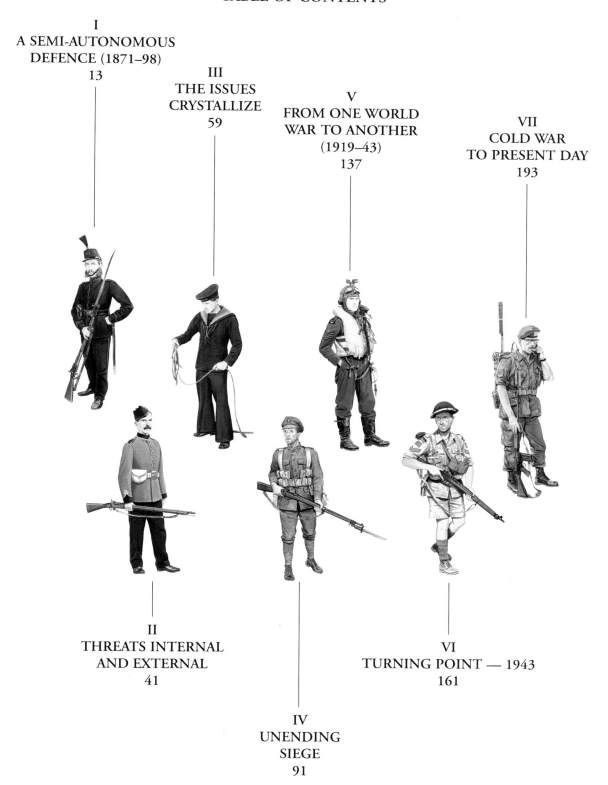

ACKNOWLEDGEMENTS

Hélène-Andrée Bizier, Jane Broderick, Isabel Campbell,
René Chartrand, William Constable, Marcel Couture, Hélène Desjardins,
Pierre Dufour, Jean-Pierre Gagnon, Lucie Grimard,
Steve Harris, Jacques Janson, Bill Johnston,
Christine Rebours, Donna Porter, Bill Rawling,
Roger Sarty, Terry Shaw, Ronald Volstad.

FOREWORD

By placing our past in perspective rather than remaining its prisoners, we make it possible to gain a clearer vision of the future. If we are to avoid repeating costly mistakes, therefore, our look backward must be critical. Such an approach requires us to highlight both successes and failures, to attack certain myths, and to throw light on some of the stupidity that is an inevitable element in any country's history. Yet this is not always a good way to win popularity.

Total objectivity and absolute truth—the latter sometimes requires some reconstruction—will always be our goals. But however true our reconstructed account may be, there is one fact that will never change: It is the task of the historian to re-interpret history, for history is not a static subject. In fact, by the time you reach the final lines of this book, Canada's military history will already be replete with new experiences and fresh research will have been carried out.

It is our hope that this third and final volume of *Canadian Military Heritage* will fulfil its purpose: to give the reader an interesting account of almost 130 years of Canadian military history, enhancing your knowledge and understanding of this period.

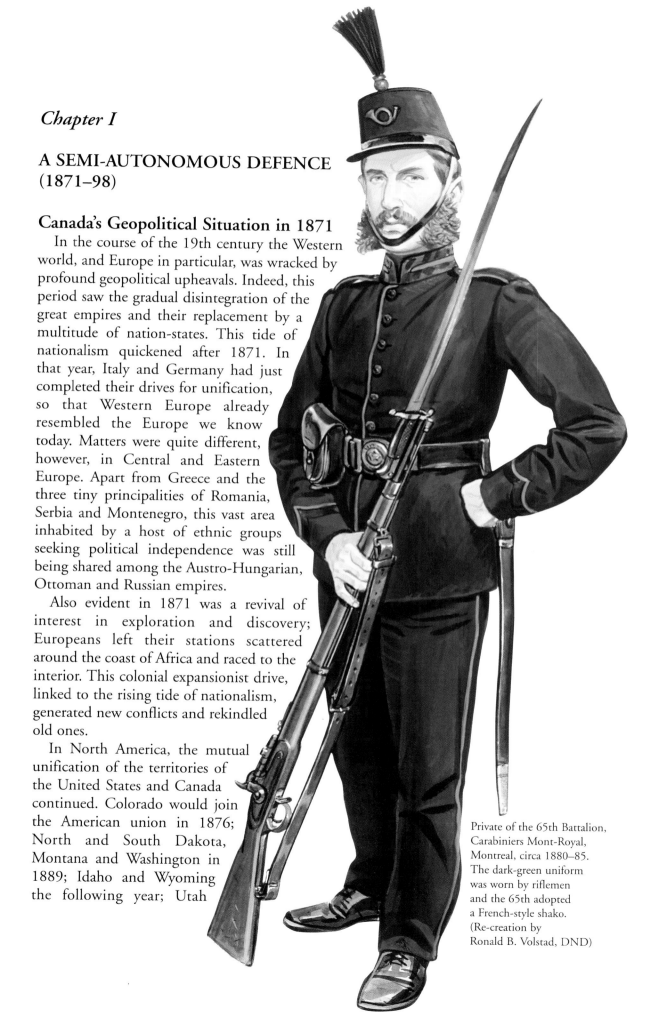

Chapter I

A SEMI-AUTONOMOUS DEFENCE (1871–98)

Canada's Geopolitical Situation in 1871

In the course of the 19th century the Western world, and Europe in particular, was wracked by profound geopolitical upheavals. Indeed, this period saw the gradual disintegration of the great empires and their replacement by a multitude of nation-states. This tide of nationalism quickened after 1871. In that year, Italy and Germany had just completed their drives for unification, so that Western Europe already resembled the Europe we know today. Matters were quite different, however, in Central and Eastern Europe. Apart from Greece and the three tiny principalities of Romania, Serbia and Montenegro, this vast area inhabited by a host of ethnic groups seeking political independence was still being shared among the Austro-Hungarian, Ottoman and Russian empires.

Also evident in 1871 was a revival of interest in exploration and discovery; Europeans left their stations scattered around the coast of Africa and raced to the interior. This colonial expansionist drive, linked to the rising tide of nationalism, generated new conflicts and rekindled old ones.

In North America, the mutual unification of the territories of the United States and Canada continued. Colorado would join the American union in 1876; North and South Dakota, Montana and Washington in 1889; Idaho and Wyoming the following year; Utah

Private of the 65th Battalion, Carabiniers Mont-Royal, Montreal, circa 1880–85. The dark-green uniform was worn by riflemen and the 65th adopted a French-style shako. (Re-creation by Ronald B. Volstad, DND)

in 1896; Oklahoma in 1907; and Arizona and New Mexico in 1912. In Canada, meanwhile, the vast expanses of the Northwest Territories had still not been organized. Manitoba was acquired from the Hudson's Bay Company in 1870, though representing only a minuscule portion of its possessions, to become the fifth province. In 1871 it was the turn of British Columbia to join the Canadian Confederation. While on the one hand England was gradually relaxing its hold over its North American colonies, on the other hand an emerging Canada was slowly crystallizing from sea to sea.

The Empire

The imperial British influence did not disappear in Canada after the bulk of the British troops left in 1871. Rather, in the second half of the 19th century it became entrenched in Canada, permeating the country and, in particular, its political, economic and military elites. It even reached a kind of apogee in 1897 on the 60th anniversary of Queen Victoria's accession to the throne.

This full-blown imperialism is hard to define with any degree of accuracy. It comprised an economic dimension that drove the British and other Europeans to capture new world markets. It was also racist, enshrining white superiority. This sense of superiority was qualified by a willingness to effect social change in England, change that would embrace those "inferiors" whose redemption was the "white man's burden." Of all whites, the Anglo-Saxons supposedly occupied the highest rung. These widespread notions were undeniably important, but they harboured, one imagines, their share of contradictions and matters left unsaid. In Canada, the current of imperial feeling that made the Anglo-Saxons a united and superior race ran up against three obstacles. The first comprised everyone who was not Anglo-Saxon, particularly the Aboriginals, Métis and French-speaking Canadians who together accounted for over 35 percent of the population. The second was represented by the United States, whose population, though predominantly Anglo-Saxon, nursed its own dream of imperial expansion, a dream which posed a threat to Canada. The Anglo-Saxon bloc was not as monolithic as some might have wished. The third obstacle stemmed from Canada's own nationalistic feelings, which were developing partly in response to American "manifest destiny" and partly in opposition to the grip the British continued to maintain on the country.

Imperialism, as it was occasionally understood in London and within certain Canadian social circles, consisted in strengthening the British Empire by reinforcing the economic, military and naval ties binding together the various lands it comprised. Yet for many Canadians this cementing of ties was a vehicle for change that would eventually give the colonies some influence in implementing the Empire's foreign policy and, by doing so, boost Canadian nationalism. As for imperial trade, that was about to be eclipsed by trade between Canada and the United States.

Two events, in 1871 and in 1897, best illustrate these divergent trends within the Empire. The 1871 Treaty of Washington made it quite clear to Canadian Prime Minister John A. Macdonald, who participated in the Anglo-American discussions, that Canadian interests could be jeopardized by the British strategy of neutralizing the American threat to allow for better use of their resources in the rest of the world.

One small example: Canada was ordered to pay for the damage caused to banks in St Albans in the course of a Confederate raid staged from Canada during the American Civil War, but Britain refused to lay a claim with the Americans for damages caused during the Fenian raids, the last of which had just taken place. Under the 1871 agreement, Canada would lose economically, politically and geographically, and both England and Canada would sustain a blow to their pride.

In 1897, on the other hand, amid celebrations marking Victoria's lengthy reign, the British Colonial Secretary, Joseph Chamberlain, staged a Colonial Conference at which the splendid formal ceremonies cloaked the host's real intentions. "The informal discussion of many questions of the greatest imperial interest"[1] to which Chamberlain summoned his guests actually focused on the concept of an imperial connection to be forged by a Great Council of Empire, headquartered in London, where problems would be studied and decisions taken. Chamberlain also made allusions to a genuine partnership based on the sharing of the rights and responsibilities pertaining to defence. Canadian Prime Minister Wilfrid Laurier's response was more or less that the status quo suited him just fine. Laurier admitted that the Dominions did want some say in imperial decision-making, but he was unreceptive to the idea that this should be granted in return for greater military participation in Britain's ventures around the world. Yet here was a man who loved British institutions. Wherever he went, both within Canada and abroad, Laurier's speeches glorified the Empire. But he would not go so far as to promise to defend it at all costs or to abandon elements of Canada's nascent nationalism. Laurier thus showed himself to be more a nationalist than an imperialist, and his attitude was shared by a large segment of the population, particularly the French Canadians. For, amid the imperialist frenzy that prevailed in Canada, certain voices stood out, among them that of Honoré Mercier, the premier of Quebec (1887–91), who warned that some day the fanaticism incarnated by the powerful Imperial Federation League would send young Canadians to die in foreign lands for a cause that was foreign to them.

The Colonial Conference of 1897 did generate some decisions which, though vague, were of some importance from a military standpoint. Plans were made to strengthen co-operation between the War Office and the various departments which handled defence in the dominions, a general principle that some wanted to make more explicit by requiring all the armies of the Empire to conform to a similar structure and to use standard training and equipment.

By the end of the 19th century the expression "painting the map red" so often heard at that time had long been recognized by many imperialists as referring to an impossible goal. But romanticism feeds on myths, and the myth of imperial Britain would somehow survive until the First World War, drawing in its wake a fair number of young Canadians who were undoubtedly attracted more by the promise of adventure offered by the imperial dream than by the dream itself.

The Defence of Canada by Canadians

In Canada the pivotal year of 1871 was marked, from a military standpoint, by the pacification of the border with the United States, which has endured to this day. This new state of affairs brought stability to Britain's finances both through the cancellation of plans to build fortifications in Canada against a potential American invasion and through the departure of British troops from Canadian soil, except for Halifax, which continued to occupy an important place in British naval strategy.

Thus, from 1871 on, Canada somewhat unwillingly shouldered full responsibility for its own defence. It had been doing so increasingly since 1855, as we have seen, and the British North America Act of 1867 included a section on "Militia (Military and Naval Service) and Defence." Why the urgency? In 1867, the possibility of attack from without—that is, from the United States—was quite real and had to be taken into account. The threat posed by violent domestic movements also had to be weighed, along with possible threats to the sprawling British Empire of which Canada was ultimately a part. The latter two options tended to predominate up until 1945, although the vision of the strategists of 1867 did not extend this far into the future.

An analysis of the situation, constraining factors of an economic and social nature, and the myth of the militiaman's or citizen soldier's invincibility initially resulted in a system of defence based on British regular troops backed by 40,000 volunteers from the Active Militia signing up for a period of three to five years. Although mention was made of a naval militia in this Act of 1868, the Active Militia would retain the basic responsibility for land defence until the 20th century. It should also be noted that the principle of compulsory service was preserved, although it would never be used.

The Non-Permanent Active Militia could enlist men aged 18 to 60, who were divided into four categories: 18- to 30-year-old bachelors or childless widowers; 30- to 45-year-old bachelors or childless widowers; 18- to 45-year-old married men or widowers with children; and, finally, 45- to 60-year-olds. Canada was carved up into nine districts and 200 regimental divisions, each commanded by a lieutenant-colonel. There was to be an annual drill period lasting eight to 16 days. Every militiaman had to contribute $12 towards an Enfield-Snider rifle, with the government paying the difference. Exempt from militia duty were judges, priests and teachers in Holy Orders, policemen, penitentiary or mental asylum guards, persons with disabilities, only sons, and sons supporting families.

With an initial budget of $900,000, Canada's department of militia and defence was established in 1868. The old provincial or Canadian militias were disbanded in 1869, with recruitment beginning immediately in the new military districts. Officers were not compelled to re-enlist, and they had to take a new oath of allegiance if they did so. This procedure helped to get rid of some of the dead wood encumbering the pre-1867 militia.

The Ontario districts were the first to gain official acceptance, but by April of 1869 some 10 battalions plus a few independent companies comprised mainly of French Canadians made their appearance in Quebec. The Active Militia would rapidly enlist 37,170 volunteers, 3,000 short of their authorized strength. The Sedentary Militia—which amounted to a list of all men eligible for service—would run to 618,896 names.

The lawmakers of 1868 sought to avoid upsetting Canadians, whether Anglophone or Francophone, who were largely opposed to a professional soldiery. Under the appropriate circumstances, they told themselves, the militia would rise in support of the British troops to drive out any invader. However, this assumption was challenged by the departure of the British military in

Various aspects of a summer training camp for volunteer militia units are depicted in this 1875 illustration.
(NAC, C-62933)

B Battery of the Canadian artillery at firing drill on the ice of the St Charles River, Quebec City, in the winter of 1873. Because of the climate, the field guns are mounted on special sleigh-carriages and the gunners are in winter uniform.
(NAC, C-59098)

the fall of 1871. To replace these soldiers, Canada immediately took moderate steps, an approach that was probably justifiable under the circumstances, since the United States was not the threat it had been four years earlier. Thus, in October 1871, even before the British garrison left Quebec City, the country established two field artillery batteries whose duties would include protecting the fortifications at Quebec City and Kingston. These few hundred men would also deliver training to the gunners and infantrymen of the Non-Permanent Active Militia. In Kingston and Quebec City, respectively, A and B batteries formed the initial nucleus of a regular Canadian army or, to use the term of the day, Permanent Active Militia. The first commander of B Battery was Lieutenant-Colonel Thomas Bland Strange. He spoke French and had an impressive service record, having served in India, England, Ireland, Gibraltar and the West Indies before arriving in Quebec. He was a good choice, since B Battery (six officers with 153 non-commissioned members and men) included a number of Francophones from Quebec City's volunteer militia. This battery covered the fortifications at Quebec City, Lévis and Île Sainte-Hélène. In 1874 a detachment was sent to Grosse Île as the garrison artillery. A and B batteries exchanged positions first in 1880 and again in 1885. In 1883 the new C Battery would be created and stationed in Esquimalt to defend that stretch of the west coast. The three batteries would henceforth form a regiment. In 1893 this regiment was reorganized into three field batteries and two garrison companies. The field batteries would later be combined to form the Royal Canadian Field Artillery, which in 1905 became the Royal Canadian Horse Artillery. The garrison companies would become the Royal Canadian Garrison Artillery.

In the meantime, however, the Militia Act underwent a number of changes, the most important of which were the amendments of 1883. A central section of the act reads as follows:

It being necessary in consequence of the withdrawal of Imperial regular troops, to provide for the care and protection of forts, magazines, armaments, warlike stores and such like service, also to assure the establishment of Schools for Military Instruction in connection with corps enlisted for continuous service, it shall be lawful for Her Majesty to raise…one troop of cavalry, three batteries of artillery (of which two shall be "A" and "B" Batteries of artillery now embodied) and not more than three companies of infantry—the whole strength of which several corps shall not exceed seven hundred and fifty men.[2]

Thus it was that a cavalry school corps appeared in Quebec City (to become the Royal Canadian Dragoons) along with another infantry corps (the Royal Canadian Regiment), which would maintain companies in Fredericton, Saint John and Toronto. These formations would have an approximate strength of one commanding officer, three officers and 150 non-commissioned instructors and men. In 1885 a mounted infantry school was established in Winnipeg; it would later take the name Lord Strathcona's Horse.

This restructuring exercise gave the permanent force a stable nucleus, a fact the minister of the day, Adolphe Caron, tried to downplay, emphasizing instead the instructional duties performed by these regular soldiers. Caron explained that this move would help strengthen the civil government, thus enabling it to enforce its laws, forestall domestic disturbances and repel potential attackers. It can be seen that between 1867 and 1883 the main focus of the defence pro-

The Armouries, Toronto, Canada.

Beginning in the 1870s, the government built large numbers of armouries for training volunteers. Their architecture is often reminiscent of medieval fortifications, as seen in this photo of the Toronto armoury.
(Postcard from a private collection)

gramme shifted from external to domestic threats.

In 1886, following the problems with Louis Riel in the North-West, the Militia Act was amended once again to raise the number of infantry companies from three to five and the total strength of the regular force from 750 to 1,000 men.

This military machine required leaders. From 1867 to 1874 its commanding officer, provided by the British army, held the rank of Adjutant General. In 1874 the new position of General Officer Commanding was created, to be used until 1904; the incumbent was also a British professional holding the rank of colonel and above, although in Canada he could become a major-general or even a lieutenant-general. The position of adjutant-general remained on the organizational chart, and from that time on it was held by a Canadian.

One might have hoped that the British officer assuming control of Canadian defence would display some degree of objectivity with respect to the two major political parties that took turns governing the country. In theory, his professionalism should have led him to work in favour of a better militia rather than to pursue narrow partisan interests. Unfortunately the objectivity displayed by the General Officer Commanding in his dealings with Canadian politicians quite often resembled subservience to the grand imperial objectives of British politicos. As can be imagined, this attitude occasionally clashed with the nationalism of the Canadian ministers, timorous though it might have been at the turn of the century. In his annual report, the General Officer Commanding would frequently allude to concerns that had little to do with Canada. For example, General Edward Selby Smyth wrote in 1877 that "we must not for one instant let commu-nism make with impunity some great experiment in the least corner of the British Empire."[3] The good general spoke about Canadian independence, which naturally had to be protected, and about another enemy, much more distant than Canada's immediate neighbour, an enemy he made only subtle reference to but which was already becoming a problem: Russia, a country with whom Britain had frequently come into conflict.

Were these men sent to Canada by Britain—these men who, often with justification, confronted Canadian ministers over certain appointments redolent of patronage—the best of their profession? As we shall see, not necessarily. What is more, they found the Canadian system of defence generally incomprehensible. How they would have loved to take it in hand and mould it into an instrument dedicated to the achievement of British objectives!

Faced with the more or less universal apathy of Canadians, fluctuating budgets tied to the vagaries of the economy and a degree of animosity displayed by incumbent ministers, the General Officers Commanding tried to get things moving. Between 1890 and 1895, for example, Major-General I.J.C. Herbert reorganized the militia by increasing the staff at his headquarters, which comprised only three officers and an aide-de-camp, and reducing the number of officers in the districts. As for the permanent force, he reorganized into regiments the infantry and cavalry schools that had emerged over the years, sent a number of their officers to train in England, raised the criteria for recruiting and selecting men, and endeavoured to modernize their equipment.

Still, the efforts of these British generals, abetted by the occasional spark of interest shown by Canadian ministers who were often moved by political reasons or domestic crises that revealed the weakness of the existing system, slowly yielded results. As we have seen, the number of regular soldiers increased between 1871 and 1898. But there was more. The year 1876 saw the establishment of the Royal Military College of Canada (RMC), which would supply officers to permanent and non-permanent units as well as to the North-West Mounted Police. Under the national policy of the Conservative Party, Canada was prompted to build a cartridge factory, Dominion Arsenal, in Quebec City. In 1882 it began producing bullets and artillery shells. In 1885 the Arsenal supplied the troops deployed to the country's North-West and in 1888 turned out some 2.5 million cartridges. In 1885 a railway connected the Atlantic to the Pacific exclusively through Canadian territory: This primarily commercial resource also served as a strategic tool. In 1897 came authorization to appoint honorary chaplains for every battalion—with the understanding, however, that this would cost the Treasury nothing. Very slowly a payroll service developed, employing fewer than 10 officers; in 1898, all its operations, until then conducted at the district level, were centralized in Ottawa.

In 1871 Canada was without the support troops essential to an army in the field: medical, transportation, supply and engineering corps. Before then, the British army had supplied these elements whenever the militia had been mobilized. After that year, crises spawned hasty improvisations that met with varying degrees of success, as was evident during the North-West Campaign.

The House of Commons was the scene of occasionally bitter debates on the physical organization of the militia, particularly its budget; never broached, however, was the fundamental issue, the defence policy of Canada, which, other than expressing a desire for emancipation, still remained dependent on Britain.

Who were the volunteers? Jean-Yves Gravel has drawn us a portrait for the period 1868–98 in the 5th Military District (Eastern Quebec, including Quebec City). The rural battalions consisted of 45 percent farmers, 30 percent businessmen (tradesmen and clerks) and 24 percent labourers. This percentage of farmers, applicable to 1868, decreased slowly but steadily after that year.[4] Industrialization was at work here, but it was not the sole factor. Indeed almost all studies of recruitment in the Western world have reached similar conclusions: Rural communities resist all kinds of military service more than cities and towns.

The urban battalions were made up of 62 percent workers and 27 percent businessmen. After 1873 and the disappearance of the American threat, the percentage of workers declined, their bosses being largely opposed to this type of military service. The business and student communities stepped in to take their place. In short, in a country that would remain chiefly rural until after the First World War, it was the urban milieu that built Canada's defence force from its beginnings.

The Militiaman and His Training

The life of the Canadian militiaman was shaped by the size of the budgets allocated to the organization in which he enlisted. These appropriations rose from $937,513 in 1869 to $1,654,282 in 1873, then fell to a low of $580,421 in 1877. Between the years 1878 and 1881 they fluctuated between $618,136 (1878) and $777,698 (1879). Between 1882 and 1886 they rose from a low of $772,811, reaching a peak of $4,022,080 during the North-West

Campaign. After that, total annual budgets ran slightly above $1 million.

It can be seen that the situation deteriorated in the second half of the 1870s, when an economic crisis hit the industrial world. The politicians' time-honoured solution, then as now, was to cut the defence budget. There was no shortage of critics in Parliament. The most common argument ran as follows: Since Canada's security is not at stake, what good will military spending do? More detailed criticism related to the wastage of money on uniforms (which were not provided to volunteers until 1876) and weapons, the over-abundance of officers in headquarters and, after 1876, the virtual absence of Francophones at the RMC in Kingston.

The cuts in the training budget had a considerable impact following 1876, even when the RMC had been added to existing institutions. During the 1871–72 fiscal year, 34,414 men underwent 16 days of training—a peak that would not be reached again until 1905. The authorized number of volunteers for annual training had been set at 40,000 in 1868 but was cut to 30,000 in 1873. The drill period was reduced to eight days in 1876; it was raised to 12 in 1877, but this training had to be delivered at battalion headquarters rather than at camp. In 1888 the maximum authorized strength was increased to 43,000 men, but to save money only 37,000 were allowed to enlist. The city corps assembled 10,000 men for the 12-day annual exercise, while the rural corps gathered together 27,000 for 12 days of training every two years. Between 1877 and 1886, however, the number of men attending annual training rarely exceeded 20,000, the average being around 18,000.

These figures were not linked solely to budgetary factors. Volunteer enthusiasm also played a role. The Act of 1868 provided for training at least as many men as the 30,000-strong U.S. regular army. But in 1873, for the first time, the volunteers occupied only 75 percent of the 40,000 positions available. After 1874, once the law was changed to provide training to no more than 30,000 men, 97 percent of available positions for volunteer militiamen were occupied.

That said, the waxing and waning of the government's enthusiasm for military matters may have had more lasting effects than the era of low budgets, which after all was limited in duration. During the down cycles, when training was limited, volunteer interest and effectiveness declined, particularly in the rural regiments that trained only every two years. In the districts, the budgetary constraints were such that the names of the units attending camp had to be chosen by drawing lots. In such an environment, the tiny military flame sustained through pain and misery among a few volunteers often flickered out forever. Moreover, these constraints stemmed the flow of new blood that the economic crisis might have supplied had the training provided between 1877 and 1883 remained at previous levels. Budgets edged upwards after 1882, but the economic situation improved as well, making it difficult for the military to attract volunteers in the numbers the government wanted to train. Furthermore, by suddenly increasing the number of trainee openings, the government invited a flood of raw and therefore inexperienced recruits.

Annual training camps, when they did take place, were held at very specific locations. In Quebec, for example, units from the western part of the province (including Montreal) trained at Laprairie; in the east (including Quebec City) they trained at Lauzon, more precisely at the old camp set up by British engineers while fortifying

Point Lévis between 1865 and 1871. We will be commenting on the real value of these training sessions later on. The units themselves would sometimes hold reviews, particularly in the cities, to mark some joyful or sad event. This gave many people, including a number of MPs and MLAs from all parties, an opportunity to don their uniforms.

Apart from these rare moments, which were often nonexistent in rural battalions, the volunteer had little contact with the military. People's daily lives, the many efforts to reorganize units whose companies varied in number for all sorts of reasons, the determination and enthusiasm of each unit's captain being its main source of motivation, the lack of interest in the highest reaches of political life—all of these factors conspired to make the volunteer a being apart, poorly supported by a society that was far from militaristic. For those units that participated, the North-West Campaign changed all this, but the dullness of routine quickly reasserted itself after their return to quarters.

The militiaman serving in a headquarters was paid $1 a day if he was an officer and 50¢—climbing to 60¢ in 1876—for all other ranks. Men attending camp were subject to daily scales based on their ranks that showed little variation between 1868 and 1898. It is well to remember that a day labourer in the mid-1870s earned about $1 a day, and even more in summer and fall, when militia camps were normally held.

Daily Camp Pay by Rank

Rank	Daily Camp Pay
Lieutenant-Colonel	$4.87
Major	$3.90
Captain	$2.82
Lieutenant	$1.58
Ensign	$1.25
Sergeant-Major	$1.00
Sergeant	70¢
Corporal	60¢
Private	50¢

In the wake of serious budget cuts, unpopular restrictive measures could not be avoided. Rations were free for everyone until 1875, when the decision was made to increase daily pay by 10¢ but to charge everyone for meals. The men were no longer paid for their days travelling to and from the camps or for the Sundays they spent in camp. In 1883, to stem general discontent, payments for these days were resumed. With the economic situation improving, staff officers were now paid for 15 days and company commanders for 12. That same year, the pay for soldiers serving in headquarters was also adjusted to reflect their ranks.

Even though officers in the Permanent and Non-Permanent Militia were better paid than their troops, they too needed a certain capacity for self-sacrifice to agree to serve their country. An officer-candidate for the Non-Permanent Militia had to ponder the uncertainty of his future status. After all, he was required to purchase his own uniform and provide his own barracks furnishings, and when he went on a course he had to be able to get away for 57 days to obtain his 2nd Class certificate or for 72 days to get a 1st Class certificate. Of course he was expected to be able to take dictation accurately and to keep accounts.[5] And afterwards, in a number of units, his pay or a large portion thereof would go to the regimental fund. All the same, the company captain was given $40 over and above his camp pay for keeping the weapons and uniforms of his men. Battalion commanders received $100 a year against expenses incurred in the performance of their military duties (stationery, postage, recruiting advertisements in the newspapers, and so on), and a further $100 if they added a band (always a draw at annual camps), as well as $40 per company to cover pre-camp training. This latter amount, however, was generally used

for other activities: the band, the regimental fund, or else the commander would simply appropriate it for services rendered.

Throughout the year, and during the weeks or month immediately preceding the camps, volunteers were trained in their companies or, sometimes, at the battalion level. Their curriculum included drill and shooting practice. They learned to march, deploy in various ways, change fronts, execute movements by echelon, form lines of attack and fire at random. The training schools for officers and non-commissioned officers that proliferated after 1883 helped improve the quality of this kind of training.

The courses they offered lasted three months and concluded with a series of tests comprising some 40 questions dealing with manoeuvres, 10 with weapons and internal economy, and 20 with the articles of war, the Militia Act and the regulation for calling up troops in aid of the civil authorities. The written examination lasted six hours and concluded with a one-hour oral exam administered at camp. Books, notes and conversation were banned during the written test and no one could leave the room. The examiner gave three points for perfect answers, two for partly correct answers and zero for wrong answers. Candidates had to obtain two thirds of the maximum score to pass. One interesting provision in the regulation covering the courses tells us something about the real value some people attached to them: *"A corps commander or military doctor who sends a candidate to a course when he cannot read or is infirm shall pay for his return trip."*[6]

Candidates for the Permanent Militia were required to take courses as well. A young man could hold a temporary commission but could not be officially accepted without passing a series of tests. For artillery candidates, the courses and tests dealt with

The Royal Navy gunboat HMS *Thrush* was typical of the small British patrol vessels based in Halifax and Esquimalt during the 1870s and 1880s. This was the first command offered to the Duke of York, one of Queen Victoria's sons, when he was stationed in Halifax.
(Private collection)

The port of Halifax as seen from the Citadel, circa 1875. Although Britain had removed its troops from Canada in 1871, it maintained its two naval bases: Esquimalt in British Columbia and, more importantly, Halifax.
(Parks Canada)

ballistics (theory and practice), dynamic and static calculations, the resistance of materials, equipment, field artillery (theory and practice), the pieces used in garrison or in the field, aiming, firing, and use of the tackle, gin and crane. The RMC also offered a three-month introductory course on surveying, bridge-building in the field, demolition, land and underwater mines, and basic strategy and tactics. Elements of military law and administration appeared in subsequent promotion examinations. After this, the young officer returned to one of the batteries, where he was taught to assemble and work the guns. All told, he was required to progressively serve in all the positions held by his men in order to achieve a full understanding both of their duties and of his field gun—generally a rifled, muzzle-loaded 9-pounder firing ordinary shells, shrapnel, point-detonating and air-burst fuses and canister shells.

was only one running-water outlet to serve everyone, and it was located in the basement. Light was provided by kerosene lamp in the mid-1880s, and the privies were outdoors.[7] Furthermore, unless he was of independent means, the married officer with children might face some anxious moments. While attending a six-month training course in England in 1893, Oscar Pelletier left his family with his father, for his pay was insufficient to support them during his absence.[8]

The Value of the Militia

The Act of 1868 contained provisions for implementing conscription; in actual fact, this was changed to an inventory taken in 1869, 1871 and 1873 prior to its being abandoned.

Each census cost $50,000, and following the budget cuts of 1875 the decision was

Census of Men of Eligible Age for Service[9]			
Province	1869	1871	1873
Ontario	315,352	330,886	322,145
Quebec	215,216	222,854	236,285
Nova Scotia	69,876	80,345	84,746
New Brunswick	55,622	59,923	65,805
Total	656,066	694,008	708,981

Mess life was pleasant but difficult. In winter, a wood stove heated the room, but in the Quebec Citadel, for instance, there

made to conduct them only once every five years, with the next scheduled for 1880. In actual fact, the final census was held in

1873, except in New Brunswick where the exercise would be repeated until 1879.

The fact that conscription was never introduced did not stop a number of people from pressing for it. These included three lieutenant-colonels—Irumberry de Salaberry, A.C. Lotbinière-Harwood and L.G. D'Odet d'Orsonnens[10]—all of whom could be considered Francophone. But this traditional levy under French rule ran counter to British tradition. For their part, the General Officers Commanding pressed for a regular force larger than the Non-Permanent Militia. Their vision, which met with only limited success, reflected the British tradition, which emphasized the development of a professional army, rather than common practice on the European continent at that time, which involved the conscription of young men for long periods.

The supporters of conscription had a number of arguments in their favour. The first of these, which surfaced during the years when the United States still posed a threat, concerned the inadequate numbers of volunteers. In 1868–69 the Eastern Quebec Military District had a quota of 5,035 volunteers but managed to raise only 59 percent of this number. In 1871 the 6th Military District (Montreal and Western Quebec) had an authorized strength of 3,228, but less than 50 percent of that number (1,512) participated in exercises; the 4th Battalion had four officers and 46 men, below the eligible number for a company, and the 65th of Montreal mustered only 17 officers and 158 men. When the 65th Battalion was inspected in December 1873, one company, that of Member of Parliament A. Ouimet, was absent—an example, to the 18 other officers and 194 NCOs and men in attendance, from someone in a senior position. Furthermore, 66 percent of Francophones did not

serve past their first year despite their three-year contracts. Among Quebec's Anglophones, the rate of non-renewal was 33 percent, while in Ontario it was 25 percent. For Canada as a whole in 1870, 88 percent of militia positions were filled; by 1873 this figure would fall to 73 percent. One of the problems here was the full mobility of the eligible population, mainly young, unattached day labourers. Nonetheless, the conscription of the number of militiamen permitted under the Act through the drawing of lots would never take place. It is hard to see how, in the virtual absence of any threat to Canada, it could have been justified or, more importantly, accepted by the people.

That said, what was the real value of the training received by these volunteers—on whom Canada was relying, let us not forget, both to defend the country in the event of threat and to maintain and restore order within its borders? Let us look first at the permanent force, which grew to its authorized strength of 1,000 in the 1880s. In the first place, these 1,000 positions were never completely filled; in 1890–91, for example, only 886 were occupied. In any case, a large percentage of the men reporting were new recruits or inexperienced soldiers who would have found it difficult to deliver professional training to volunteers (in 1891, for example, General Herbert commented that 54 percent of his army had less than two years of service). Then there were all the militiamen who became unavailable in the course of the year. Another report from 1890–91 informs us that 103 bought out of their contracts and left during the year, 201 terminated their contracts, 41 were dismissed for various reasons, eight died, 152 deserted and 28 were in prison for various terms, which cost them periods of service. And during this same year, which was not exceptional, the regular army had to train tens of thousands of militiamen, of whom a large percentage were recruits.

But this training was also being delivered by qualified officers within the volunteer corps. In some cases this was somehow successful; in others the training was of poor quality. A large number of these officers were too old: A lieutenant could serve past age 40, and it was quite common to find majors over 50 and lieutenant-colonels over 60. The least effective training officers were those in the rural corps, since in the cities training was often in the hands of professionals.

The problems of the rural corps were immense. A battalion could comprise several companies separated from one another by 30 or 50 kilometres of badly marked road, which made it all but impossible to assemble the battalion except for the annual camp. In 1869, for example, the Rimouski Provisional Battalion was formed of five companies, including one in Matane, 100 kilometres from Rimouski over an almost impassable road. The company captains thus played a cardinal role in their organizations. They were the ones who recruited their men, often with a blend of charm and half-truths that made it virtually impossible to impose military discipline. Indeed, the recruiter's popularity was often of greater importance than his military skills. The Act left the responsibility for training in the hands of commanding officers, but on occasion these men would "still sign today [1874] a certificate of competency for themselves."[11] Naturally, they were paid to deliver training: $40 in the infantry and cavalry and up to $200 for field artillery. In the towns, an allocation for each battery or company trained would be paid to the brigade or battalion commanders. This explains the large numbers of compa-

nies, each with very few members: at $25 per company per year to the commanding officer, plus the $40 paid to the company captain, no one was interested in seeing them disappear. Not surprisingly, this led to all sorts of problems. After inspecting Montreal's 65th Battalion in December 1873, Lieutenant-Colonel A.C. Lotbinière-Harwood noted that it was "impossible to give merit points. Target shooting has not been adequately practised...the 65th Battalion has used only a very small number of cartridges."[12] To obtain its funds, a unit had to pass inspection. In the countryside, the men were hastily assembled, after which their captains went to some surprise location, often a barn or a cave, and brought out the weapons, which were hurriedly shined up at the last moment. The inspecting officer, who was placed in a difficult position, would recommend payment, "which he basically knew was undeserved."[13] But if he "[is] concerned about his duty, looks at the guns, finds them rusty inside and has a malfunctioning firing mechanism stripped, he is told that if he is that particular, volunteer corps will never be maintained." Disillusioned, D'Orsonnens added that the people who hurled these criticisms at inspectors were "*legally qualified* officers who fully intend, with the government's allocation, to spend as little as possible to maintain our arms; they generally take few pains to drill and train our soldiers."[14]

Only a few of them went through the military schools, which, it must be admitted, did not automatically qualify them as instructors able to convey their expertise, particularly to men they had often coaxed into enlisting. Moreover, a number of men who did attend military school were content to pocket their completion bonus and disappear. According to Jean-Yves Gravel, who has thoroughly examined this issue, approximately 75 per-

Officers of the 6th Duke of Connaught's Regiment of Hussars, Montreal, circa 1880–90. These officers unconventionally wore the steel helmets associated with dragoons.
(H. Bunnet, private collection)

Officer and private of the 5th Royal Scots of Canada, Montreal, circa 1880–90. This Montreal regiment was the first in the volunteer militia to wear Scottish dress.
(H. Bunnet, private collection)

cent of Non-Permanent Militia officers in the mid-1870s knew practically nothing of military matters. After 1883 the situation did show considerable improvement, but this did little to make the units more effective. The fact is that urban units were expected to train twice a week from 7 pm to 10 pm during the two or three months prior to annual inspection. There was also a firing day and one or two parades in conjunction with religious services. In practice, men were often recruited at the last minute, so that a number of volunteers had not even been sworn in when the annual inspection finally took place. When the degree of disorganization was too great, the unit would be denied the right to exercise, and its officers and men would accordingly not be paid. Thus many companies and even battalions would disappear for a few years before coming back to life under the vigorous hand of an ambitious new commanding officer.

In addition to training at the unit level, training was provided in the camps. Following passage of the Act of 1868, there was a strong movement in this direction. But since budgets had remained more or less static and expenses had mounted due to, among other things, the formation of A and B batteries in 1871, some activities had to be cut. For example, between 1 July 1873 and 30 June 1874 units were obliged to train in their own headquarters rather than in the brigades and camps as had been the case since 1868, prompting remarks that they had begun where they ought to have left off. In theory, they trained for 16 days, with at least three hours set aside each day. For the rest of the 1870s, conditions would not be favourable for the large assemblies that were useful mainly to the rural corps.

Even when a camp was held, how much value did it actually have? Following the 6th Military District's 1872 camp, one

of the largest camps held prior to the 20th century, Lieutenant-Colonel Lotbinière-Harwood wrote to his superior that, despite the camp's success, "it is my duty to inform you that most of the present volunteer corps could barely rely on two thirds of their strength in the event of immediate necessity, and in more than one locality it would not be prudent, because of the transient population, to rely on even half of the enrolment."[15] The situation was often worse than this report would lead us to understand. Indeed the company rolls often included people absent due to illness or for other reasons. The absentees, who were relatively high in number, received the same pay as attendees, which resulted in skewed camp statistics, not to mention what it did to morale. For example, in 1882 the Quebec City district reported that 1,706 militiamen had been trained when only 1,049 had attended; the discrepancy amounted to 657 men, or 38 percent. The results for the country as a whole were not much better. Brigade majors were allotted $8 for every company reporting and were therefore reluctant to dismiss companies with fewer than 30 men in the field. In 1870 one particular battalion reported 363 men trained out of 125 present. Although this sort of abuse became less widespread after 1878, with the introduction of fixed salaries for staff officers, the gap between the number of men attending the camps and the number trained would remain wide until the end of the century.

If, at the very minimum, the three-year term of service had actually applied, "trained" militiamen would have been of some use in subsequent years. However, these militiamen really served only one year before defecting for various reasons. Towns and cities would see the recruitment of a highly mobile worker population. In the

Private of the 4th Hussars from Eastern Ontario, circa 1880–90. Most Canadian cavalry regiments at this time wore uniforms similar to those worn by Britain's 13th Regiment of Hussars. However, the headdress of the Canadian volunteers was often limited to a white pith helmet or pill-box. (Re-creation by Barry Rich, Parks Canada)

Sergeant of a Canadian hussars regiment in town dress, circa 1880–90.
(Watercolour by H. Bunnet, Anne S.K. Brown Military Collection, Brown University)
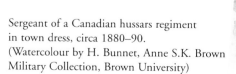

countryside a corps leader eager to maintain his political relationships and his popularity with his men would do nothing about a three-year contract being abandoned after one year of service.

Gravel has compiled revealing figures for the year 1880 (see Table 3).

In any case, "the general orders governing [camps]...are minor masterpieces of planning and foresight," Lieutenant-Colonel d'Orsonnens cynically reported.[16] In fact floods of directives were issued relating to camp organization, transportation, the type of training to be provided, and discipline—

Volunteer Strength and "Trained" Militiamen

Province	Urban Corps	Rural Corps	Total	Trained Militiamen
Ontario	4,085	12,902	16,987	9,400
Quebec	3,245	8,970	12,215	7,000
New Brunswick	540	2,140	2,680	1,500
Nova Scotia	1,148	2,798	3,946	2,200
Manitoba	207	505	712	450
Prince Edward Island	170	405	575	400
British Columbia	181	122	303	300
Total	9,576	27,842	37,418	21,250

Yet 1880 was a "good" year. It is estimated that between 1876 and 1898 an average of 18,500 soldiers were trained annually. This figure must be tempered somewhat to account for the exceptions—men who were paid but not trained. In the urban battalions these included musicians and buglers, signalmen, ambulance men and a prodigious number of NCOs who did nothing. In the rural battalions they included officers' servants, grooms, waiters, cooks and so on. In actual fact, training was being provided to approximately 14,000 men a year.

for example, on matters of dress (no civilian dress), leave and evening passes.

Ultimately, what is most shocking about the entire system is that the country's defence relied heavily on the rural units, and these were the weakest of all. In 1891 the General Officer Commanding, Major-General Ivor Herbert, again reported: "The training of rural units is very shaky, but their organization is even more so."[17] And the measures taken were not always effective. Accordingly, between 15 and 26 September 1891 the 7th District

Officer and gunner of the Halifax Garrison Artillery, circa 1880–90. The dress of Canadian gunners was virtually identical to that of the regular British artillery. However, Canadian gunners preferred the white pith helmet. (H. Bunnet, private collection)

Officer of the 2nd Queen's Own Rifles of Canada, Toronto, circa 1885–90. (H. Bunnet, private collection)

THE 2nd QUEEN'S OWN RIFLES (CANADA)

assembled its units at Rimouski instead of Lévis. This meant that the Trois-Rivières and Lévis battalions, among others, had to travel dozens of kilometres further than necessary. In addition, the site selected at Rimouski was less suitable than the Lévis site. However, the Lower St Lawrence battalions were better served in terms of proximity.

In 1896 it was the turn of Major-General W.J. Gascoigne, who had succeeded Herbert in 1895, to report that none of the troops were ready to take the field. Reforms had indeed been carried out over the years: Under Herbert, for example, the military schools had been formed into regiments, permanent sites had been chosen for the annual camps and a medical service had been set up, along with six-week qualification camps for officers and NCOs. But there were still no quartermaster's stores, and the militia was generally disorganized and demoralized.[18] Yet the public seemed satisfied with its defence forces. The militiaman's annual pay had become a well-accepted allocation, particularly in rural districts. Defence was already playing an acknowledged and appreciated role in the regional economy.

One of the few advantages of the Non-Permanent Militia was that it gave recognition to those men who were willing to serve. There were a number of disadvantages, however. The defence force not only suffered from a lack of arsenals, but also had a tendency to lose uniforms and equipment. Moreover, its headquarters were invested with insufficient power for fear of infringing on the authority of several politicians playing soldier within their communities. There was also some abuse of the system of ranks.

Furthermore, the volunteer was required to pay fees and make sacrifices. If he joined his unit to maintain public order because the police force was weak—if indeed there was one—he might wait months before being paid. If he left for weeks or months in the field, his employer might not guarantee that he would have a job upon his return. He would also be leaving his family to public assistance agencies hastily formed for this purpose. If harm befell him, his family was not assured of a pension. This in addition to the constant reshuffling that moved battalions from one brigade to another and from one military district to another, made ranks disappear and reappear, and abolished and revived units without anyone really understanding the reason behind all the changes.

Anyone examining the issue in any detail would come away with fairly negative results. Anyone imagining how the country might deal with aggression could not be very optimistic. In the *Journal of the Military Service Institution,* an American publication, an anonymous, but clearly Canadian, foreign correspondent described a mobilization plan for a Canadian Militia abruptly assigned responsibility for defending the border from Quebec City to Detroit. In issues 29 and 30 (March and June 1887), he explained that the country was far from capable of mobilizing the 150,000 men that would be required. Moreover, the cause would have to be popular among both Francophones and Anglophones. Although it did end on some positive notes, the long article let it be known that Montreal, the industrial and economic heart of Canada, would be virtually indefensible.

Some solutions were suggested, particularly by the successive General Officers Commanding who over the years managed to gradually improve the entire system, focusing their efforts on the permanent force to the extent that their ministers would allow.

Many Canadian militiamen proposed their own solutions. Consider those advanced in 1874 by Lieutenant-Colonel Gustave D'Odet d'Orsonnens, whose many appointments during his career in the Permanent Militia included commander of the military school founded at St Jean in 1883. In his view, the schools (which were few in number in 1874) should have been replaced by permanent regiments in which candidates for ranks in the volunteer Non-Permanent Militia would be required to serve three months in the element of their choosing. This approach would be more or less implemented in the 1880s and 1890s through a series of reforms rooted in the Act of 1883.

D'Orsonnens would also have favoured a regular army composed of several special corps whose captains could be commissioned as militia lieutenant-colonels and commanders of militia regiments on active service. This army would in a sense serve as a staff school, its officers forming the staff of the Confederation. In peacetime this army could be kept busy on major public works. The militia would rely on conscription except in towns and cities, where there could be volunteer corps recruiting for a four-year term with annual training periods lasting from 10 to 14 days.

These volunteer militia units would be divided proportionately among Canada's various regions, but since the "volunteers" would be conscripts, the battalion rosters would be full, offering a countrywide total strength of 15,040 men in 1874. During their first two years of service the militiamen would train in their respective headquarters; in the third year a camp would be held at the brigade level; and in the fourth year a camp would be held at the divisional level.

D'Orsonnens was especially partial to proportional representation, advocating 82 regimental divisions in Ontario (with 6,560 men), 70 in Quebec (with 5,600 men) and the remainder of the country in proportion: "Assuring each Province its right to provide its contingent would be a fair and reasonable political act...but assuring the

Permanent Militia Officers in 1888		
Units	Anglophones	Francophones
Infantry schools	17	4
Mounted infantry	4	1
Batteries in service	22	2
Cavalry schools	2	1
RMC	16	1
Total	61	9

rights of its fellow citizens (nationals) by a well-ordered Constitution would be further to fulfil a sacred duty to nationality. This is why the army's ranks must be maintained in the proportions given above, as a guarantee of the future of each Province."[19]

The Role of Francophones

Indeed a Francophone problem already existed within the Canadian defence system. Forming approximately 35 percent of Canada's population up to 1914, Francophones accounted for only 20 percent of its military manpower and about 10 percent of its officer positions (depending on the year). Between 1876 and 1898, RMC trained 10 or so Francophone officers (4.7 percent) out of the 255 obtaining commissions there. The figures for Permanent Militia officers on the Militia List of the Dominion of Canada for 1888 are shown in the table.

"We do not have the percentage of officers we require," concluded an admirer of minister Adolphe Caron, adding: "Yet this is the fault of neither the minister nor the officers, but is due to the fact that our people do not give military service the attention it deserves."[20]

In the 6th Military District (Montreal), the records for 1868 through 1873 reveal no French-Canadian officers in the artillery or the engineers. In 1871, however, when the Fenian threat was still alive and George-Étienne Cartier was the minister of militia and defence, Colonel Robertson Ross, the Adjutant-General of Militia, estimated that over 2,000 of the 5,310 officers and men from the 5th and 6th Military districts then training in the Laprairie camp were Francophones. The threat posed by the United States subsequently faded, and throughout Canada, as we have seen, the

militia saw both its role and its budgets shrink for about a decade.

At the same time, British traditions were becoming more and more entrenched. A proposal to establish Zouave units to deal with the Fenian threat was refused—which was hardly encouraging for the Francophones who had made the suggestion. In fact, the entire military system was being modelled on that of the British Empire: uniforms, military regulations, and exchanges of officers and instructors. In the Militia Report of 1878, Selby Smyth pointed out that the British government approved and even desired "the assimilation at all points of the Canadian Militia with the British Army."[21] The General Officers Commanding laboured mightily to promote this cause.

The regular army, which delivered training to the Non-Permanent Militia, harboured a great many former British soldiers who had decided to serve in Canada after their British army contracts expired. The working language was English. Commands were issued in English, and correspondence between Francophones was in English. Annual exercises were also conducted in English, which created problems for the prodigious numbers of unilingual Francophones. In the camps, improvised translations for unilingual Francophones simply hampered their progress. The Francophone officers, who were militarily no more competent than their Anglophone colleagues, generally spoke poor English, which frustrated their efforts. Translated manuals were rare and always late in arriving. Since governments showed interest in the militia only when it was needed, everyone soon learned to manage on their own. At his own expense, Louis-Timothée Suzor translated a drill manual published in 1863 and 1867. He had not finished translating the second edition before it was superseded, in 1877,

Tunic of an infantryman in the Canadian volunteer militia, 1870–76. (Canadian War Museum)

Except for a few details, the full dress uniform of officer cadets at the Royal Military College in Kingston, Ontario, has remained essentially the same since the college was founded in 1874. As shown in this 1954 photo, only the shakos and pith helmets worn on parade by first-class officer-cadets have disappeared, to be replaced by pill-boxes. (DND, ZK-2049)

by a new *Field Exercises* manual. In 1885 this new manual was translated by David Frève, on his own initiative. In 1888, however, the British launched a new series of manuals that even in 1914 were not to be found in French. If a translation did exist, the Francophone officer was required to pay for it, while his Anglophone colleague got his book free of charge. All this led to problems, including the introduction into the French used by Francophone soldiers of a host of poorly integrated English terms. Most importantly, this state of affairs drove Francophones out of the army.

Among the officers of the Non-Permanent Militia—who became instructors, it will be remembered—matters grew even more complicated. At first, courses were delivered in English. Then, beginning in the 1880s, battalions frequently opened their own schools, offering mandatory officer courses culminating in district examinations. This meant that a candidate could be taught, in French, the rudiments of a profession that was really practised only in English.

Yet for 18 of the 31 years between 1867 and 1898 the department of militia and defence was headed by Francophone ministers, three in all. The position of deputy minister was held by Francophones from 1868 to 1898—in fact, this was true until 1940. One has to wonder exactly how determined these men were in promoting the use of their language within the Militia. Just in terms of getting the training manuals translated, it took years of ministerial pressure to get permission from the General Officer Commanding to publish Frève's work.

According to d'Orsonnens, at least one other reason militated against Francophone participation in the Militia. When he asked some of his own people why they were forming fewer volunteer companies than Canadians of other backgrounds, he got this answer: "It's fine for the English. They're rich. We're poor. We can't afford to waste our time *voluntarily* in this way—they'd cut our allocations. So let them force us. We'll bow to the law like all the others. We'll even submit gladly."[22]

This reply neatly summarizes the response to the conscriptionist message that d'Orsonnens articulated at greater length elsewhere, so we should not take it too literally. All the same, we may conclude that a French Canadian who enlisted despite the hostile conditions described above had a sense of military duty far above average. In any case, the key problem of Francophone under-representation in the Canadian defence forces following Confederation would have major repercussions. No one seemed prepared to deal with this issue while there was still time.

The Infantryman's Weapons: His Rifle
During the War of 1812, Canadian militiamen used a smooth-bored, muzzle-loaded musket, usually a Brown Bess, with an extremely limited range and a level of accuracy that left much to be desired. A British officer of the period left this description of the effectiveness of this weapon:

The soldier's musket, if it is not too badly calibrated, which is very often the case, can strike a man at a distance of 80 yards and even up to 100 yards. But a soldier has to be very unlucky even to be wounded at a distance of 150 yards, this on condition that his adversary aims well. As for firing on a man at a distance of 200 yards, you might as well aim at the moon hoping to strike it.

Moreover, the Brown Bess permitted only two shots a minute, or, occasionally, in the hands of an extremely well-trained soldier, three.

A century later, during the First World War, the descendant of the militiaman of 1812 found himself on the battlefields of Europe with a rifle that was much easier to load, with remarkably improved accuracy and considerably increased range. With its rifled barrel, the Canadian infantryman's Lee-Enfield Short Rifle (S.M.L.E.) could fire at a range of over 2,000 yards (1,830 m) at an average rate of 10 shots a minute, even 15 in the hands of a highly skilled shooter.

In fact the S.M.L.E. was not an invention in itself but the result of a series of technological innovations that emerged primarily in the second half of the 19th century. At about mid-point in the century the new industrial ability to rifle gun barrels contributed to the spread of such rifles. Spiral grooves cut into the rifle bore imparted a rotating movement to the projectile that persisted throughout its trajectory, delivering both greater accuracy and greater range. The early 1850s also saw the development of the self-contained metal cartridge with a central percussion unit containing powder, bullet and bore. This invention helped to make breech loading more common during the 1860s: Gone was the lengthy and inconvenient process of forcing the bullet into the rifle's bore with a metal rod driven home with a mallet. Soon projectiles would take on a cylindro-conical shape that made them even more effective.

At this stage in its development, the rifle still contained only a single shot: Each cartridge had to be inserted manually. During the last quarter of the century a more rapidly firing rifle was developed. It had a locked breech that combined the cartridge chamber with the firing system. Both simple and strong, the lever locking made it possible to clear, open, extract and eject the spent clip, load a new cartridge, lock the system and arm the firing pin. The subsequent appearance of the clip magazine containing several cartridges successively introduced into the breech by a spring system gave birth to the repeating rifle. Finally, during the 1890s the Swedish chemist Alfred Nobel invented cordite, a smokeless powder containing nitroglycerine, and a powerful explosive that was immediately adopted as a propellant for projectiles. This invention was the last in the list of refinements characterizing the rifle used by troopers in the First World War, a weapon that had become vastly more deadly than its predecessor of the early 19th century.

The Machine Gun

Who is not familiar with the famous revolver, the cowboy's companion, a hand gun equipped with a cylinder containing a number of chambers—usually six—revolving around a central axis? Invented in 1836 by the American Samuel Colt, the revolver remains essentially the same today, although some improvements have been made, particularly with respect to the resistance of metals.

In the mid-19th century an American farm machinery manufacturer by the name of Gatling used the revolver principle to develop a new weapon. He grouped several gun barrels around a central axis; a simple, hand-operated crank was used to rotate the whole group around the axis while a cam system opened and closed the gun breeches at each revolution. Though still very rudimentary, the machine gun was born. At the end of the century Hiram Stevens Maxim, a self-taught American electrician, radically modified the Gatling gun: Henceforth, the energy used to rotate the barrels would be derived from the gases released by the explosion, with no further human intervention required. The Maxim automatic machine gun spread rapidly. In 1904 the British developed a lighter and quicker-firing version of the Maxim gun called the Vickers. Finally, in 1911 a U.S. Army colonel introduced the first true light machine gun. Faster and cheaper than the Vickers, the Lewis gun could be operated by one man.

Canadian troops used machine guns for the first time in the North-West Campaign of 1885. At that time they had two Gatlings whose effectiveness left much to be desired. Nicknamed "rababou" (meaning noise-maker) by the Métis, the Gatling seemed capable of accomplishing little more than irritating the eardrums. During the First World War, however, Canadian soldiers used the latest machine guns. Equipped with motor vehicles protected by light armour and fitted with Vickers and Lewis guns, the first Canadian motorized machine-gun brigade built an enviable reputation.

Coupled with the power of the rifle, the machine gun played a decisive role from the very beginning of the 1914–18 war—a role most military strategists had not foreseen. With a slightly longer range than the rifle, this weapon provided much greater firepower at as much as 600 rounds a minute. Just a few men with a heavy machine gun entrenched in a "nest" and shielded by barbed wire could keep a large party of soldiers at bay almost indefinitely.

Chapter II

THREATS INTERNAL AND EXTERNAL

Events Leading Up to the North-West Rebellion

Between 1871 and 1898 the event that had the greatest impact on Canada's young defence force was unquestionably the second Métis uprising that rocked the North-West Territories in the spring of 1885. This crisis stemmed from conditions closely resembling those that had prevailed in the Red River region in 1870. The seeds of

the conflict were sown in 1872 when government emissaries passed over the heads of the Métis and signed a treaty with the Aboriginals of the Qu'Appelle district.

Close behind them came the surveyors who began carving up the big free spaces into settlement lands. Between 1878 and 1884 the Métis sent dozens of demands to Ottawa, calling for recogni-

tion of their right to the land they had been occupying for, in some cases, more than a generation. But nothing was done. The first land registry office in the Territories opened in Prince Albert in 1881 while disputes and fraud cases still dogged the 1870 Manitoba agreements.

This situation exasperated the Métis, many of whom had drifted back west from Manitoba, where the land was being overrun by settlers threatening their way of life. In May 1884 the Métis Council of Batoche held a meeting at which its leader, Gabriel Dumont, managed to get a motion passed inviting Louis Riel to come to the defence of his brothers.

Married, Riel was now living in Montana, where he taught at the Saint Pierre Mission. The Saskatchewan Métis delegation arrived there on 4 June. Five days later Riel resigned his position, beginning his journey north the following day. The Riel of 1884 was more fanatical than the previous

Infantryman of the volunteer militia during the 1880s. The infantry wore the scarlet tunic with a white braid cloverleaf over the facing from 1876 on. The "Glengarry" cap shown here was the only headdress provided by the Department of Militia, but many units bought helmets, sometimes dark blue with a point but mainly white pith helmets similar to those worn in the British army. (Re-creation by Ronald B. Volstad, DND)

one. He believed it was his mission to lead the Métis and Indians and ensure they became united as a single people.

Between the time of Riel's arrival in Batoche and the end of the winter of 1884–85, Ottawa's failure to respond to Métis claims stirred up unrest that reached a peak when a Hudson's Bay Company employee returning from Winnipeg informed the Métis that police were being sent to crush their revolt and clap Riel in irons. On 19 March, when the Métis traditionally gathered for the feast of St Joseph, their patron saint, they formed a provisional government led by Riel with Gabriel Dumont as adjutant-general. Batoche became the capital of this government and, very soon, the objective that the Canadian government authorities wanted to smash.

The group referred to as the "rebels" were planning to take action; their main goal now was to persuade the Indians to make common cause with the Métis. This diplomatic manoeuvre had only limited success; in the end, very few Amerindians actually supported the Métis. Seeking complete control over the territory, the Riel-Dumont government demanded that the North-West Mounted Police cede Fort Carlton and Fort Battleford. All the pieces were in position for the tragedy to occur.

Provisional Government Rule

The police were obviously not prepared to obey the rebels. Assistant Commissioner Lief N.F. (Paddy) Crozier commanding Fort Carlton was no man to give in. He also controlled the Duck Lake trading post located between Carlton and Batoche where there were stores of food and ammunition. Though the post was of some importance locally, it was hardly worth an ill-prepared battle. Crozier was advised not to move

before the arrival of reinforcements; however, urged on by a few zealous volunteers and certain of his strength and his cause, he took to the road at the head of 55 men. This initiative would cost him dearly.

On 26 March, while moving towards Duck Lake, which he knew to be already under Métis control, Crozier was ambushed by a Métis party under Gabriel Dumont. The fight was brief and violent, leaving 12 policemen dead and 11 wounded. The bloodshed surprised and unsettled Riel, who did not want Dumont to pursue a police force who, in their haste to retreat, had abandoned some of their casualties and equipment in the field.

Dumont's victory set several Aboriginal groups on the warpath. Divided, the police would be easy prey. On 28 March, abandoning Fort Carlton, they fell back on Prince Albert. Further west, in the Battleford area, other law enforcement officers barricaded themselves in their post along with the white population, leaving the surrounding area to Cree and Blackfoot groups. Even further west, at Frog Lake, the Aboriginals massacred some settlers.

In early April 1885, as Ottawa finally began to see that it had lost control over events on the North Saskatchewan River, the Métis leader realized that his Indian allies were not entirely under his control.

Canadian Government Mobilization

If it was true that Riel had changed, it was also true that the Canadian West had changed; the situation in 1885 was not what he had known in 1870. The American adventurers might again fuel the flames of conflict, but these disruptive elements constituted less of a threat than the Fenians who had played but a minor role in the Red River affair. The real change lay in the means avail-

Driver from B Battery of the
Canadian artillery, circa 1885.
During the North-West Campaign,
the gunners' white helmets were
dyed brown.
(Watercolour by R.W. Rutherford,
private collection)

Canadian artillery officer in field dress,
circa 1880–85.
(Watercolour by R.W. Rutherford, Parks Canada)

able to the Canadian government for suppressing rebellion. The most important of these was unquestionably the railway, the military effectiveness of which had been amply demonstrated in the American Civil War and the Franco-Prussian War. The transcontinental railway would represent a key element in Ottawa's response; the authorities now knew it was possible to reach the West in a few days without having to travel through American territory.

On 23 March, four days after Riel's provisional government was proclaimed, Prime Minister Macdonald responded by assigning Major-General Frederick Middleton, the General Officer Commanding the Canadian Militia, the task of organizing a counterattack. The local militia were the first to receive the order to be prepared to leave. Middleton travelled to Winnipeg and on 27 March, one day after the clash at Duck Lake, left for Qu'Appelle at the head of the Winnipeg Rifles. Within a few weeks more than 8,000 men from Quebec and Ontario would congregate under his command. Some of the western units would be commanded by General Thomas Strange, first commander of B Battery and the artillery school, who had pulled back in proximity to Calgary; others would be commanded by Colonel William Otter.

Middleton's strategy was simple: He would deploy his forces in three columns heading north. The commander personally led the group that left Qu'Appelle for Batoche. Otter led the Swift Current column towards Battleford, while Strange left Calgary for the North Saskatchewan River, where he would follow its course eastwards.

Middleton's Column

General Middleton had somewhat limited confidence in his citizen soldiers, undoubtedly because he was familiar with the shortcomings of the training most of them had received, while the military qualifications of the remainder went no further than a willingness to serve. Prior to setting out, therefore, the troops received minimum mandatory training. Given these circumstances, many militiamen executed their first shooting drill with weapons that in many cases were badly maintained, improperly stored or damaged through long disuse. The skills and experience of the men detached to Otter and Strange were similar, and less than reassuring.

Middleton moved very slowly towards Batoche. The British general was suspicious, remembering the fate of Lieutenant-Colonel George Armstrong Custer at the hands of American Indians on the Little Big Horn in 1876, and the lesson so recently administered to Crozier and his men was fresh in his mind. When it was reported to him that the Métis had dug in on both sides of the South Saskatchewan River, he ordered nearly half his troops across the river, deviating even further from a principle of war he had already violated by forming up in three columns: the principle of concentration of force. It is not always a mistake to proceed in this way, but in this case it was. On 24 April the troop on the east side of the river, where Batoche was located, was ambushed at Fish Creek. After suffering some losses, Middleton ordered a retreat and took a break that lasted two weeks.

During this period, Riel sent a message to his Indian allies asking them to join him at Batoche, where a decisive confrontation was shaping up. Since the Indians took their time responding, Middleton, who had consolidated all his men on the east bank of the river, was able to resume his advance in early May. He was now better prepared. His forces had been reorganized and given additional training. Their logistical strength had

44

Gabriel Dumont, "military" leader of the Métis forces in 1885, was
a brilliant tactician. Historians generally concede that had Dumont fully
controlled Métis operations the Canadian volunteers would have faced
a much tougher campaign.
(NAC, PA-178147)

Fort Pitt, a North-West Mounted Police post, was besieged and taken by the Cree
on 15 April 1885. (Parks Canada)

been augmented with the arrival of a small steamboat which, stationed across from Batoche, would lay down supporting fire for the militiamen attacking Métis land positions. The siege of Batoche commenced on 10 May, and the federal troops settled in for a war of positions that was frustrating for many militiamen who knew they possessed superior strength in terms of men and weapons—artillery pieces, a Gatling gun and hundreds of rifles. When the firing slackened they realized the Métis were short of ammunition. On the 12th, two regiments, unable to stand the inactivity any longer, followed their colonels in an attack: The entrenchments and the village yielded easily. The whole operation cost the Métis 12 dead and three wounded. Middleton's army counted eight dead and 46 wounded.

At the moment of truth, Louis Riel and Gabriel Dumont were no longer with their people. On 15 May, having refused to follow Dumont into American exile once again, Riel surrendered.

Otter's Column

Leaving Swift Current, located west of Qu'Appelle, Otter and his men headed north. By the third week of April they reached Battleford, where their first act was to secure the safety of the white inhabitants. The column then veered southwest, where scouts had located some Indian marauders responsible for murder and extortion in and around Battleford. Advancing by night towards the Indian camp near Cut Knife Hill, Otter was discovered before he could attack, thereby losing the advantage of surprise. On 2 May, after a day of indecisive fighting, the soldiers fell back on Battleford.

Under Poundmaker, who was following Riel's orders, the Indians made their way towards Batoche. They seized a supply con-

voy en route to Battleford on 14 May, the very day the Métis were beaten at Batoche; realizing there was no way out, the members of Poundmaker's band began to scatter. After nine days playing a dangerous game of hide and seek, the Indian leader reached Battleford, where he surrendered.

Strange's Column

Strange had left Calgary for the North Saskatchewan River, intending to follow its course back to Battleford and to tighten the net as Middleton had ordered. At the end of May he reached Frenchman's Butte, where he surprised the Cree. Big Bear's party moved quickly and dug in at that location, which overlooks the strategic points of the river and Fort Pitt. If they wished to fight it out man to man with Big Bear's 600 warriors, the militiamen would have to cross some swampy ground, leaving themselves exposed. At the very moment when Strange was making the decision to retreat, despite having much greater firepower than the enemy, the Cree were preparing to do the same. On 1 June, after receiving the supplies he had been lacking, Strange returned to attack Frenchman's Butte only to discover that it had been abandoned. Since the Cree had begun to disperse, Strange did not pursue them. Two days later he was joined at Fort Pitt by nearly 900 men under Middleton. The general immediately organized a hunt but kept all his men close by, including the light cavalry, and began another slow advance. The wagons, with 120 soldiers on board, sank into the half-frozen ground north of the Saskatchewan River.

This initiative came to naught. On 4 June, Colonel Sam Steele's troopers exchanged a few rounds with Big Bear's warriors at Duck Lake. This would be the last fight in the campaign, as the Cree had elected to aban-

The Battle of Fish Creek, 24 April 1885. (Parks Canada)

The Battle of Cut Knife Hill, 2 May 1885. (Parks Canada)

don the cause. On 2 July, Big Bear surrendered near Fort Carlton.

So the brush-fire ignited by the Métis insurrection had been contained and put out. Momentarily eclipsed by military activity, law and politics would reclaim their rightful place. After a highly controversial trial and verdict, Riel would be hanged on 16 November 1885. This event caused the first significant rift between the Conservative Party and the French Canadians, many of whom had taken up the defence of the Métis and their leader. In 1887, Quebecers removed the Conservatives from power and installed the nationalist Honoré Mercier as premier.

An Assessment of the Campaign

The Métis and their Indian allies were ill prepared and therefore incapable of measuring up to the military force quickly deployed against them. Despite some well-conducted battles and a few isolated victories, their chances of winning had been virtually nil from the start.

Though the government celebrated this military triumph, it was not unaware that its own indecisiveness had contributed to the tragedy that had just occurred. From the time of its initial reaction to the Métis uprising, Canada mobilized 8,000 men, 2,648 of whom were employed on logistics duties. Ontario provided 1,929 of these men, Quebec 1,012 and Nova Scotia 383. They were joined by 2,010 militiamen and 500 police and local civic guard members from the West. On 27 March, A and B batteries and the 65th Montreal Rifle Battalion, the first militia unit to be mobilized in this conflict, were called into combat. The following day saw the list of participating units grow longer, and soon every region of the country was represented.[23]

The minister, Sir Adolphe Caron, made every effort to institute a logistics and transportation system that relied almost exclusively on private enterprise. The Militia's lack of preparation was apparently behind this solution, one in which patronage and politics were the best of bedfellows. The government had to foot a steep bill of $4.5 million, an enormous amount for the late 19th century.

Almost nothing had been done to prepare for such a campaign. The military medical and supply services were thrown together in four days. The variety of weapons issued was of no concern. Men left for war with Snider, Winchester and Martini-Henry carbines and rifles. Similarly, they carried three types of ammunition that had to be distributed, at times with difficulty, to units that were sometimes far apart. Some of this ammunition turned out to be unusable or non-existent; for example, General Strange reached Frenchman's Butte with only 22 artillery shells. Leadership was extremely weak, but Middleton would ascribe his slowness and procrastination to the inexperience of his subordinates; he had no confidence in them nor they in him. It was the general's view that he had prevented the Batoche engagement from ending in failure, but people could not forget that he had been unable to use his mounted forces or manoeuvre his troops, or that his timid approach was the cause of the lack of fighting spirit in his men.

Facing this fighting force, which could easily have been beaten by a vigorous enemy, were scarcely 1,000 insurgents, badly armed and short of food and ammunition. The courage of the handful of troops fighting for a lost cause at Batoche surprised Middleton, and he was impressed by the strength of their position and the ingenuity and care with which their trenches had been

The guns of A Battery of the Canadian artillery in position during the Battle of Fish Creek, 24 April 1885. This picture was taken by Captain James Peters of A Battery, an amateur who took his camera to the North-West and recorded the very first photographs in history of a battle in progress. (NAC, C-3461)

Thick smoke rises from the Métis village of Batoche during the battle of 9 May 1885. (James Peters, NAC, C-3464)

Staff and wounded militiamen (two of whom have lost an arm) in the field hospital installed in a Moose Jaw building in 1885. (Army Museum, Halifax)

constructed. The weakness of the vanquished would enable the victor to indulge in some flag-waving, but 40 years after these events the Métis Historical Society accurately foresaw that "the time is not far off when the Canadian West will salute [the Métis of 1870 and 1885] as precursors and liberators."[24]

Middleton would give an accounting of his expedition. Five years after serving as a witness at Louis Riel's trial in 1885, he appeared before a special Commons committee to explain his actions in connection with a North-West Mounted Police seizure of furs. The furs belonged to a Métis who was unable to reclaim them on his release following the events at Batoche because they had vanished. Based on the plaintiff's statement, the trail led right up to Middleton, who claimed he had had the right to order the seizure of pelts stolen by someone else. The committee pronounced the seizures unjustified and unlawful, and Middleton's conduct in the affair was characterized as unspeakable. Middleton left Canada under a cloud of almost universal disapproval. He was not the first of Canada's military "heroes" to be judged for both what he did—conduct a campaign—and what he did not do—steal furs. In 1896 the British government gave him the prestigious office of Keeper of the Crown Jewels—"sweet revenge on those who had driven him out of Canada like a thief."[25]

Oscar Pelletier, Militia Officer

Oscar Pelletier was a typical Non-Permanent Militia officer. His father, Charles Pelletier, a Liberal senator who had been minister of agriculture in the Alexander Mackenzie government (1873–79), was opposed to his son's taking up a military career. All the same, Oscar enlisted in the Queen's Own Canadian Hussars in Quebec City, before transferring to the 9th Battalion of Carabineers, later the Quebec Regiment of Voltigeurs. In June 1884, after some three years' service, Pelletier registered at the St Jean d'Iberville infantry school to obtain certificates confirming his rank as an officer. He was surrounded by generally bilingual officers of Canadian and British stock; D'Odet d'Orsonnens was commander of the school.

At the outbreak of hostilities in the North-West, Pelletier was a lieutenant on an artillery course at RMC Kingston, where B Battery, a permanent unit, was stationed at the time. Eager to enter the field of battle, he was determined to get a transfer to that unit. He approached his uncle, P.-B. Casgrain, the Liberal MP for L'Islet whose family connections included the Conservative minister of militia and defence, Adolphe Caron. The B Battery commander had no choice but to accept Pelletier, whom he attached to one of the two field artillery troops. When the force formed up in three columns, Pelletier and his artillerymen were placed with Otter. In the battle of Cut Knife Hill, a bullet passed right through Pelletier's left thigh, without, however, breaking the bone. While serving in the B Battery ambulance service, Pelletier became acquainted with Gaston Labat, a Frenchman who had come to Canada after the Franco-Prussian War; his is a name that will appear again in these pages.

When the units were being repatriated, Pelletier was in Winnipeg with the medical convoy. Now on the mend, he was able to walk. During his travels, he ran into some members of the 9th Battalion, his original unit. It suddenly occurred to him that it would be nice to go back to Quebec City as a hero instead of to Kingston with an unfamiliar unit. Pelletier's leave to visit the 9th was good for only two hours—a minor problem that was once again quickly resolved. It was laid before the regiment's commanding officer, Lieutenant-Colonel Guillaume Amyot, who, like eight other colonels on that campaign, was a Member of Parliament. Amyot, who represented the Quebec riding of Bellechasse and was a personal friend of the minister, immediately telegraphed Caron, who, according to Pelletier, replied without delay: "Authorization to detach us from the convoy that brought us here was communicated to Major Short."[26]

One may wonder what authority a commander could exercise over his unit when a capricious minister had the power to impose or remove men. Poor Middleton's command included nine MP-colonels and one MP-private who were in the habit of communicating directly with Caron.

The 9th Battalion in the North-West Campaign

A number of battalions have testified in one way or another about their role in the North-West Campaign. The 9th of Quebec City was typical of these battalions. The unit was commanded by Guillaume Amyot. His entourage consisted mainly of French Canadians whose compatriots were opposed to the fight against Louis Riel's Métis.

The battalion's mobilization order was received on 31 March. By 2 April its 236 men, including 28 officers, were ready to leave. Yet between 13 and 25 March the 9th Battalion had trained with 22 officers and 336 men. Political views and educa-

tional and job commitments had deprived the battalion of approximately one hundred militiamen who would not be accompanying it on its way west. Its officer ranks, however, were swelled by the arrival of the scions of the aristocracy: At the last minute, they had been joined by the sons of Judge Adolphe Routhier, MLA Joseph Sheyn and MP P.-B. Casgrain, and by two sons of Senator Jean-Baptiste Fiset.[27]

In a campaign journal he later published, Private Georges Beauregard alluded to the ambiguous situation of the French-Canadian soldier: "The government has decided to disrupt our quiet little lives to set us against Indians and Métis: It has its reasons, which have nothing to do with us, since we are not involved in politics and do not question the orders of the military authorities."[28] Meanwhile, the volunteers were reminded by a number of their acquaintances that they were going to "make war on our brothers, Frenchmen like ourselves."[29] This was not a very happy prospect, and the formation of a committee to help volunteers' families, itself made up of volunteers, served as a reminder that the army did very little for the men it sent into combat.

The trip west gave the men lots to think about. They were packed into rail cars that were sometimes open to the elements. Where the railway was unfinished, they were transferred into wagons; and north of Lake Superior they suffered the miseries of a spring that announced its arrival with heat, cold and frequent blizzards.[30] The 9th had not even seen combat when two of its pri-

vates succumbed to the hardships of the journey. One of them left a wife and several children whom the aid committee had to help before the government pension was paid, and even after the paltry sum was paid.

The 9th Battalion's basic assignment was to secure the lines of communication. Split up into small squads, the men were scattered between Calgary and Fort McLeod, their only shelter a tent that slept six. The battalion's 3rd and 4th companies took up positions at Gleichen, Crowfoot and Langdon along the Canadian Pacific Railway line. In this area they would have many encounters with Indians, whose abject misery they longed to ease. This humanitarian attitude prompted the historian Jean-Yves Gravel to compare, quite correctly, the role of this unit with the role that Canadian soldiers have been playing for more than 50 years as peacekeepers to the

Photo Journalists

An officer in the Canadian artillery, James Peters was also an adept amateur photographer. Mobilized for the North-West Campaign, he lugged his unwieldy camera nearly 9,000 kilometres and took 120 photographs. The 63 that turned out "are generally recognized as being the very first photographs ever taken on a battlefield."[32]

Peters had a talented imitator in the person of Henry Woodside. While serving as an officer in the Non-Permanent Militia, Woodside was primarily a journalist. However, the experience he acquired in 1885 enabled him, six years later, to become an amateur photographer. We are indebted to Woodside for numerous shots of the militia on duty in Canada and of units departing for the Yukon and South Africa.

These two men, trail-blazers in an occupation they pursued on their own initiative and without pay, led the way for the many photographers and cameramen who would record Canada's military operations in the 20th century.

As early as the 1880s, a few volunteer militia regiments had auxiliary companies consisting of women like these members of the Ladies School Cadet Corps in St Catharines, Ontario, in 1891. Since they were unofficial, there is very little information about these formations.
(Ontario Archives, Toronto, S-4821)

Cadet Guy Thorold of Guelph High School, circa 1882. The Scottish uniform includes a black velvet tunic with white piping and a Royal Stewart tartan kilt. The long Peabody rifle is from militia surplus issued to cadet corps.
(D. Blyth Collection, Guelph, Ontario)

Members of the "Amazons" Company of the 62nd Saint John Fusiliers gather around their instructor in Saint John, New Brunswick, in 1901.
(Private collection)

world.[31] Not surprisingly, after a month-long journey to reach Calgary and two months spent at isolated posts, not one 9th Battalion volunteer wanted to remain in garrison. The men in most of the other units were just as eager to return home.

The Yukon Campaign

The discovery, in the late 19th century, of gold-bearing ore in the Yukon forced the Canadian government to take steps to maintain peace in this part of its territory, where they knew the situation could easily deteriorate. The wild scramble for gold in Oregon around 1840 had not been forgotten. Already present in the Yukon, the North-West Mounted Police might quickly have been swamped, especially if the greed of the American expansionists prompted them to raise questions of territorial jurisdiction. In the minds of Canada's political leaders, territorial protection had to be based on military strength. A unit of volunteers recruited from the permanent force was therefore assembled in Vancouver.

On 14 May 1898 this contingent of more than 200, nearly one quarter of the total permanent force, left Vancouver for the Yukon. The group was joined by six women—a journalist, four nurses from the Victorian Order of Nurses and the wife of a Mounted Police officer on duty in the Yukon. They travelled by boat and on foot along badly marked tracks and paths over ground which, even in summer, was frozen to 50 centimetres beneath the surface. Escorted by clouds of mosquitoes, the unit reached Fort Selkirk on 11 September. A few weeks later one of its contingents was sent to Dawson.

The following spring, with the gold rush over and the Yukon population dwindling, half of the men took the road back to Vancouver. In 1900 all but one volunteer, kept there until 1901 to give evidence in a trial, had returned home. They were replaced the next year by a Non-Permanent Militia unit raised in Dawson City.

Thanks to this energetic action and despite a few minor hitches, the Yukon gold rush was very orderly. In particular, it helped to reinforce the principle of Canadian sovereignty over a region virtually unexplored before the discovery of gold. For example, leaving from Vancouver, the expedition used an access route which, though difficult and much slower than the route through Alaska, had the advantage of being almost entirely on Canadian soil. For the return journey they would simplify things by using U.S. territory: 10 days from Fort Selkirk to Vancouver instead of the four months on the way out.

On this occasion, for the first time—and the situation would not be repeated for half a century—Canadian troops ventured and wintered north of the 60th Parallel, where a third of Canada's continental area happens to lie.[33]

Among the members of the expedition were Captain Harry Burstall, who would become a major-general and army chief of staff, and Superintendent S.B. Steele of the Mounted Police, who had been on the North-West campaign and whose career would later take him to South Africa.

Assistance to the Civil Authorities

Between 1867 and 1898 the militia acted on 67 occasions to support the civil authorities and twice in penitentiaries. Called on by local authorities, soldiers responded with varying degrees of good grace, since each had to abandon his occupation and renounce his wages for an indeterminate period of time. What is more, up until

One of the many cadet corps established in schools during the latter years of the 19th century included these students from Quebec City High School. (Photo taken on 11 June 1890, NAC, PA-99974)

The Canadian militia in 1898. (Private collection)

Cadet corps of the Papal Zouaves from Sacré-Coeur Parish, Chicoutimi. In French Canada, cadets were often attached to the Canadian Papal Zouaves. It was felt at the time that this totally Francophone religious paramilitary organization was more attuned to the French-Canadian community than the Anglophone-commanded militia.
(Lemay photo, 1924. Archives nationales du Québec à Chicoutimi, 68810)

1879, when the Canadian government began to fully and quickly reimburse communities for their costs, citizen soldiers knew that some of the towns requesting assistance would be unable to pay them. So long as the police were not formed into solidly structured forces, militiamen would be called in to restore order, and they would be uneasy in the role.

The annual militia report for 1878 listed the difficulties connected with these ad hoc interventions: "Unrest often occurs every year. The militia lack the necessary knowledge, the police are too weak, militiamen are forced to fight people from the same part of the country: a permanent military force is required."

The practice of casting votes by a show of hands caused 13 actual or apprehended riots between 1867 and 1883, 11 of them in Quebec. Amendments to election laws would put an end to militia activity in this area. However, quarrels over language, religion and education, along with annual Orange parades, also served as pretexts for calling in the troops. The hardest events to control were strikes. Raised on the spot, the control party was often made up of men living near the site of the demonstration or related to the people they had to fight. As a rule, militiamen were called in after an initial violent outbreak against persons or property. In over 90 percent of cases their presence alone prevented things from getting out of hand. The lack of real police forces created the need for these militia actions.[34]

The Nile Expedition, 1884–85

The ability of the Canadian armed forces to function outside their national territory was tested in 1884, when Major-General C.G. Gordon was under siege in Khartoum on the Upper Nile in Sudan.

Britain organized a relief expedition under General Garnet Wolseley. In 1881 and 1882, as army chief of staff, he had fiercely opposed the old plan to build a tunnel under the English Channel that was being strongly revived by French and British businessmen. This position did nothing to tarnish his reputation as the conqueror of Ter-el-Kebir or his title of Lord Wolseley of Cairo. In Canada, Wolseley had led the Red River campaign, and he had positive memories of the Canadians who enabled the British troops to take on supplies during that 1870 march and conflict.

From its beginnings and for the year following, the Sudan affair had reverberations in Canada, where colonels declared their readiness to raise their militia regiments to fight in the distant Upper Nile. Cautiously, the British government took the Canadian pulse regarding the willingness of the volunteers, but then advised that the territory of New South Wales in southern Australia had offered a contingent. Thus Prime Minister John A. Macdonald could easily resist the few enthusiasts eager to go to Khartoum, even if he thereby disappointed the British and offended some of his countrymen.

In 1884, however, Macdonald agreed that the British could recruit a few hundred Canadian "voyageurs" to help with the logistics of the combatants going up the Nile. In other words, Wolseley, who had been favourably impressed by his Canadians, intended to have them play a role similar to the one they played in 1870, though on a foreign stage, in an alien climate and for a cause that had nothing whatsoever to do with them.

Nearly 400 Canadians, a great many of whom knew nothing whatsoever of what awaited them, would sign six-month contracts: The age of the voyageur was almost past. The volunteers going to Africa would wear no uniforms, bear no arms and take no part in the rare skirmishes engaged in by Wolseley. Gordon and his troops would be wiped out even before their rescuers reached them.

These volunteers included several notable personalities. One of these was Lieutenant-Colonel Fred C. Denison, Wolseley's aide-de-camp in 1869–70. The Denison family has participated in Canadian military activities since the mid-19th century, with some members still in the Reserves today. Another was Captain A. Bouchard, a Catholic chaplain who had been in Khartoum as a missionary and was prepared to return as an interpreter and to watch over the souls of the Canadian soldiers. Hospital sergeant Gaston P. Labat, who would be on board *Saskatchewan* a year later with a brother of Fred C. Denison, accompanied Major T.L.H. Neilson, surgeon-major of B Battery and also a Red River veteran.

The 386 Canadians left Halifax on 14 September 1884. Fifteen days later they landed at Gibraltar. One of the men had succumbed to sickness at sea. The group reached Alexandria on 7 October and then, travelling by train and steamer, passed Luxor and Aswan, to finally reach the first cataract. By November 1884 they were at work. On 1 December the expedition was halfway between Khartoum and Alexandria. At each of the 14 cataracts, which extend over 15 kilometres and form 40-metre drops, the Canadian voyageurs awaited the arrival of British troops to help them over these obstacles. The Iroquois Louis Capitaine and a few others would lose their lives in these tests of courage and endurance.

The voyageurs were offered a new six-month engagement beginning on 6 March 1885, but only 86 men, commanded by Denison, accepted. For the others, the mission ended before it had really begun. On 10 January, shortly after their contracts expired, most of the Canadians began the journey home. They headed for Alexandria, where in February they would begin the embarkation.

This experience enabled the Canadian volunteers to observe what other participants in British wars would also notice: The British treated their officers and men very differently. Like the British privates, the Canadian privates were less well-fed than the officers. Reacting to this injustice, one Canadian dared to open a tin of cheese, for which he was sentenced to three months' imprisonment. However, the Canadian claimed that a British soldier committing the same offence could have been handed down five years' hard labour.[35]

Writing to the Governor General of Canada in April 1885, Wolseley congratulated the Canadians. In August the British Commons and House of Lords passed a vote of thanks for their services. All the volunteers would receive the special British medal commemorating this expedition. Those who renewed their contracts would add the bar for the battle of Kirbekan, even though they had not participated in the fighting.

Venezuela and Canada

Canada's membership in the British Empire could have further repercussions. So it was with the dispute that arose in 1895 between Britain and Venezuela over the boundaries of British Guiana. President Grover Cleveland of the United States seemed inclined to come to Venezuela's defence against Britain. Pushed to the limit in this matter, Britain might well have decided to go to war against the Venezuelans. For Canada, the prospect meant potential confrontation with the United States, which in turn could possibly be tempted to invade this corner of the British Empire.

The Canadian government reacted immediately to this possibility by investing $3 million in rearmament. The single-shot Snider rifles were replaced by 40,000 Lee Enfield .303 repeaters. A few modern machine guns were purchased and artillery was refurbished.

Although this crisis had no violent outcome, it did prompt the authorities to act out of panic. A poor advisor in the area of crisis management and administration of a country's military affairs, panic would be heard from on several more occasions.

In 1897, for the first time since 1876, an annual training period was made compulsory for all volunteer regiments. The year 1896 had seen the publication of the first mobilization plans for the Canadian forces in the event of war. The militia was organized into divisions, brigades, detachments and so on, and each unit was assigned a mobilization centre. The composition of units was kept secret and headquarters had to be designated at the last possible moment, which easily could have caused confusion in an emergency. This initial plan, despite its foibles, is notable for the mere fact of its existence.

Chapter III

THE ISSUES CRYSTALLIZE

Canadians in South Africa

Less than 15 years after the North-West Rebellion a crisis erupting on the fringes of the southern hemisphere brought new upheaval in relations between Canadians of British and French origin.

Britain had long been at daggers drawn with the Boer republics of Transvaal and Orange Free State, located in present-day South Africa. In late summer 1899 all of Britain's dominions except Canada proclaimed their readiness to lend a hand to the mother country. In Canada a coalition formed in part by the ethnic British population, working through their Members of Parliament and the small but influential Imperial Federation League, demanded that the Laurier government take a stand. The coalition was dominated by the voice of Governor General Lord Minto, who gave Laurier to understand that Canada's support might prompt London, in turn, to support the Canadian viewpoint in discussions over the boundary between Canada and Alaska (this question would not reach arbitration until 1904, with an outcome somewhat unfavourable to Canada).

Despite the tensions and pressures that this matter generated within his party, Prime Minister Laurier played for time, fearing a crisis

A member of the Royal Canadian Navy in 1910–20.
The Canadian naval uniform was identical to that of the
Royal Navy except that, instead of "HMS," the ribbon on the Canadian headdress read
"HMCS," for "His Majesty's Canadian Ship."
(Re-creation by Ronald B. Volstad, DND)

like that which had erupted after the hanging of Louis Riel. While he temporized, a confrontation between Britain and the Boer republics became seemingly unavoidable. Major-General Edward H. Hutton, General Officer Commanding of the Canadian forces, used all his influence to secure a firm Canadian commitment at Britain's side. On 5 September he sent a "private and confidential" letter to Oscar Pelletier of the Permanent Militia assuring him that in the probable event of Canada's offering troops to Britain he would suggest that Pelletier command one of the infantry battalions Hutton intended to form. In fact he let it be understood that the Canadian announcement would follow in two days. Yet Laurier continued to procrastinate: To get him into a corner, Hutton devised a stratagem that would cost him his job.

On 3 October Hutton had the *Canadian Military Gazette* publish mobilization plans for potential contingents for the South African conflict. That same day, the British press published an announcement by Colonial Secretary Joseph Chamberlain to the effect that Canada's commitment had already been studied: Britain would assume control of the troops when they landed in South Africa and would be responsible for paying them. Laurier was still eluding journalists' questions. His unease grew when, on 11 October, both Boer republics declared war on Britain. Two days later, acting against his personal convictions, Laurier gave in—though in his own way. Although the proposal had not been debated in Parliament, the government announced its readiness to equip a maximum of 1,000 volunteers and pay the costs of transporting them to South Africa. Thus Laurier would not have to answer such questions as: Is this a just war? Is Britain really threatened?

The order to mobilize these volunteers came on the 14th. Since there would initially be only one battalion, to be commanded by Colonel William Otter, Pelletier would go as a company commander. Here again, Canada took an idiosyncratic approach. Britain would have preferred to be sent companies it could use as it thought best. Instead, Canada formed the 2nd (Special Service) Battalion of the Royal Canadian Regiment to recruit volunteers from the Permanent and Non-Permanent Militia along with men who had never had anything to do with the army, in any capacity. These soldiers would be paid on an equal basis with the members of the Permanent Militia, a higher rate than the British troops were paid.

On 20 October the six companies were designated: Company A would be recruited in British Columbia and Manitoba, B in London, C in Toronto, D in Ottawa and Kingston, E in Montreal, F in Quebec City, G in New Brunswick and Prince Edward Island, and H in Nova Scotia.

Those opposing the prime minister's decision, most of them French Canadians, were quick to voice their disagreement and rally round the journalist Henri Bourassa. Bourassa's strong personality and ideas enabled him to publicly criticize Laurier—whom he had always supported—for giving in. He even predicted this was nothing compared to what would follow. If Canada could send 1,000 men to South Africa, how many would it be sending had the war been in Europe? Bourassa saw British imperialism as "the participation of the colonies in England's wars."[36]

Taking up Bourassa's cause in 1903, the English Canadian Goldwin Smith would recall that the purpose of the South African war had been to secure equality for the white, mainly British, *uitlanders*, to whom

Private Alexander Sinclair of the Royal Canadian Regiment's 2nd Service Battalion
in South Africa, circa 1902.
(Museum of the 48th Highlanders of Canada, Toronto)

the Boers were refusing the right to vote. "This is a strange doctrine in an Empire with a population composed five sixths of coloured races and which allies itself with Japan."[37] On 29 April 1910, when another large project with imperialist repercussions, the Naval Bill, was being discussed, Senator Raoul Dandurand would recall that the official cause of the war in Africa, namely redress for wrongs meted out to English residents, was not the real one: *"I frankly confess that this dispute aroused no enthusiasm in me, but we had nothing to say before the affair, and when war was declared the time for discussion had passed."*[38]

Despite the powerful opposition movement among French Canadians, Wilfrid Laurier's Liberals were re-elected on 7 November 1900 with strong support from Quebec voters. Was this approval of imperialist policy? In another context the French Canadians might have voiced disapproval, but Laurier's nuanced response struck them as preferable to that of Charles Tupper's Conservatives, pledged as the Tories were to support British policies. In the end, the opposition to this war benefited the Liberals, but now they would have to reckon with Henri Bourassa and the Quebec nationalists elected to Parliament, for they would be continuing their campaign against participation in the war, in however watered-down a form.

In Quebec, and especially in Montreal, the situation rekindled ethnic tensions. On 1 and 2 March 1900 a group of Anglophones, including a number of McGill University students, marched in celebration of the Canadian victory at Paardeberg. They smashed the windows of the French-language newspapers *La Presse, La Patrie* and *Le Journal* and wrecked some of Université Laval's Montreal offices. Although these tensions subsided after the 1900 federal election, they nonetheless would remain latent until the First World War.

Canadians in Battle

Whether permanent or non-permanent, Canadian militiamen were prepared for neither war nor the South African climate. Between 12 and 31 October the 2nd RCR Battalion had to be recruited, clothed, trained (though how little!), organized and shipped out. Despite a multitude of problems including almost universal amateurism, by virtue of energy and determination the bare minimum was amassed in under three weeks. As for organization, as soon as the men boarded the aptly named *Sardinia* on 31 October it became obvious the term did apply. Alterations were to have enabled this cargo vessel to accommodate and transport nearly 700 people. The 1,039 volunteers would be crammed in with the crew and the contingent's nurses, horses and dogs. The equipment, which had not even been inventoried, was stuffed just anywhere.

The voyage took them over an often rough sea that direly tested the endurance of Oscar Pelletier, even with his background as a sailor. For those who had never seen the sea, it was a nightmare.

The Canadians began training as soon as they reached Cape Town on 29 November. By mid-February 1900 they were ready for action. As hostilities began, the Boers had cornered the English in three towns— Kimberley, Mafeking and Ladysmith. In late February the British attempted to break open the bolt of Kimberley in the Paardeberg sector. There, the Canadians would experience their first important overseas battle as part of the 19th Brigade of Major-General Horace Smith-Dorrien, who in 1915 would direct the operations of the 1st Canadian Division in Belgium.

On 13 February the British army had begun a big, sweeping movement that rapidly led to the encirclement of the Boers under Cronje. On the 18th an incautious Canadian charge across deserted ground was stopped short by enemy fire after less than 200 metres. On the 26th the Canadians relieved an English battalion in a line of trenches located some 600 metres from the Boer positions. On 27 February they were ordered to advance. As they did so, they were seriously battered. Four of the six companies fell back, while the other two hung on to their new positions. Demoralized after several days, their opponents had no choice but to surrender to the Canadians, which they did in early morning. At Majuba 19 years earlier to the day, the British had met defeat at the hands of the Boers, the consequences of which included the creation of the Orange Free State and Transvaal republics north of the Cape.

The Canadians were congratulated for this feat even though it had required neither strategy nor prior organization, nor even participation by a large number of men. The exploit assumed mythic proportions that are still maintained a century later.[39]

The members of the initial contingent were rarely at the heart of the action, even when they participated in taking Bloemfontein, capital of the Orange Free State, and in skirmishes in the course of which Otter was wounded. Their one-year contract had nearly expired when, to please his imperial masters, their leader gave them to understand that the Canadians were prepared to stay until the war came to an end. The men had not been consulted about this, and when they heard the rumour they bridled. Redoubling his efforts, Otter secured the participation of 261 Canadians, most of whom had been in the permanent force before volunteering for South Africa or were

members of recently arrived reinforcement troops whose contracts had barely begun. Few were satisfied with their fate or with Otter, yet several of his officers offered to stay. Oscar Pelletier, wounded once again, boarded SS *Idaho* on 1 October 1900 at the head of over 400 men returning to Canada 11 months after they had left it. On 2 November they landed in Halifax amid euphoria. The 3rd RCR Battalion, which had been raised in Halifax to replace the British soldiers the mother country had decided to use in South Africa (another component of Canadian support for Britain), welcomed the 2nd Battalion, which paraded with its Halifax H company in the lead.

The remainder of the first contingent left South Africa on 7 November. After 22 days at sea en route to Britain, the men were entitled to 10 days' leave and were received by Queen Victoria. The volunteers then re-embarked to cross the Atlantic to Halifax, arriving there on 23 December 1900. On the 31st, the 2nd Battalion RCR was disbanded.

The capture of the capitals of the two Boer republics did not end the fighting. At this stage a complete British victory was more or less assured, though a number of Boers did not see things that way. The ones who kept fighting were viewed as rebels, not soldiers. All the same, their many attacks on the long, vulnerable British lines of communication provided the Canadians with a number of opportunities to distinguish themselves.

Canada's military commitments were no longer limited to a company or a few reinforcements: On 2 November 1899 Canada placed a second contingent at Britain's disposal. On 16 December, after reversals at Stormberg, Magersfontein and Colenso, the British accepted the offer. This time trained volunteers were used, and in contrast to the first contingent, which had been heavy and not very mobile, this one would be characterized by its mobility and striking force. A brigade of field artillery 539 strong was formed under the command of Lieutenant-Colonel C.W. Drury. Two battalions of mounted riflemen were also formed, each with a strength of 371 officers and men. The first of these, later to become the Royal Canadian Dragoons (today an armoured regiment), was led by Lieutenant-Colonel François Lessard. The second was led by Lieutenant-Colonel L.W. Herchmer. Conditions for payment of wages and provision of equipment were the same as those for the 2nd Battalion RCR.

The artillery brigade was divided into C, D and E batteries, which moved around to support various units, some of them Canadian. Of the three batteries, C, commanded by Major J.A. Hudon, saw the most action, hunting down small groups of vindictive Boers, especially in the northwestern Transvaal. On 16 May 1900, after a long and difficult approach, C Battery opened the road to Mafeking. When it left the Cape for Canada on 13 December 1900 its area of operation was still unpacified. "Enemy" homes and livestock had indeed been destroyed—though rarely by Canadians, it must be admitted—but the Boers were still putting up resistance.

D Battery would find itself in the middle of a big skirmish near Leliefontein. It was in the rear guard, accompanied by a handful of Royal Canadian Dragoons, when 200 mounted Boers attacked. The Canadians held their assailants at bay by fighting courageously with good co-ordination and flexibility. The British infantry fled, leaving them alone in inferior numbers, but this did not stop the Canadians from using the resources of the terrain to beat the Boers at

their own game. Even though this battleground lacked the strategic or symbolic value of Paardeberg, the Canadians saved their guns and baggage while preventing loss of life among the British. The action would earn three Dragoons the Victoria Cross: Lieutenants H.Z.C. Cockburn and R.E.W. Turner and Sergeant E.J. Holland. Other Canadians would be decorated for this feat of arms. For some time during the First World War, Turner would have occasion to command one of the Canadian divisions in battle.

D Battery, commanded by Major W.G. Hurdman, was the first to see action. It would campaign for 41 days and spend the rest of the year holding outposts, guarding railways and moving around. Its toughest enemy would be enteric fever. E Battery would be doomed to a similar fate in this war of skirmishes.[40]

As for the two mounted rifle battalions, they covered great distances on policing-type missions that struck them as futile. In April 1900 both of these units were incorporated into the 1st Mounted Rifles Division commanded by Major-General Hutton. After pointing out the absurdity of relying on the combat effectiveness of militiamen who lacked training, Hutton had left his position as Major-General of the Canadian Militia. He was accordingly cautious about bringing Canadians into his force. The Canadian mounted troops took part in the advance on Pretoria. Afterwards, they were in almost constant contact with Boer patrols during operations in the eastern Transvaal.

All the Canadians present in South Africa in the spring of 1900 were still far from representative of the total human effort Canada contributed to that war. Other units would go there, some of which were not raised by the Canadian government. At his own expense, Lord Strathcona and Mount Royal, Canada's High Commissioner to London, recruited a regiment of mounted rifles comprising 537 officers and men in Manitoba, British Columbia and the Northwest Territories. Lord Strathcona's Horse would be placed under the command of Lieutenant-Colonel S.B. Steele of the Mounted Police. Strathcona himself paid to recruit, organize, equip and transport the men to South Africa. He also made up the difference between the British soldiers' pay assumed by Britain and the rate Canada paid its professionals. In South Africa the unit went as far as Mozambique to cut Boer communications extending to Delagoa Bay, though without success. It then joined Sir Redvers Buller's campaign in Natal. In a skirmish under heavy fire, Sergeant A.H.L. Richardson daringly risked exposure as he retraced his steps to bring out his wounded. This act of heroism earned him the Victoria Cross.

To adjust to the war of raids which typified the fighting in South Africa towards the second half of the year 1900, the British forces frequently relied on small groups of mounted men. Every time Britain requested the recruitment of mounted police to maintain peace in various areas of the country, Canada acquiesced. More than 1,000 men were thus recruited for a three-year term and organized into 12 platoons of South African police. Some of these recruits had been in earlier Canadian contingents and returned to service for Britain when their initial contracts expired. Upon recruitment, in any case, they were all in excellent physical condition and knew how to ride a horse.

Their recruitment did not please everyone. The anti-imperialists had not altered their views, and a number of imperialists were incensed to note that the emerging Canadian identity was completely eclipsed

as soon as the policemen were signed up. Nonetheless the success of these mounted troops encouraged other Canadians to offer their services at the front lines. Lieutenant-Colonel A. Denison and Major William Hamilton Merritt both proposed the formation of fresh mounted contingents for South Africa. The War Office greeted these plans with enthusiasm, subject to the usual conditions. At length, Merritt's scheme of 29 December 1900 was accepted by the British. Assuming that he had the support of his own government, Merritt began assembling his unit. He had not reckoned, however, on the scars the police affair had left on the minds of the politicians, who prevented him from going any further until a clear policy had been agreed on for Canadian participation. On 13 May 1901 a set of conditions was finally produced, which can be summarized as follows: All requests for the recruitment of Canadians would be addressed to the government of Canada; only the minister of militia and defence could raise troops and designate their officers, even for temporary units of the type fighting in South Africa; as a rule, these officers would be chosen from the permanent force; it was prohibited for anyone to recruit police in Canada.[41]

To prove it was serious, Canada immediately offered to recruit a new contingent following these criteria. It created the Canadian Yeomanry, a unit of slightly under 600 men claimed by Britain on 25 November 1901 that would later be named the 2nd Regiment, Canadian Mounted Rifles. As was customary, on arrival in South Africa it would cease to be accountable to any Canadian authority.

The 2nd Regiment Canadian Mounted Rifles served for three months, during which time it earned distinction for the quality of its reconnaissance work. It was assigned to the southwestern Transvaal as part of the final drive to capture the country as far as Vrybierg in the west. Four of its soldiers distinguished themselves at Honing Sprint by holding 50 Boers at bay, but before they could be relieved two were killed and the other two wounded. All four, wrote General Hutton, who was sparing of his compliments to Canadians, "were from Pincher Creek...at the foot of the Rockies, a region well known for the excellence, daring and boldness of its troopers."[42]

Let us touch on a few other aspects of the Canadian contribution. Some 2,000 men in four mounted rifle regiments reached South Africa between 31 May 1902 and the end of hostilities. Theirs would be a return journey without a fight. As well, the 64 men of Canada's field hospital unit would serve various British troops. The Canadians would also provide 16 nurses, and this commitment in South Africa was an appropriate moment to establish the Canadian Nursing Service. Canada's effort extended to sending five postal clerks, 23 artificers (cobblers and blacksmiths, for example) and some 300 Canadians who joined the British irregulars either directly or at the end of their contracts with the units that had brought them to South Africa.

More than a hundred other Canadians served with the regular British troops, not to mention the hundred or so graduates of the Royal Military College (RMC) who had received British commissions. These men included Lieutenant-Colonel Édouard Percy Girouard and Major H.G. Joly de Lotbinière of the Royal Engineers and Philippe-Henri-Duperron Casgrain, Deputy Adjutant-General at British army headquarters in South Africa. Some of them, like Howard's Canadian Scouts, have passed into legend. Howard was an American who in 1885 had moved to

Canada and been taught how to operate the Gatling machine gun. Now a British subject, he volunteered for South Africa. When his contract expired he offered a unit of some 125 adventurers of Canadian origin recruited among men whose contracts were ending. Accepted by the British, these Scouts would dare all, sometimes suffering heavy losses.

Summing Up

Rudyard Kipling and J.H.M. Abbott (in *Tommy Cornstalk*) would portray the Canadian as the champion pillager and horse thief. (Among themselves, Canadians called this a sense of initiative, an especially useful gift against the vagaries of the British logistics and remount system.) For their part, British military leaders from Redvers Buller to Smith-Dorrien had only good things to say about the valiant Canadians. Hutton, who did not easily change his mind, was more reserved. In his opinion, the Canadians' great successes were due to gallant leaders (such as himself, no doubt) and previous service with professional British cavalry units. However, he added, it was impossible for militia troopers to rise to the level of regular troops.[43]

Canadians had their own opinions of their British big brothers. Lieutenant-Colonel S.B. Steele, for example, condemned their lack of initiative: Unless ordered, the British did not budge and thus missed out on some excellent opportunities. As his stay wore on, Steele grew more critical of the British generals, their tactics and especially some of their orders, which created problems and needlessly exhausted the men. In one case, for example, they had set up bivouacs right under the guns of small groups of Boers, who soon ringed the British campfires with shells. Only then was

Cavalryman from one of the six
Canadian Mounted Rifles regiments sent to
South Africa in 1900–02. All of them wore
the khaki uniform and wide-brimmed stetson.
(Re-creation by Ronald B. Volstad, DND)

The Royal Canadian Regiment in the
Battle of Paardeberg, 27 February 1900.
(R. Caton Woodville, DND, ZK-1938-1)

Cavalryman from Lord Strathcona's Horse photographed in Ottawa in
February 1900. Raised at the expense of Canadian Pacific magnate
Donald Smith, this cavalry regiment earned distinction during its brief service
in South Africa from April 1900 to January 1901. Sergeant A.H.L. Richardson
earned the Victoria Cross for heroism on 15 July 1900, becoming the first
of many Canadians to be awarded the British Empire's most prestigious
decoration. Lord Strathcona's Horse was disbanded in Canada in March 1901.
In South Africa, this dark-blue uniform was exchanged for khaki and
the wide-brimmed stetson. (Private collection)

it decided to shift camp. The British would also routinely advance without first securing the heights, which would immediately be seized by the enemy. A pointless battle would then be needed to dislodge them.[44] The records teem with examples of this type. In a situation where imperial troops were spending the night in a depression, Sam Hughes was roused by a sentry who had spotted Boers hurtling down the slope with their sights on the British soldiery. Hughes and his group, who were on the heights and passed undetected, set a trap for the Boers as they escaped into the night. The future defence minister of Canada would not be sparing in his comments on this situation and never forgave the British for an even bigger mistake: They failed to decorate him for his feat.[45]

Other aspects of imperial co-operation were destabilizing for various Canadians. Since troops were often split up into small groups, some of them were subject to British disciplinary measures without a Canadian officer being notified. For example, Lieutenant-Colonel Lessard would learn that two of his men were being court-martialled on a charge of attempting to resell to the Boers weapons they had seized from them. When Lessard got wind of this, he also learned that his two privates had been lured into their crime by a British sergeant.[46]

We can draw the following conclusions about Canada's participation in the South African War: It fostered sociopolitical division at home; the men who took part in it returned home with a stronger sense of being Canadian; and the reputation of British military professionalism, so vaunted by British officers serving in Canada, had been seriously eroded. The clear difference between Canadians and British did not escape the few thousand men and women who went to South Africa. Food and water, distributed in accordance with English procedures, were often lacking. Similarly, in British military hospitals the sick and wounded were cared for in terms of rank more than need. The Canadian response to these observations would not necessarily have only positive effects, however, as the "national" choices made afterwards would be costly.

In sociological terms, the South African war saw a growing tendency for Canadian soldiers to serve under their own officers, even in the field—a development that cemented the relationship between these officers and the politicians in Ottawa and witnessed the first halting steps in the formation of a national chain of command linking Canadian soldiers with their own government. But that process was far from complete, and would not be absolutely so for many years. Indeed the problems created by divided loyalties and parallel chains of command would persist until the demise, finally, of the neo-colonial system under which Canada's military developed during the first half of the 20th century.

Therefore, contrary to what some have argued, imperial centralization did not altogether advance between 1899 and 1902. In many respects, Canadian nationalism was also stimulated by the experience. This does not mean that the debate between nationalists and imperialists was done with, however, especially since Bourassa's Nationalist League found its origins in that war.

More than 8,000 men and women, including members of the Halifax Battalion, participated directly in the Canadian war effort in South Africa. At least 270 of them died either in battle (89) or of illness (181), and 252 suffered slight or serious injuries such as the loss of a limb.[47] After the conflict, 16 widows, 24 orphans and 72 dependents

Cavalrymen of the Royal Canadian Dragoons on manoeuvres, 1906.
(Watercolour by Ernest Smythe, Anne S.K. Brown Military Collection, Brown University)

Cavalryman of the 19th Alberta Dragoons, Edmonton, circa 1912. Most of the volunteer cavalry regiments raised in the new Prairie Provinces at the turn of the 20th century wore broad-brimmed hats and tunics of red or dark-blue serge. Today, this dress is reminiscent of the Royal Canadian Mounted Police, but at the time it was seen as a militarized version of cowboy dress and worn by numerous Canadian soldiers.
(Re-creation by Ronald B. Volstad, DND)

of the departed requested contributions from the Patriotic Fund. This organization also received 712 requests from men whose incomes had been reduced because of injury or illness resulting from the war zone: 612 of them would receive monetary compensation. It must be emphasized that illness had been a more deadly enemy than the Boers ever were: Even if enteric fever was not always fatal, it weakened both body and soul.

On their return, most of these men bore memories of the horrors of combat, illness, fatigue, privation, monotony and discipline. Those men of the first contingent added to these memories the inexperience, confusion and disorganization of those early weeks when they had to take part on foot in a highly mobile campaign carelessly waged by the High Command. A long time afterwards, these troubling images would be replaced in their memories with those of adventure, endurance, courage and eternal friendship forged in the theatre of war. The four Victoria Crosses awarded to Canadians came as compensation for the efforts made by all.

Canadian Military Life After South Africa

The lessons learned in South Africa would be useful. In particular, the experience would revive Canadians' interest in their militia and, for some, pride in their army. Canada itself would turn away from its focus on territorial defence to a gradual involvement in world affairs.

There was nothing to indicate that the conflict might be a prelude to Canadian participation in a European war, but in some respects it had been just that, including the opposition between French and English Canadians. In 1914–18 the leaders, and their arguments and political tactics, would be similar to those of 1899–1902.

The main shortcomings noted in the Canadian militia during that war had to do with planning and supply, particularly the replacement in units of men lost or concluding their contracts. There were also the improvised medical services. Some of these matters were corrected with the establishment of, in 1899, the Militia Medical Service and, in 1904, the Canadian Army Medical Corps. In 1903 the Corps of Royal Canadian Engineers appeared under the aegis of a former RMC officer cadet, Lieutenant-Colonel Paul Weatherbe. That same year saw the appearance of the supply service, the Canadian Army Service Corps and the Guides and Signals Corps. The Headquarters Corps of Military Staff Clerks appeared in 1905 and the Canadian Pay Corps in 1906, though the Pay Corps was not officially operating until 1 July 1907, with 33 members of all ranks. In 1913 the Canadian Officer Training Corps had its beginnings in various universities across the country.

During this period, budgets increased, as did maximum volunteer militia recruitment and daily pay for camp. Extensive properties were purchased for training, including Petawawa, and exercises were resumed. In 1899 new rifles and guns were purchased. Training standards and officer promotion criteria were reviewed, while the army adopted more practical field uniforms.

After 1902, pressure built up to make the militia an increasingly Canadian arm of the federal government. As early as January 1900 the minister responsible, Frederick Borden, was able to gain approval for the idea of a corps, which he described as provisional, of over 1,000 men, an eight-company battalion to be called the 3rd (Special Service) Battalion Royal Canadian Regiment of Infantry, to relieve the British garrison in Halifax, which was needed in South Africa. In 1905 and 1906 the British garrisons in

Halifax and Esquimalt were permanently replaced by Canadian men. In this process, the ceiling for the permanent force was raised first from 1,000 to 2,000 men and then, before 1914, to 4,000 men. Again in 1904, the Militia Council was formed and command of the militia passed to Canadians. This signalled the end of the precedence of British officers over Canadians of similar rank. Canadians' confidence in their military talents and abilities would encourage them to choose a different rifle and uniforms somewhat distinct from those of the imperial troops.

Sir Eugène Fiset returns to service...

Marie-Joseph-Eugène Fiset was born at Rimouski on 15 March 1874. At the age of 16, while studying at the Rimouski seminary, he joined the ranks of the 89th Regiment, where his father was the surgeon. In 1894, having completed his classical studies, Fiset enrolled in the Université Laval faculty of medicine. The following year he rose to the rank of lieutenant, and in 1897 the Royal Infantry School awarded him a 1st Class certificate of qualification. Becoming a medical doctor in 1898, he replaced his father as surgeon to the 89th Regiment in May 1899. A few months later, however, he joined the 2nd Battalion of the Royal Canadian Regiment and embarked for South Africa with the rank of major.

In mid-January 1900, Fiset wrote to his father that he had grown accustomed to caring for the sick on the battlefield without worrying too much about the bullets whistling past him. "I still have not a single scratch and am beginning to think there is no danger," he wrote. This was not recklessness on his part, however, for he added: "I am working hard to do my duty."

On 18 February, Fiset distinguished himself in the Battle of Paardeberg when Captain H.M. Arnold collapsed with a bullet to the head. Three stretcher-bearers tried to get to him but were themselves wounded. Fiset then reached Arnold, bandaged him on the spot and brought him back behind the firing line. In later confrontations, Fiset often ran risks and earned the admiration of his comrades in arms, including a future minister of militia and defence, Sam Hughes, who viewed the "little French doctor" as something of a hero. Fiset was mentioned three times for his acts of gallantry in despatches to the minister, was awarded the Queen's Medal with four bars along with the Distinguished Service Order and rose to the rank of lieutenant-colonel.

When his tour of duty ended in late 1900, Fiset spent a year interning at London's Nose and Throat Hospital and Paris's Hôpital Saint-Antoine. Back in Canada, he practised for eight months in Rimouski before being appointed, on 1 November 1902, to the position of Adjutant in the Army Medical Service. Several months later, on 1 July 1903, he was promoted to colonel and made Director General of the Service. On 22 December 1906 he was named deputy minister of militia and defence.

When the First World War broke out, Fiset was promoted to the rank of major-general. During that conflict, over and above his usual duties Fiset attended to the military interests of various Allies. In recognition, England made him first a Companion and then a Knight of the Order of St Michael and St George, and France named him a Chevalier of the Legion of Honour. Fiset also became a Commander of the Belgian Crown and an officer first class of the Order of St Sava (Yugoslavia), while Czechoslovakia awarded him its Military Cross.

Fiset retired in 1923 after serving for 17 years under seven consecutive ministers; at the time, he was the only French Canadian to hold the position of deputy minister in Ottawa. The next year, Fiset embarked on a political career that would be almost as long as his administrative one: From 1924 to 1939 he sat in the Commons as Liberal MP for Rimouski.

On 30 December 1939, Fiset was installed as lieutenant governor of Quebec, taking as his motto "J'ai servi." In January 1941 and again in February 1942 he departed from protocol by opening the legislative session in his khaki major-general's uniform rather than the ceremonial garb of a lieutenant governor to demonstrate his support for a greater Canadian war effort. As lieutenant governor, following custom, he received a number of honours: honorary doctorates from Université Laval in 1940, Bishop's College in 1941 and Université de Montréal in 1943. He was made a Knight of the Order of St John of Jerusalem in 1941 and a Fellow of the Royal College of Physicians and Surgeons of Canada in 1943.

Sir Eugène Fiset left office on 1 October 1950 and died a short time later, on 8 June 1951, at Rivière-du-Loup. On 20 May 1902 he had married Zoé-Mary-Stella Taschereau and they had four daughters.

Eugène Fiset. (Private collection)

The Militia Council

In most countries of the world civil-military relations are a source of various problems. In Canada, especially after Confederation, these were exacerbated by the British presence in running the defence system, which brought Canadian and imperial interests into the mix. An example of this was Hutton's meddling in the political process to propel Canada into the South African war. During his time in Canada, Hutton had also suggested measures that would have reduced the powers of the deputy minister and Canadian civil authorities in general. His proposals, which would have enabled him to approach the minister directly without going through the deputy minister, were received all the more reservedly in that Hutton was often lacking in tact. He was known to choose the officers to be sent on courses and to involve himself in remount contracts and a number of areas where the minister and, traditionally, patronage reigned supreme. The General Officer Commanding had no hesitation in openly proclaiming the faults and weakness of the militia. In the face of a history of such conduct, his relations with Frederick Borden came to the breaking point over Hutton's plan to mobilize the militia for South Africa.

The fact that Laurier had more or less put Hutton's proposal into effect did nothing to ease the resentment of the General Officer Commanding, which the prime minister and Borden continued to nurse. When Hutton formed a commission to buy horses for the second contingent, Laurier insisted that he be recalled. Lord Minto would attempt to protect Hutton but soon bowed to Laurier's resolve. Hutton never seemed to comprehend—and he was not alone in this—that he was merely the advisor to his minister and the government on military affairs. He acted as if he were the commander of the militia, almost totally free of politics.

The demands voiced in the House to make the General Officer Commanding a Canadian position would become more numerous and insistent. From 1900 to 1902, British Major-General R.H. O'Grady Haly occupied that office with all the diplomacy called for in the circumstances and implemented some of the reforms Hutton had suggested. In 1902 he was replaced by Major-General the Earl of Dundonald, a cavalryman who had built his reputation in South Africa with gallantry, daring, joviality and modesty. Dundonald's friends had advised him to refuse a position that had become increasingly unhealthy for its incumbents, but in the end, despite some clear reservations, he accepted. In London he was coached about avoiding blunders. Upon reaching Canada, he took command of a defence system viewed as a necessary evil by the local politicians.

Dundonald's analysis of the situation led him to suggest a first-line force of 100,000 men, based in reality on a militia 40,000 to 50,000 strong ready to react to any threat to the national territory. The second line of defence would rest on the shoulders of 100,000 more men who could be rapidly recruited and trained by officers who were supernumerary in peacetime units; hence the purchase of large training camps like the one in Petawawa. Dundonald also wanted to rebalance the arms and set up the necessary support services, reforms he was permitted to implement. It was he who suggested the regional commands that still exist in the army despite changes and a 20-year eclipse. Naturally these serious labours came at a price. Acceptance of his plan would entail initial expenditures of $12 to $13 million and an annual $5-million investment for upkeep. The outcry in the press did not

Head nurse of the Canadian Nursing Service in winter uniform,
circa 1908. Canadian military nurses served in South Africa, and the
Nursing Service was formed in 1901. Initially dressed in khaki,
they were given more appropriate uniforms in 1907.
(Re-creation by Ronald B. Volstad from a photo by Georgina Fane Pope,
a woman of exceptional talents who was the Service's first head: DND)

stop the minister from implementing some of Dundonald's proposals while keeping the whole picture from the public. Two of his recommendations would not be acted on: compulsory service in cadet corps by all young boys and the enlistment of a surplus of officers and men, a move that would have doubled militia strength in times of emergency.

Nonetheless, between 1902 and 1904 the militia underwent a major reorganization that had been begun by Dundonald's predecessors. These years saw the creation of an Intelligence Service and a Central Records Office and the construction of arsenals and indoor ranges. A new Militia Pensions Act supported the Permanent Force, which was receiving more and more RMC graduates.

Dundonald was the first commander since Wolseley to arouse the militiaman's enthusiasm. Soon, however, things would turn sour between the Earl and Frederick Borden. Dundonald had taken up one of Hutton's habits and was speaking publicly about the militia and its problems. Even though his 1902 report had not been made public, it had largely been accepted, whereas the 1903 report was revised by the minister. Dundonald grew annoyed at delays, especially when it came to creating the central camp, and at the constant political intrusions into his world.

Dundonald, who cultivated relations with the Conservative opposition, ended his career, lamentably, over a patronage matter. In June 1904 he was shocked when the acting minister, Sidney Fisher, crossed out the name of a Conservative chosen by Dundonald to command a new regiment in the Eastern Townships of Quebec. The major-general protested publicly, and on 14 June an order in council dismissed him from his post. Before leaving the country, he took advantage of the election campaign to get up on any platform that would have him and deliver stinging attacks on the outgoing Liberal regime. These goings-on would not hurt Wilfrid Laurier's team, which was returned to power, but they did bring the public to the realization that Dundonald had been right on the issue that ended in his dismissal.

The circumstances surrounding Dundonald's departure augured well for a reform that had been gathering momentum for years, one that would replace the General Officer Commanding with the Canadian minister of militia and defence as the government's principal advisor on military matters. Borden, who had already set in motion a review of the Militia Act, now brought it to a vote, and the new system came into effect in November 1904. An order in council immediately established the Militia Council (similar to the British Army Council), to include the minister, his deputy minister and the departmental accountant, along with the chief of the general staff, the adjutant-general, the quartermaster-general and the master general of ordnance. Though less powerful than the General Officer Commanding had been, this Council would in fact be more influential. The minister was its unchallenged master. He could vet the agenda for discussion and was better informed about his department's requirements. As for the military members, they were finally made aware of the minister's problems. The first Chief of the General Staff, Brigadier-General P.H.N. Lake, was of British origin. Others of his ilk would follow, but the function would very soon be reserved for native-born Canadians.

Canada and the Imperial Connection

The rise of Germany prompted Britain to concentrate more of her energies around the

OFFICER 64TH CHATEAUGUAY AND
BEAUHARNOIS REGT.
4

3RD NEW BRUNSWICK REGT.
GARRISON ARTILLERY ST. JOHN.
41

ROYAL CANADIAN HORSE ARTILLERY
KINGSTON
32

P.E.I. LIGHT HORSE
CHARLOTTETOWN
49

DUKE OF YORK'S ROYAL CANADIAN
HUSSARS MONTREAL
18

10TH REGT. ROYAL GRENADIERS
TORONTO
30

53RD SHERBROOKE REGT.
SHERBROOKE. Q.
11

42   8TH ROYAL RIFLES QUEBEC.

ROYAL CANADIAN ENGINEERS
HALIFAX
51

OFFICER. 72ND RECT. SEAFORTH
29 HIGHLANDERS OF CANADA. VANCOUVER.

66TH PRINCESS LOUISE FUSILIERS
54 HALIFAX, N.S.

22ND SASKATCHEWAN LIGHT HORSE
45 LLOYDMINSTER

OFFICER QUEEN'S OWN RIFLES
9 TORONTO

OFFICER. 38TH REGT.
15 DUFFIRN RIFLES OF CANADA

CANADIAN ARMY SERVICE CORPS
8 MONTREAL

PIPER 48TH HIGHLANDERS
TORONTO.

31

SERGEANT. 1ST GRENADIER GUARDS
MONTREAL.

2

3RD MONTREAL. BATTERY
14   FIELD ARTILLERY.

28   OFFICER 7TH FUSILIERS
LONDON   ONT

QUEEN'S OWN CAMERON HIGHLANDERS
7   WINNIPEG

heart of her Empire. The initial reverses suffered in South Africa had put the admiration professed by her colonies in a more realistic perspective. There had been reforms in London as elsewhere in the Empire. The Royal Navy was recalled to European waters, and Canada agreed to assume the defence of Halifax as of 1 July 1905. It did the same for Esquimalt in 1906, if only to provide supplies for the Royal Navy when it was on the move. Halifax became Canadian in 1906; Esquimalt would not follow until 1910. The British orders in council officially authorizing this transfer of power would not be signed until October 1910 and May 1911.

In spite of the raise in basic pay from 40¢ to 50¢ per day, Canadians were disinclined to sign up for the expanded, 4,000-man force. At the outset a number of British troops ending their contracts in Canada would form part of the new Canadian garrisons at Halifax and Esquimalt, but they did not provide enough manpower to meet current need. In 1908 only 2,730 of the 4,000 permanent army positions were filled.

More than ever, Britain needed allies. The Entente Cordiale with France stands as an example of what she sought in order to manage Germany. A substantial rapprochement with the colonies was also on the agenda. At the 1902 Colonial Conference in London, Joseph Chamberlain had asked the dominions to attach some of their troops to a special imperial reserve to be placed under the orders of the British government for service anywhere in the world. Canada, along with Australia, refused to relinquish its authority. Undiplomatically, the British criticized Canada for the weakness of its defences and its meagre participation in the common cause.

This rejection would not stop Britain from returning to the charge five years later with a different approach. Now, with a less centrally minded Liberal government and with Chamberlain out of the Colonial Office, Britain was trying for maximum uniformity in the Empire's armed forces, to be ruled over by an imperial general headquarters. There would be only one navy, however, under a single command, and standardization would apply to training, organization, equipment, supplies and ammunition.

The governments attending this 1907 Colonial Conference passed a noncommittal resolution calling for the creation of an imperial headquarters, which would, without meddling in national issues, advise the governments of the Empire "as regards the training, instruction and organization for war of the military forces of the Crown."[48] This agency would collect intelligence to be disseminated to these various governments and would make defence plans based on a common principle. In London, a chief of the imperial staff would run the central headquarters. This embryonic formal alliance within the Empire closely resembled the commitments that Canada and other members of the North Atlantic Treaty Organization would make from 1949 on.

In 1909 a special conference on imperial defence dealt with naval and military problems in terms of the basic principle of standardization. As far as possible, this uniformity was to extend from the make-up of units to the weapons they used, including their transportation. Here we find complete Canadian autonomy coupled with the quick and easy integration of Canada's forces should they have to rally to Britain's defence.

Although less obvious than it had been at the turn of the century, imperial centralization was nonetheless coming to pass. After the 1909 meeting, some British officers came to Canada to take part in the labours of the Canadian section of the general headquarters whose creation had been approved in 1907. At the same time, some Canadian officers travelled to Britain to familiarize themselves with British methods. Mobilization plans were drawn up both for defending Canada and for sending an expeditionary force overseas to assist London. Neither Laurier's resistance to all centralization nor the largely ineffectual trumpetings for imperial federation would impede this quiet integration, which would form a single school of thought. Despite the advantages of this development, factors that might deprive the Canadian soldier of his distinctive character were already in evidence. Rather than preparing for the defence of their own country—conducting winter manoeuvres, for example—Canadian militiamen were rehearsing to be as British as possible.

The Colonial Conference of 1911 revolved around the coronation of George V. Relegated to second rank, military discussions focused on details arising from implementation of the decisions of 1907 and especially 1909. Beginning in 1912, the imperial general headquarters absorbed Canadian and Australian officers within the Dominions Section, an initiative that saw Canada more fully involved in the defence of the British Empire. In 1914, Canada, without being fully aware of it, was poised to expand an effort that would far exceed the wishes of its most fervent imperialists. On the one hand it was moving towards greater autonomy, while on the other hand the various colonial conferences that had been taking place since 1902 had helped to cement the Anglo-Canadian rapprochement.

The Naval Bill

Many Canadians think the Naval Bill cropped up suddenly in 1909–10, but the fact is that the principles of Canada's maritime defence were present in the first Militia Act of 1868, when George-Étienne Cartier was the incumbent minister. This embryo of naval defence resulted only in the building of a few gunboats and cutters to defend the Great Lakes and seacoasts and protect the fisheries: Canada's actual naval force was British. After 1871, there were scarcely any significant problems with its only neighbour, and the Canadian government quickly abandoned its slender naval commitments, some of which had been made prior to Confederation by colonies like Nova Scotia. After 1867, however, lacking resources and following the death of its creator and champion, B. Weir, the Nova Scotian naval brigade foundered. In Quebec, the naval units established at Bonaventure and New Carlisle in 1868 and at Carleton after 1869 were ill equipped and viewed by militia leaders as anomalous. Less than a decade later they would have vanished: The facility at Bonaventure was dismantled in 1878.[49] As for the British-supervised fisheries police on the Atlantic coast, their usefulness was cast in doubt after the U.S. Congress ratified the Treaty of Washington in 1873.

When British Columbia entered Confederation in 1871, Peter Mitchell, the minister of marine and fisheries, and Hector Langevin, the minister of public works, suggested that Canada defray the costs of maintaining the British warship that had been posted at Esquimalt for years. The suggestion of the two ministers was set aside as soon as Canada was no longer haunted by the prospect of Fenian raids.

The year 1886 saw new disputes between Canada and the United States over fishing zones. As Britain wanted to avoid diplomatic problems arising from Royal Navy intervention concerning U.S. fishermen, a

Canadian fisheries protection service was re-established. This civil agency had limited responsibilities, which were mainly to assert Canada's presence and legitimacy while avoiding direct confrontation with the Americans. In 1892 the government strengthened this service with three vessels: one on the Great Lakes, one in the Bay of Fundy and one in the Lower St Lawrence. Its men wore a uniform that was practically identical to that of British seamen. The vessels, which flew the White Ensign with the Canadian coat of arms, were commanded by British officers. The real force was still the Royal Navy's Halifax-based North American and West Indies squadron.

In the meantime there was a flurry of panic. In 1878 a Russian steamship, *Cimbria,* landed at Ellsworth, Maine, with a complement of 60 officers and 600 men. Some thought its mission was to purchase from the Americans small, fast steamers that could attack Britain's seaborne commerce. The apprehended crisis did not materialize, but Major-General Edward Selby Smyth continued to believe that in the event of an Anglo-Russian war the weapons and guns that might be installed in *Cimbria* could serve as well on land as at sea. It was in view of such a contingency that, in a letter to his minister on 3 May 1878, Smyth suggested forming a small armada of steamships in the Gulf of St Lawrence.

In February 1879 this danger was a thing of the past. Smyth was inclined to favour a naval reserve based on one or two old British vessels on which, even at anchor, numerous Canadian sailors, idled by winter, could train. Landlocked naval militia units could use them in summer.[50]

At first the British Admiralty expressed no interest, but in 1880, in one of the about-faces Canadians would have to get used to, came the announcement that it was prepared to give Canada *Charybes,* a vessel suitable for what the Canadians wanted. The Canadian government had other concerns, however, and turned *Charybes* over to the department of marine and fisheries, which had a refit done at a cost of over $20,000. Afterwards, not knowing what to do with the ship, they towed it to Halifax, where it was left with the Admiralty. This fiasco would result in long-term moth-balling of the naval force.

If Canada was still feeling its way on naval defence, it was no further ahead with its general perspective on maritime affairs. A department of marine and fisheries had been formed in 1868, then split into two separate departments in 1884, only to be reconstituted in 1892 as the single department it had been in the first place. It would be split again in 1930, and then, in 1936, the marine section would be transferred to the department of transport. In 1995 the marine section would be moved to the department of fisheries and oceans.

This indecisiveness would have no negative effect on plans to create a Canadian navy, which continued to hatch until the late 19th century. Almost all these plans were based on data that are still valid at the end of the 20th century—the immensity of Canada's coastlines, for example—or would remain important for decades and even up to the Second World War. During the 1880s fears were voiced more or less as follows: Lacking naval batteries or vessels, Canada's coasts were left undefended. The nearest British squadron was also responsible for Bermuda and would be recalled immediately in the event of war in Europe.

In these circumstances, a Canada desiring to arm rapidly would see its defence contracts competing with those of the Royal Navy. However, that navy, though still the most powerful in the world at the end of the

19th century, was less dominant than it had been 50 years earlier. Canada even stood to be threatened by a small armed mail ship which, launching an attack on maritime trade, could do significant damage to a country that had no means of pursuing and destroying it.

Among the projects submitted to ward off such possibilities were those of Colin Campbell and Andrew Gordon. Campbell wanted to build a naval reserve with seamen from the deep-sea fishery. These men would have first-rate fishing vessels armed with guns from the Royal Navy and would be trained by Britons lent to Canada and invited to settle here. Approximate cost of the operation: $150,000. Gordon would submit a number of proposals to the Honourable Charles Tupper between 1888 and 1891. His 1888 plan focused on better coastal batteries and the purchase of vessels of average tonnage and torpedoes for port defence. In 1891 Gordon was advocating the use of Canada's numerous seamen to form a naval reserve. In the event of armed conflict, these militiamen would be integrated with the men of the imperial navy. Even so, Gordon wanted to be able to rely on two vessels of average tonnage built in Britain, one for patrolling the fishing zones and the other for training.

Despite interest voiced by a number of key people, these projects came to naught, the reasons being the continued presence of the Royal Navy and the fact that the Canadian land militia captured what little money was available for Canada's defence. As the 20th century drew near, the possibility of a threat to Canada grew especially improbable: Steam navigation and its corollary, armour-plated warships, had increased naval reliance on fuel sources and supplies. These developments dampened the ardour of Britain's enemies who, unlike her, did not have bases all over the world. Any bases on Canadian soil were available to the British, distant from the European countries and virtually invulnerable unless attacked from the United States, another increasingly remote possibility. Any wooden or sailing vessels would be stopped by the coastal artillery batteries that were slowly increasing in number along Canada's coasts in the late 19th century.

In 1895, however, pressure mounted. In Britain, the competition with Germany over the number and quality of new ships, including the famous and extremely costly Dreadnoughts, prompted the naval lobby to form the Navy League. It purpose was to help the government persuade the people of the British Isles to accept the sacrifices needed to maintain naval superiority. By founding sections in the colonies, the Navy League hoped to press local governments, including Canada's, to share this British vision.

Branch No. 6 of the Navy League was founded in Toronto in 1895. On 20 June 1896, three days before the federal vote that would bring Wilfrid Laurier to office, a naval defence plan drawn up by H.S. Wickham, the branch's honorary secretary, was published in the *Globe and Mail*. In the circumstances, it could hardly go anywhere, but the proposal was not without interest. Wickham argued for a naval militia partnering the land militia with the equivalent of a General Officer Commanding, permanent and reserve forces, schools on both coasts and, lastly, the adaptation of the Fisheries Protection Service to the requirements of coastal defence.

In December of the same year, Wickham submitted another idea to the Governor General and the prime minister. This time Canadians were to be provided to the Royal Naval Reserve as part of a programme the

The first seamen recruited by the Canadian navy, for HMCS *Niobe*, November 1910:
Niobe is in the background.
(NAC, PA-132835)

Advertisement for "Twin Navy" tobacco, circa 1911. For the Canadians of the day,
their new fleet was clearly one with the Royal Navy.
(Private collection)

Admiralty had set up to help small merchant vessels convert to warships in a crisis.[51] This suggestion was not picked up, but Wickham would persistently press for government action in this area until 1910.

As with the rest of Canada's political and military life, imperial and colonial conferences had an impact on the development of Canada's naval defence. In the meetings of 1887, 1894 and 1897, the Canadian ministers rejected any idea of participating in this defence, even though the Royal Navy was not what it had been 40 years earlier.

In 1902 the Admiralty supported the idea of a centralized imperial navy that could strike the enemy wherever he might be. This view ran counter to earlier plans in which the priority had been to defend Canada and in doing so defend the Empire. Canada was looking more and more seriously at the plan for a naval reserve to support the British forces. Other colonies chose to vote credits which Britain would use for maintaining the vessels assigned to their defence. In either case, there was opposition to the idea of a centralized imperial navy run by London. In 1904, when the Militia Act was under review, the Canadian government drafted a Naval Militia Bill that never got beyond that stage.[52] Meanwhile, the Alaska boundary negotiations ended to Canada's detriment, in large part because it lacked a presence in the disputed area.

Why was a Naval Militia Bill not brought forward at that crucial moment? A number of reasons could be cited. The government had the Dundonald affair on its hands, and influential ministers, including Clifford Sifton, were arguing that the settlement of the west should take precedence over the fisheries protection force. The department of militia and defence, which questioned the usefulness of defending the Great Lakes, advocated the status quo on the coastal issue. Total control of Canada's maritime defence would involve significant costs at a time when the takeover of Esquimalt and Halifax, pushing the defence budget up by 40 percent, had already been announced.[53] Finally, this issue, which seemed capable of winning a consensus, aroused the nationalist and imperialist passions that had just clashed over South Africa.

However, the department of marine and fisheries did acquire two small, British-built patrol vessels on the torpedo-boat model. In 1905 one of them, *Canada,* took part in military exercises with the British squadron deployed to Bermuda.

At the Colonial Conference of April–May 1907 the Admiralty softened its position on the "single navy" idea. Though prepared to accept a degree of colonial participation, it still insisted on retaining total control. During this conference, Canada, once again accused of not putting enough muscle into naval defence, drew up a long indictment summarizing its contribution to Britain's total military effort in North America since 1871. Among the initiatives it wanted credit for were the takeover of land defence and the Halifax and Esquimalt bases, along with the fisheries patrols beginning in 1885. After these exchanges, the British admitted that Canada had contributed substantially to British naval affairs.

In 1907, though it was decided to make some repairs to the vessel *Canada,* naval defence was still not foremost among the country's concerns. That December, however, the U.S. fleet made a world tour, one purpose of which was to impress Japan, a British ally. Even from afar, Canada again felt threatened, so that in 1908 it reviewed its naval defence position. L.P. Brodeur, the minister of marine and fisheries, headed the review, the report of which was available early in the new year. With his own deputy minister and marine commander taking early retirement and U.S.-Japan tensions ebbing, Brodeur named Georges Desbarats to the position of deputy minister. Rear Admiral Charles E. Kingsmill, a Canadian who had served in the Royal Navy, was made available to his native country as of 15 May 1908. To the informed observer, this surprising appointment came as an indication that after many false starts Canada's naval militia might well, finally, come to pass. What made it even more likely was the fact that 1908 saw a grand celebration, with French and British warships present, to mark the 300th anniversary of the founding of the city of Quebec.

The fall of 1908 and the following winter, when Australia was establishing its own naval militia, saw discussion about equipping Canada with such a force, though the plan was not debated in the 1908 federal election that returned Laurier's Liberals to office. In the 1909 parliamentary session the Conservatives put forth a motion that Canada assume responsibility for some of the burden of its naval defence. Over the two months while the Conservative Party's Francophones tried to prevent this motion from being sent to committee, Kingsmill completed his plan for a naval militia, which, while not being overly ambitious, suggested the establishment of a school at Halifax to prepare crews for service on board the military vessels Canada would be acquiring over the years.

None of this had yet been made public when Britain erupted in what became known as the Dreadnought Crisis. Though dominating all other navies, Britain had just realized that it could no longer call on as many naval units as the total that could be arrayed by any two European continental powers. Germany was making swift progress. A debate on the matter that began in London on 16 March 1909 preceded by 13 days the debate on Conservative George Foster's motion already scheduled for the Commons in Ottawa. The Canadian parliamentary debate thus began in the glare of what Britain was to have handled as an internal matter.

In Canada, discussion reflected two complementary concerns: the need to help the mother country (imperialism) and the desirability of a Canadian navy for this purpose (national feeling). On Brodeur's orders, Kingsmill put the finishing touches on the naval militia plan that Borden took to London in July 1909. The British authorities improvised a special imperial conference on "military" and naval defence. Two suggestions were made regarding navies. Colonial participation could take the form of financial contributions or focus on creating local naval forces that could be added to the imperial naval strength in wartime. Australia, which had offered to defray the cost of a Dreadnought, was told by the Admiralty that creating an Australian navy would be more acceptable to Britain. This option was perfectly suitable to Canada, where, since it had become a matter of destroyers and battleships, discussion revolved around not a naval militia but a genuine navy, and produced the Naval Bill of spring 1910.

Although it was passed on 4 May 1910, this legislation triggered the tough national debate Laurier had foreseen on coming to power in 1896. Fourteen years later, protective of Canadian interests, he proceeded with caution. His Majesty's first two Canadian ships, HMCS *Niobe* and *Rainbow,* were used to patrol fishing zones and provide training.

Since recruiting Canadians proved difficult, the men who agreed to serve were mainly seamen from the Royal Navy.

Imperialists denigrated this minimal effort as essentially useless to the mother country in any real crisis. Outmoded technologically and at the end of their useful lives, *Niobe* and *Rainbow* were called "tin-pots." Meanwhile, nationalists scoffed at their "comic-opera navy." *Rainbow,* a cruiser built in 1890, had been retired from active service as outmoded in 1905: Canada acquired it for $243,000. The more modern *Niobe* cost $1.075 million and still required expensive repairs. According to the nationalists, this tiny navy, non-threatening in battle, was but the visible portion of the considerable and limitless effort Canada could be induced to make in the event of a European war. From this standpoint, the Naval Act was contemptible.

Others voiced their opposition. In 1913, Christopher West wrote in *Canada and Sea Power* that Canadian politicians were being hypocrites. The little Canadian navy was dangerous and would drag the country into all kinds of wars. Canada would have been better advised, wrote West, to send Europe a mission of pacifists to calm everyone down.[54] By shifting from a naval militia to a trifling Canadian fleet subordinate to the imperial navy, Laurier lost in both national and imperial terms.[55]

The Naval Act was clear in the sense of enabling the Governor in Council to place the naval force on active duty in critical situations as well as make it available to His Majesty for service in the Royal Navy. Hence the quite justified nationalist fears stirred by Wilfrid Laurier's remark in the heat of debate that when Britain was at war, so was Canada. Indeed there was no place for an independent Canadian foreign policy. A number of the threats directed at Britain—the one in the Sudan during 1884–85, for example—posed absolutely no danger to Canada. On the other hand,

the nationalists led by Henri Bourassa, who had founded *Le Devoir* in 1910, held that Canada's sole potential enemy was the United States. Now Britain had shown itself prepared to make any accommodation to avoid conflict with that country, which position had already cost Canada vast acreages in disputes with the Americans.[56] "With the exception of an Asian aggression, which would be possible only with United States consent, all we have to fear is the wars England saddles us with."[57]

In short, the Naval Act did not reflect general agreement. The Atlantic region preferred the status quo, while Pacific Canada would have supported a cash contribution to the Admiralty. Ontario, however, stood by Laurier. The Act was also attacked as overly expensive, with the nationalists estimating its cost at $20 million. Meanwhile, the imperialists maintained that an annual expenditure of about $18 million was excessive for what Canada was getting. There would be more point in simply giving the $18 million to Britain: That would fetch more than two useless old wrecks and a few hundred sailors. In fact, this was now the solution preferred by the British. In the event, the Laurier government held to the course it had chosen, and it made all the necessary arrangements in the summer of 1910, before the two cruisers were officially turned over to Canada on 21 October, to integrate them and their crews with the Royal Navy in case of need.[58]

In the summer of 1911, Laurier called an election for 21 September. There was general dissatisfaction with the country's support to Britain and the form it was to take, and the Naval Act became an election issue, albeit a minor one. The victorious Conservatives, though they had supported the legislation, now refused to put it into effect. They suspended construction of the new ships and the training of seamen, though allowing *Rainbow* to continue its fisheries patrols.

In July 1912, Prime Minister Robert Borden attended a naval review in Britain that included some 315 vessels. His hosts made a point of reminding him that all the colonies but Canada were a part of this show of power. After discussions with Winston Churchill, who since 1911 had been the First Sea Lord of the Admiralty, Borden returned to Canada. In December 1912 the Borden government tabled a bill to assist the Royal Navy to the tune of up to $35 million. Despite strong opposition that included some of the Quebec nationalists allied with the Conservatives in the House, the bill was passed in the Commons on 15 May 1913, only to be rejected by the Liberal-dominated Senate.

The only recognized legislation remained the Act of 4 May 1910. However, its virtual abandonment by the Conservatives took the Naval Service to the verge of extinction. Indeed in August 1912 the British seamen on loan to Canada returned home. Given their uncertain fate, the Canadian recruits deserted in large numbers. In October 1912 the two cruisers were mothballed and recruiting ceased. The few remaining seamen of all ranks were transferred to the Royal Navy. In 1913 the Naval Service became the Fisheries Protection Service, even though Kingsmill made sure that basic naval training was maintained in Canada. Dating from 1880, two small vessels remained in service: *Constance* and *Rebel,* minesweepers useless even for training.[59]

At the time that the affair became political, most Canadians would have been incapable of gauging the military significance of this planned flotilla. The issue had scarcely changed when the country went to war in August 1914. The Canadian navy was then so weak that it could neither lend support to the Royal Navy nor even protect its own shores, and the anticipated Canadian naval industry was still on the drawing board.

French Canadians in the Defence Forces

Just before going to war, Canada was bitterly divided over the naval issue. Socially, no serious effort had yet been made to get French Canadians involved in the country's defence forces despite the obvious lessons shown to the leaders in both the South African war and the debate on the Naval Bill.

In the 1899–1902 conflict, it is estimated that Canada's Francophones accounted for only three percent of all contingents taken together. In the first contingent, however, drawn from the permanent force, they represented 5.4 percent of total strength. As soon as he arrived in Canada in 1898, Major-General Hutton had spotted the absence of French Canadians as a problem. One of his responses was to issue a directive, in February 1899, recommending that staff officers and instructors be able to command and train French-language militiamen in their own tongue. Apparently Hutton had grasped the obvious: To get French Canadians to participate in the Empire's military undertakings, the authorities would have to go to them. Hutton, who spoke French, had to defend his regulation in Toronto.[60] During the summer of 1899, two further directives were issued laying down conditions for language tests.

The South African war interrupted Hutton's efforts in that direction, while he paid dearly for some of his mistakes made in other sectors of his activities. Nonetheless one of Hutton's officers, Oscar Pelletier, always regarded him with a "sentiment of strong attachment, admiration and gratitude"[61]—either because Hutton had promised him a battalion in South Africa or because of Hutton's approach to the Francophone issue.

After Hutton's departure and while the militia were being reorganized to reflect some of the lessons learned in South Africa, the French fact was left in the background. "Only English was used officially, although two artillery units out of 18 and 27 of the 166 infantry regiments (battalions) were Francophone on the eve of the Great War."[62]

When the Canadian Naval Service was being founded, in spite of the presence of the deputy minister, Georges Desbarats, and of L.P. Brodeur, who was replaced as minister between August and October 1911 by Rodolphe Lemieux, the French-language issue was ignored. Most of the British officers serving in Canada paid no attention to it, although they were reminded that Canada was "a bilingual country [where] French and English are on an equal footing."[63] Brodeur wrote to Desbarats in August 1910 that if training was not made available in both languages, which would require bilingual instructors, unilingual Francophones would be excluded. This vision would go no further in the navy as it was in 1910, with neither a body nor a soul. The Conservative minister of militia as of 1911, Sam Hughes, was far from friendly to Francophones and their language. A year after Hughes arrived, in fact, the sole ranking Francophone at headquarters, Colonel François-Louis Lessard, Adjutant-General since 1 April 1907, was replaced by an Anglophone. When Canada went to war, its militia was barely nine percent Francophone and 20 percent of its officers were British. To conclude, no one seems to have been sensitive to the French fact. No affinity appears to have developed between the two majority peoples of European origin in Canada, even though it had supposedly been built on two languages, two cultures and two peoples.

Chapter IV

UNENDING SIEGE

Canada in 1914

In July and August 1914 several countries, including France, Great Britain, Russia, Belgium and their colonies, went to war against the Central Powers of the German and Austro-Hungarian empires. Italy joined them in May 1915. In December 1917 Russia signed a separate peace treaty, but the United States was already replacing it on the battlefields, having been at war alongside the Allies since April of that year.

At the end of this violent upheaval, empires would disappear, new countries would be created and a League of Nations would revive the ideal of universal peace. The great enigma of this war between peoples has never found a satisfactory explanation: How was it that so many millions of combatants could be kept on the battlefields under such horrible conditions? They were not, after all, warriors by trade. A vortex of death would crush them in battle and drag them into the great post-1918 mass movements that would hatch another cataclysm.

When Britain went to war in August 1914 the Canadian economy had still not recovered from the harsh depression that had surfaced in late 1912 against a background of industrial overproduction. Unemployment rose and there was a severe credit squeeze. Farmers abandoned their land in the hope of finding city jobs that did not exist. At best, for-

Infantryman of the Canadian Expeditionary Force in France, 1915–16. During the first years of the war, Canadian soldiers wore the khaki tunic adopted in 1903. Badges on hats and collars often took the form of a maple leaf. Infantrymen carried the Canadian Ross rifle rather than the British Lee-Enfield. Many of these distinctions disappeared in 1916, when the Force was equipped with iron helmets, Lee-Enfield rifles and uniforms patterned on the British model. (Re-creation by Ronald B. Volstad, DND)

tune smiled on them in the form of some small amount of material assistance. In 1914 even the companies that owned the two transcontinental railways were in difficulty.

Canada's colonial status meant that it was automatically at war as well. Clausewitz had written in the first half of the 19th century that war was the continuation of politics by other means. Yet Canada was at war with no foreign policy worthy of the term. In 1914 most people hoped that this conflict, the true scale of which was grasped by only a few, would be over quickly. Nonetheless the government vested itself with exceptional powers. On 18 August it introduced a War Measures Bill in Parliament that would enable it to govern by decree. The bill would be passed the following month.

When it went to war, the British Empire was not as united as some might have believed. Sinn Fein, already active in Ireland, fully intended to seize this opportunity to advance its cause. In South Africa the Afrikaners, just as white as their English countrymen, were divided over a proposed attack on Germany's South West Africa colony. In Canada their chief supporters were the Quebec Francophones, who would themselves refuse all-out participation in the hostilities.

From the first weeks of conflict, whites throughout the Empire voiced their loyalty to Britain's cause. Yet a murmur of division persisted. It would abate without altogether disappearing when the liner *Lusitania* was sunk in 1915; the Empire turned with virtual unanimity against Germany and her allies, beginning with Austria-Hungary and swelling over the months by the addition of Turkey and Bulgaria. People everywhere were asking the same question: At what price must this war be fought?

In general, the British colonies went to war relying on imperial experience. Later,

the game would turn to slaughter and the colonies would give it their best. The end of the massacre, in 1918, would come as a great relief.

Canada's Participation in the War

Canada was distant from the sense of total war felt across the European continent and the British Isles. Nothing here was preventing people from leading peaceful lives. Since 1912, Ontario had been debating the notorious Regulation 17 to dismiss French as a language of instruction in its separate schools, while at the same time, once war broke out, criticizing Quebec Francophones for refusing to fight for the Empire. The Quebec nationalists proclaimed their readiness to fight for the Franco-Ontarian victims of Regulation 17 instead of making an all-out effort overseas.

The pursuit of grand political objectives was not conducted without internal strife. To the Quebec nationalists, conflicts at home were more urgent than those on the battlefield. They asked why they should fight for France when a century and a half earlier France had negotiated away its interest in Quebec; they wondered if the war of 1870, less than half a century earlier, had meant anything at all.

However, not everything was negative. Britain undoubtedly would have preferred a stronger mobilization of her Empire, but in 1914 British and Canadian forces did work closely together—though Canada remained independent. The British faction in Canada was less than confident about Canada's citizen soldiers and their embryonic navy, which had just picked up two submarines from the U.S. for coastal patrols; these joined the two outmoded cruisers that Canada had owned since 1910 and that now fell under British command. Despite

Sir Sam Hughes, the controversial Minister of Militia and Defence
when the First World War began.
(DND Library)

its insignificance, however, the navy was the first of Canada's two military arms to see combat. HMCS *Rainbow* sailed off into the Pacific in an unsuccessful search for German raiders.

With his 1910 Naval Act, Prime Minister Wilfrid Laurier had envisaged an independent Canada building its own navy, because Canada could hardly rely fully on the British navy in the event of an attack. He was right, and the First World War would make Laurier and hundreds of thousands of other Canadians long for a totally independent country.

Canada's efforts on land forces. The result was that fewer than 5,000 men would serve in Canada's naval forces during the First World War.

In August 1914, with some 3,000 professional soldiers and 60,000 men in the Non-Permanent Active Militia, the army was far from representing a threat to the Central Powers. Canada was able to manufacture ammunition for personal weapons along with artillery shells and some small arms, but its usable armaments could hardly equip two divisions, and military aviation was nonexistent.

Career's End for Oscar Pelletier

In 1912, after 27 years' service and growing increasingly hard of hearing, Oscar Pelletier decided to retire. He was living quietly in Kamouraska, Quebec, when, in August 1914, he was entrusted with a special mission: to go to Anticosti Island and secure control of a Marconi radio unit that might be a target for the Germans. Even before the war officially began, Pelletier was on his way to the island, located in the mouth of the St Lawrence River, with a small party of men. He remained on Anticosti until October when he was relieved by a permanent team.

Pelletier then resumed his retirement, but the war was not over for the Pelletier family. His elder daughter became a volunteer nurse, and one of his sons, also a volunteer, would die in September 1916 as a result of wounds sustained in combat.

Canadian territorial waters were unprotected against the dangers of war. To curb the activities of German submarines, Canada built up a fleet of 134 small patrol vessels that would mainly cruise along the Atlantic coast. The British would assume its command.

The British were asked whether Canada should build a real navy. The answer was a resounding no—better to concentrate

Though Canada was automatically at war, it was up to Canadians to decide what its effort would be. Precedents going back to 1867 indicated what route it should take. Voluntary enlistment would be the basis for recruiting the forces to be sent overseas. In a miscalculated fit of imperialism, however, all these volunteers would be sent into battle, with new divisions being created over the months rather than reserve troops used

Cavalryman from Lord Strathcona's Horse, 1918.
(Re-creation by Ronald B. Volstad, DND)

Private of the 2nd Construction Battalion, circa 1917.
This unit, the first in the armed forces to recruit Canadians of
African origin, was made up of volunteers who came mainly
from Nova Scotia.
(Re-creation by Ronald B. Volstad, DND)

to make up losses. By late 1915 enthusiasm for the front was flagging, and, beginning in 1917, the numbers of volunteers enlisting each month were no longer sufficient to offset casualties. Thus conscription followed, and it caused deep wounds that would never completely heal.

In 1917, French and English Canadians were already firmly rooted in their positions. Francophones were indifferent to a war being fought far from home, for an outcome that was unlikely to affect them. For French Canadians, the struggle for their own survival had to be waged, and it had to be waged at home, on their own soil. Meanwhile Canadians of British extraction volunteered in large numbers, accusing the Francophones of not pulling their weight. This position overlooked a number of important facts. For example, nearly 70 percent of the first volunteer contingent was made up of young men born in the British Isles; without the conscription of 1917–18, it is likely that more than 50 percent of the volunteers Canada sent overseas would have been men born outside Canada. Also, the United States would remain aloof from the deadly game of war until the spring of 1917. The reaction of the French Canadians, who had been settled for generations in North America, was similar to that of their southern neighbours—a fact that many of their countrymen refused to acknowledge.

When conscription was announced, Quebec Conservatives hastened to point out that this policy would come at a heavy cost to them personally and to their party. When the bill received first reading, on 29 August 1917, the government stonewalled Laurier's demand for a referendum on the issue. Facing the backlash that swept the country, mainly in French-speaking Quebec, Prime Minister Robert Laird Borden suggested to Laurier that they form a coalition government. Despite the inclination of certain Liberals to accept this offer, the former prime minister refused. A Union cabinet would finally be formed, comprising 15 Conservatives, nine pro-conscription Liberals and a worker representative.

The Union government won the general election of 17 December 1917, taking 153 of 235 seats. Quebec isolated itself by giving 62 of its 65 seats to Laurier's Liberals. Borden offset this outcome by naming a French-Canadian senator to his cabinet. Canada might have escaped the ravages of war, but the conflict divided it politically.

From 1914 to 1918, Canada taxed its physical strength to the limit. Cultivated farmland doubled and industrial production saw remarkable expansion, mainly through growth in the wood products and paper sector as well as munitions plants, shipyards and aircraft factories. Canada's financial effort was considerable as well: Its national debt rose from $336 million to $3 billion. War expenditures amounted to $1.5 billion.

Mobilization

According to the German plan, an attack based on a broad, wheeling movement to contain the French armies would seal France's fate within six weeks. Having invaded Belgium, the German wheeling flank would advance into northeastern France, its objective being to take Paris and pin the French combatants between this flank and the almost stationary wall created in Alsace-Lorraine. Things did not go as expected. The French did retreat, but in an orderly manner punctuated by costly counterattacks. So the Germans narrowed the invasion zone by passing to the east of Paris. Thus exposed, the German flank became the target of an attack, celebrated in history as the Battle of the Marne, that forced them to yield part of their conquered territory. It was followed by some mutual outflanking moves that left no immediate victor but did make it possible for the French to liberate a large tract of occupied France and a small part of Belgium. Soon there were two lines of trenches facing each other between the Swiss border and the North Sea.

The manoeuvre warfare begun in August shifted to siege warfare in mid-October, with the Central Powers as the strong points to be surrounded.

Canada, which had not had time to intervene during the first phase of the conflict, still had laid the foundations for its role in the events to follow. The Militia Act of 1904 empowered the Governor in Council to call up part or all of the militia for active service either in Canada or externally. According to the 1911 mobilization plans, which were drawn up to reflect British views, Canada could, in circumstances deemed critical by its government, send a contingent made up of an infantry division and a mounted brigade to fight in a country in the civilized world—in the language of the time—with a temperate climate.

However, these plans were cloaked in such mystery that Sam Hughes, minister of militia and defence since 1911, was unaware of their existence until 1913.

At that point, the Active Militia was the largest Canada had ever been able to form in peacetime: 59,000 men were trained, and there were plans to increase their numbers to 64,000 in 1915. Purchased by the Canadian government, Camp Petawawa received nearly 34,000 men during the summer of 1914. Training exercises would often take place before an audience of elegant women—guests of the officers.

One might wonder what the eight million Canadian civilians thought of the train-ing-camp circus. In 1943, Father Alphonse Fortin described the pre-1914 militia packs rallying at Camp Lévis as training in "form-less exercises that meant nothing to grown men at that time. Canadians had lived so long in peace that they had lost even the memory of a military tradition...we had the impression of a *paper militia, comic offi-cers*—in short, a kind of waste."[64]

It was with these militiamen and this population, ill-prepared but enthusiastic, that Canada plunged into the conflict. On 1 August 1914, three days before Britain entered the war, Canada offered assistance. Britain accepted the offer on 6 August. Sam Hughes had already triggered the mobilization process, though without re-gard for the plans of 1911. On 10 August an order in council officially authorized the creation of an expeditionary force.

By this time, militia headquarters had already begun to contact units directly. The men the units recruited were sent to Valcartier, which would be the assembly point for the expeditionary force. Vol-unteers were redistributed in new battalions identified numerically. These battalions had little or nothing to do with tradition. Volunteers from the 89th Regiment of Témiscouata and Rimouski, for example, were dispersed in new units. Despite every-thing, however, the result was impressive. By 8 September some 32,000 men were in place. On 3 October the 1st Division left Gaspé for England. It was reckoned at 33,000 men and women and 7,000 horses aboard 31 vessels in a convoy protected by seven British cruisers. When they landed on 14 October, however, the Canadians were still far from the battlefield.

On 30 October 1915 the number of Canadians having crossed the Atlantic reached 250,000. Enthusiasm was running so high that on 30 December Borden and

Hughes, who were attending a conference in London, promised the British half a million men. It is still not known today whether they were referring to 500,000 for the front, which Canada would have been unable to provide, or a total effort of 500,000, including all lines of communication, garrisons in Canada, the navy and various other services. If the latter, Canada amply fulfilled its promise: It mobilized more than 600,000 people.

In 1916 the Canadian forces deployed in northwestern Europe comprised an army corps of four divisions, each with three brigades of four battalions about 3,000 men strong. For a country with a population of just slightly under eight million, this European presence was as remarkable as its record of casualties: 59,544 dead and 172,950 wounded. The human cost of this war was much higher than its financial cost.

Princess Patricia's Canadian Light Infantry (PPCLI)

Canada's initial military effort, intended as an all-out drive, reflected the original and even eccentric mind of Sam Hughes, the minister of militia and defence.

The Royal Canadian Regiment (RCR), Canada's only professional infantry regiment, was sent to Bermuda to relieve an English unit recalled to Europe, where the real action was centred. Replaced in turn by inexperienced militia units raised in Canada, the RCR would later rejoin the professional fighting force.

The creation of Princess Patricia's Canadian Light Infantry was an exception to the recruiting methods used by Hughes. On 1 August 1914 Montreal industrialist Hamilton Gault offered Hughes a cavalry regiment. At a distance of 15 years, Gault seemed inspired by Strathcona's initiative, though unlike his predecessor he wanted to fight with the regiment he bought.

On 2 August the minister accepted, with the proviso that the formation be an infantry regiment. Its first commanding officer would be Francis Farquhar, military secretary to the Duke of Connaught, the governor-general of Canada and brother of the King. The Duke was the father of the Princess Patricia who would lend the battalion her name. Gault put up the $100,000 needed to establish the regiment, which recruited mainly veterans, especially veterans of South Africa. It was believed that these experienced men could be trained more quickly, and the fact that they came from a small population segment would not impede recruiting for the rest of the Canadian Expeditionary Force.

The PPCLI assembled in Ottawa, and on 24 August the men took the train to Montreal where a ship was ready for them. The regiment was ordered to stop at Quebec City to await a convoy that was to leave for England in early October. In the meantime the PPCLI trained at Lévis, not Valcartier, thus displaying a spirit of independence that was not in keeping with Hughes's expressed determination to have a Canadian force.

Integrated with the British 27th Division, the PPCLI was the first unit from Canada to reach the front and suffer terrible losses. In the fall of 1915 the division was called to Salonika with brigades of four battalions rather than five. Having to choose between a new British brigade and an equivalent Canadian formation, the PPCLI opted for the latter, which would simplify the replacement of its casualties. On 25 November 1915 the transfer was completed. By that stage the PPCLI had many more young Canadian recruits than when it had reached the front. Inspecting her regiment in London on 21 February 1919, Princess Patricia would recognize only 44 men out of the 1,000 militiamen she had seen in Ottawa in 1914. Among them was Hamilton Gault, with one leg amputated.

The Hughes Method and Camp Valcartier

In 1912 the minister of militia and defence sought to acquire a central camp for militia training in Quebec. Five different sites were evaluated. That November, the matter was handed over to a land agent named William McBain. The following June, McBain acquired a 4,931-acre property located over 20 kilometres northwest of Quebec City. To avoid speculation, the agent registered the transaction in his own name. Five thousand men were to be trained there every summer.

When the war began, the government needed an area that could accommodate 25,000 to 30,000 men. The minister negotiated the expropriation of 125 farmers, to whom he paid $40,000, thus adding some 8,600 acres to McBain's property. By 1918 Camp Valcartier would occupy 12,428 acres and have cost $428,131, including McBain's commission. On 10 August 1914, Sam Hughes—ever generous in awarding honorary ranks to himself and those who pleased him—made William McBain an honorary lieutenant-colonel, with pay.

Just as war broke out, firing ranges for individual weapons were under construction in the Ottawa area. At the department's request, the contractor momentarily left the work in progress to go to Valcartier, where a firing range with 15,000 targets was needed. Work began on 8 August and five days later some 1,000 targets were ready. The world's largest and most successful firing range, including shelters, firing positions and notices, was completed on August 22.

The minister was triumphant, but he wanted more, and to get what he wanted he approached some wealthy businessmen. William Price accepted the task of supplying the camp with potable water. He ordered the instalment of one pump that had a capacity of 500,000 gallons of water a day and another that brought in a million gallons. These pumps were connected to a 50,000-gallon tank encased in a steel frame 16 metres high. Thanks to Price, it was now possible to deliver water simultaneously to 200 four-metre-long washing tables and 80 shower stalls. Like McBain before him, Price was soon rewarded for his generosity. In 1914 he was made an honorary lieutenant-colonel and on 1 January 1915 he was knighted.

Lighting for the camp's roads was provided by the Quebec Light and Power Company. Telegraph and telephone networks linked Valcartier to Quebec City, and a railway was laid on bridges watched by pickets of armed guards living in tents that were raised by the riverbank.

All of this cost only $185,000 to set up and maintain until the Armistice. Throughout the war, the gates of Camp Valcartier would be closed for the winter. Beside the temporary shelters, the rare permanent buildings included the minister's residence and the pump house with a water chlorination system. The camp would accommodate 33,644 men in 1914. With the decentralization of basic training, however, there would be only 8,737 in 1915, 14,924 in 1916 and 1,811 in 1917. Total operating costs from 1914 to 1918 would amount to $590,278.24.[65] *From the spring of 1915 on, virtually all reinforcements were taken to Halifax, where, unlike Quebec City, ships could sail year-round.*

Daily Ration for Soldiers Training at Valcartier

Pepper and salt	*1¼ pounds bread*
1 ounce tea	*⅓ ounce coffee*
1 ounce cheese	*2 ounces jam*
2 ounces beans	*2 ounces butter*
2 ounces sugar	*6 ounces fresh vegetables*
1 pound fresh meat	*1 pound potatoes*
1 ounce oil	*1 cubic foot wood*
Fruit is extra	

The daily ration for horses was 19 pounds of hay, 10 pounds of oats and 2 pounds of straw.

The Canadian Combatant

The training programme for Canadians and members of other imperial armed forces had been modified since the South African war. Though the parade ground was essential, battalions had been split up to create half-companies and platoons subdivided into 10-man sections. Non-commissioned officers had gained importance in battle management. In Canada, where the myth that militiamen were superior to professionals continued to flourish, there was a particular reliance on the soldier's initiative and intelligence. From 1906 on, he was taught the rudiments of the profession and then trained in sections, platoons and companies.

In 1911 the permanent force held a large exercise at Petawawa. It would be the last exercise, as Sam Hughes, the apostle of the citizen soldier, was convinced that Canadians could do without them. Result: The real amateurism of the militia and the defective resources available to the professionals were the two major liabilities Canada would take into the war.

The volunteer's enthusiasm was immediately dampened by an inescapable fact that cost him valuable time: a shortage of qualified instructors in Canada. Not until 1917, when the flood of volunteers had dried up, would there be a basic 14-week training programme.

Thus far, the volunteer's daily round scarcely prepared him for action. He rose at 6 am. After a period of gymnastics, ablutions and inspection, he had breakfast. Training began at 8:30 and ended at 4:30, with a one-hour break for lunch. In this typical day, the recruit learned to parade and to charge with a bayonet, one of the favourite exercises of Sam Hughes, who liked to demonstrate it himself. The men did a lot of marching while carrying 60 to 80 pounds of equipment. They got little use out of their weapon and attended numerous theoretical courses that had little to do with combat as it was practised in 1914.

The volunteer wore a peaked cap decorated with a bronze maple leaf; a tight jacket of khaki serge with a rigid high collar fastened by seven bronze buttons; trousers also made of khaki serge; brown boots with woollen puttees from the ankle to the knee—troopers wrapped their puttees from the top; a collarless grey shirt; thick woollen socks; woollen undergarments; a sleeved vest; a long, heavy coat for protection from the cold and rain; and two coarse grey blankets.

The army supplied the volunteer with a razor and shaving brush; a brush each for his teeth, hair and boots; a mess tin with utensils; two towels; a pair of woollen gloves; and a balaclava. Added to this was his Oliver equipment, a complicated set of leather belts with various pockets that could hold ammunition, food, a water bottle and certain articles of clothing. Around 1890 a British army doctor in the Halifax garrison had persuaded the government to provide militiamen with Olivers. As the pocket for ammunition was next to the stomach, this equipment was impractical for crawling. This was not its only failing: The shoulder straps irritated the armpits; the water bottle and several of the pockets were tiny; and the tapes for bullets lost their shape, resulting in loss of ammunition. When it had been soaked, the whole mishmash would crack while drying out.

For attack or defence, the infantryman received a Ross rifle with bayonet, a bottle of oil and a kit for cleaning the bore of his weapon.[66] The Ross rifle was not without its flaws: Its magazine held only five bullets; the rod that the soldier had to pull to get the cartridge out soon grew red-hot; and the bayonet fixed to the barrel would sometimes fall off during firing. The Ross was also very long (50½ inches), but it weighed 450 grams less than the shorter and safer British Lee-Enfield that would replace it.

So much for the training, knowledge and equipment of the young recruit departing for England. Once there and under experienced warriors on Salisbury Plain, he would be readied for the real shock of combat. It would not take long for the young man to discover that more than his training had been botched. His tunic came apart at the seams and his cotton and wool coat protected him from neither rain nor cold. His boots, made hastily to meet the needs of an army expanding at a frantic pace, fell apart in the mud. To offset their flimsiness, the soldier slipped on rubber overshoes sent by the defence department.

Most of the problems would be corrected. In South Africa the British had discarded the Oliver equipment in favour of the Webb, which was more practical for an overladen infantrymen. This made Britain a supplier to its Canadian colony, which had failed to back up its determination to run its own military show. In addition to the Webb, the British provided more durable boots and looser tunics.

At this time, an infantry division would have some 6,000 horses, most of them used for drawing wagons. Once in England, the Canadians were surprised to find that the harness provided by their British allies (designed so that horses wounded or killed could easily be unhitched) did not fit their water wagons. Even their wagons were unsuitable: The wood used for their manufacture in Canada was too green and thus tended to split, break and rot; and they could not be drained or cleaned. Canadian motor vehicles were soon off the road because spare parts were unobtainable in England.

In all these cases, Britain came to the rescue of her colony. Grappling with a rearmament problem themselves, the British were periodically faced with the sometimes pitiful stubbornness of Canadian politicians refusing to replace the Ross rifle or the Colt machine gun. The MacAdam shovel was to be used as a shield against bullets while soldiers used a hole in the upper corner to observe the battlefield. Too heavy at nearly 5½ pounds and virtually useless for digging, especially in mud, the shovel was abandoned.

The Canadians training on Salisbury Plain hardly lived it up. Every morning they were served porridge and tea. At noon they received a serving of stew they would long savour. The evening meal of bread, jam and tea recalled a Canadian breakfast. Delicacies were rare.

The rules of order and discipline governing Canadian soldiers on British soil were those of Canadian military law. Their British counterparts were subject to British civil law as long as they were still in Britain. Offshore, however, they observed a military code identical to that observed by the Canadian troops. This code governed officers and men alike, but it appears not to have been applied very fairly. Between 1914 and 1918, for example, some 25.4 percent of officers, but only 10.2 of other ranks, brought before a court-martial were acquitted. Of the numerous officers tried for cowardice, desertion in the face of the enemy and other offences punishable by death, none was brought before a firing squad.

The Canadian Officer

To become an officer, a volunteer had to hold a militia commission and have his colonel's permission or the approval of a militia commanding officer. Infantry offi-

Motorcycle courier, 1917. (Inglis Sheldon-Williams, DND Library)

Sergeant of the Fort Garry Horse, 1916. (Inglis Sheldon-Williams, DND Library)

cers were trained less stringently than their gunner colleagues. The theoretical part of their training became sketchy when it took place in armouries in small communities; their city brethren fared better in this department.

Of the 44 senior officers in the first two contingents that left Canada in 1914 and 1915, only nine belonged to the Permanent Militia. Of the 1,100 officers who left, more than 200 had no known qualifications, and 184, including 27 lieutenant-colonels—those in command of fighting units—were not qualified for the ranks they held.

Our picture of the First World War officer is still hazy. Using information collected and analysed during and since the war, however, we can note a few common character-istics. Most of the officers were apparently professionals or bank employees, but there were also farmers, workers and students. A slim majority of officers were Canadian-born.

There were some basic criteria governing officer status. For example, one had to be at least 5'4" tall and 18 years of age. The vol-unteer had to be able to survive the tough living conditions imposed by war. A future lieutenant took courses that would suppos-edly teach him to lead his platoon with con-fidence. He was initiated into military law and trained as much for coping with health problems among his men as for leading a march or patrol. The lieutenant had a good knowledge of the weapons that would be used (including the machine gun) and the

Casualties[67]

Battles	Number of Men Involved (approx.)	Casualties	% Casualties (approx.)
Ypres, 1915	16,500	6,104	37
Somme, 1916	77,000	24,029	31
Vimy, 1917	81,000	13,477	16
Passchendaele, 1917	81,000	16,404	20
Amiens, 1918	91,000	11,725	13
Arras, 1918	46,000	6,836	15
Drocourt-Quéant, 1918	46,000	7,218	15.5
Canal du Nord, 1918	68,500	13,672	20

German bombardment of Arras, 1914. The destruction of Arras, a town with
a priceless architectural heritage, along with many other historic Belgian and
French cities, helped reinforce Allied propaganda likening Germans to barbarians.
(G. Fraipont, private collection)

various types of trenches. He could gauge distances with accuracy, see that his men got fed and organize guard parties. For assimilating all this knowledge and putting it into practice on the battlefield under conditions that were almost always complex, dangerous and arduous, he received $2.60 a day.

Casualties

Canada has not made detailed studies on the causes of death or types of injury sustained on the battlefields of 1914–18. The British statistics are as follows: 59 percent of deaths caused by mortar and cannon fire, 39 percent by rifle bullets and 2 percent by myriad other factors. We may assume that Canadians fighting under British command or in sectors where the British were operating sustained comparable losses. Loss of life due to artillery fire seems to have been heavier among the Germans, where it apparently accounted for 85 percent of the total between 1916 and 1918, a period during which the coalition of Allied countries held a growing material superiority.

Though these percentages show that the casualty rate decreased with combat experience, the figures also show clearly that the rates were terrible and that the turnover at the front was considerable, especially among the infantry units hardest hit in numbers and percentages.

Reaching the front, an infantry battalion comprised 800 to 1,000 men. Some 4,500 to 5,500 men would pass through each fighting unit, which gives an idea of the scale of this steady replacement activity. In the 4th Division: the 44th Battalion, in two years of combat, received 5,640 men of whom 1,193 would be killed; the 38th Battalion saw 3,512 march in and 691 die; the 22nd Battalion had some 5,584 march in and 1,147 killed.[68]

These figures illustrate why the Canadian Army Medical Corps, established in 1901, had more than one occasion to prove its worth. The Corps would grow from 13 doctors and five nurses before 1914 to 1,525 doctors, 1,901 nurses and 15,624 NCOs and soldiers at the height of the war. A Canadian peculiarity was that nurses were entitled to officer ranks and privileges. The top-ranked Major Margaret Clothilde MacDonald had already served in South Africa.[69]

The Burdens of War

Of the 59,544 who died in the Canadian Expeditionary Force, 6,767 succumbed to sickness and 13,289 to injuries sustained in battle or as the result of an accident. Another 154,361 soldiers were injured but survived. The approximate success rate for the care given to these wounded men was an impressive 90 percent. One phenomenon noted in most of the armies involved in the conflict is worthy of mention: This was the first major war in which disease proved less fatal than battle.

In 1916, when the Canadians were involved in the vast offensives on the Somme, the infantryman carried a load that, in proportion to

Nurse Blanche Lavallée at the Canadian Military Hospital in St Cloud, 16 June 1916. Nicknamed the "Bluebirds" by the wounded because of their sky-blue uniforms, more than 2,500 Canadian nurses served overseas. As early as 1899, Canadian nurses were accorded officer rank to confirm their professional standing. This was not the case with American military nurses, and the energetic Blanche Lavallée campaigned with them until they made their point in 1920. She also demanded pay equity with men of the same rank, which was finally granted during the Second World War. (Colour drawing by R.G. Mathews, DND, PMR-C-86-419)

his weight, was heavier than mules were made to bear. He bore a rifle, 220 cartridges, four bombs, rations for 24 hours, a winter coat or waterproof poncho, signal equipment, bags for sand and a pick or shovel (sometimes both). He found it difficult to walk, let alone rush at the enemy. If in addition, as was often the case, there was mud clinging to his boots, he was virtually paralysed. An infantryman might be carrying as much as 120 pounds of clothing and equipment. The officers and men admitted that this was unreasonable and many attempts were made to get rid of the excess.

By the 1917 battle of Vimy Ridge, the load had been reduced to about 40 pounds. The soldier now carried a poncho, gas mask, weapon, ammunition, pliers, protective gloves for cutting barbed wire, signal fuses, bags for sand and a pick or shovel. Some soldiers also carried large pieces of stiff leather with which they could throw themselves on barbed wire to make a bridge for their comrades to cross. Units provided, after the first light waves that could now move at a run, consignments of picks and shovels so the men could consolidate positions taken.

By August 1918 at Amiens, each man carried a day's rations, his rifle, 250 bullets, a gas mask, a water bottle, two grenades, two bags for sand and a pick or shovel. Compared to his comrade of 1915–16, the infantryman of 1918 was as light as air. And by a quirk of nature the ground was dry at Amiens—so there was no mud![70]

From Canada to Britain and France

The Canadians' apprenticeship to war and the war itself fell under British tutelage, at least for the first two years. In 1915 a third of the Canadian staff officers, whose work it was to plan and prepare for combat, were British. Several years would pass before Canadians occupied the majority of these positions. Upon arrival in England, the first contingent headed for camp at Bustard on Salisbury Plain, a 200-square-mile tract that had long been used almost exclusively for military manoeuvres. Being near to Stonehenge, it was also a mecca for tourists. Some of the men lived in tents, others in barracks. The Canadians were not alone. Part of "Kitchener's army"—a term used to describe British conscripts—was training there too. Training was conducted in companies. The first stage lasted five weeks, followed by two weeks at battalion level and a further two weeks at brigade level. Finally, on 11 December 1914, the division drilled in formation for the first time.

Two events caught the attention of the Canadians on Salisbury Plain. They saw the King himself on the two inspections he conducted...and it rained on 89 of the 123 days they spent there.

In January 1915 the lessons the British had learned on the battlefield were passed on to the Canadians. Their allocation of Colt machine guns went from two to four per battalion and the 30 men responsible for serving them received special training.

On 6 February 1915 the first group of Canadians crossed the Channel. Leaving from Bristol, they landed at St Nazaire and headed for their billets at Hazebrouck in northeastern France. The 2nd Division reached the front in September 1915 and, with the 1st Division, formed the Canadian Army Corps. They were joined shortly afterwards by the 3rd Division, including the PPCLI and the Royal Canadian Regiment, the latter back from a year's garrison posting in Bermuda. The 4th Division would arrive in 1916. Each of these divisions was made up of three brigades of four battalions. Until 1917 the Army Corps would have British commanders: Lieutenants-General E.A.H. Alderson (September 1915 to late May 1916) and Sir Julian Byng (to 23 July 1917). From then until the end of the war the command would be in the hands of a Canadian, Lieutenant-General Sir Arthur Currie.

The 18,000 men of the 1st Division were gradually initiated into combat. Between 17 February and 2 March each of the three brigades was detached for one week with a British division, where it became acquainted with the routine surrounding the siege that the First World War had already become on its western front. Under the British procedures that the Canadians had adopted, approximately 2,000 men from the same division would be at the front at the same time. A battalion was in the front line for four days and then moved to direct support for four days. After this came four days of rest away from the front, though their time was actually spent working and training. As they moved into battle, the Canadians would experience tension and boredom, action and terror.

At Neuve-Chapelle from 10 to 12 March 1915, the 1st Division saw its first engagement. Supporting an Anglo-French attack, the Canadian artillery played the role expected of it, but the infantry, paralysed by the Ross rifle that jammed all too often, were unable to produce rapid fire. With sheer initiative, however, they succeeded in filling this gap in the system: A number of them grabbed Lee-Enfields abandoned on the battlefield by the English dead and wounded. In August 1915 the Ross Mark III was modified by fitting the Lee-Enfield chamber on it. The 1st, 2nd, 3rd, 4th and 5th divisions (the 5th, which never left England, was later disbanded to provide reinforcements for the other four) would receive this modified rifle. In 1916, however, the Lee-Enfield would replace the Ross, which was used thereafter only by snipers, who could take advantage of its greater accuracy.

Ypres Defended

The siege war was punctuated by attacks launched by the besieged seeking to break out of their prisons and attacks by besiegers eager to conquer.

In April the 1st Division was given two miles of front on the far left of the British Expeditionary Force and beside a French colonial division. From 20 April to 4 May 1915 the Germans would attempt to break through at this junction of the Algerian and Canadian "colonials."

In addition to heavily bombarding this sector, the Germans used gas for the first time. The Allied troops were unprepared for this. The Algerians fled and the Canadians fell back in order: Despite the suffering

(3,058 casualties on 24 April alone), by engaging their reserves they managed to re-establish a continuous front. In this strictly defensive role and in a space of two weeks, the Canadians suffered 5,975 casualties: more than a thousand killed, with the remainder wounded, captured or listed as missing; of this total, 5,026 were infantrymen.

Givenchy and Festubert

The British used Canadians for a summer 1915 offensive. Conditions were unpromising, all the more so because it would be impossible to surprise the enemy. Major-General Arthur Currie commanding the 1st Canadian Division was not unaware of this, but the orders were clear. The attack, which would last five days, would give the British control over a piece of land approximately 600 metres deep by 1.5 kilometres wide. The price of this lot: 2,323 Canadian casualties. Later, when the British asked the Canadians for other troops, Sam Hughes, who never missed an opportunity to point out the incompetence of the professionals, would comment on the events at Givenchy by saying that Texas cattle rather than human beings should be provided for such fighting.

At Givenchy, 3,000 Canadians opted for the equipment of the motherland by exchanging their Ross rifles, whose superiority over the Lee-Enfield had always been defended by Sam Hughes, even when he was in the Opposition.

The 2nd Division underwent its baptism of fire in an attack in the Saint-Éloi sector in early April 1916. After some initial gains, a vigorous German counterattack pushed the Canadian brigades almost back to their starting point. This action cost the Canadians 2,000 casualties.

At Mt Sorrel from 2 to 13 June, some-thing of a reverse scenario was played out as the Germans attacked the 3rd Division. The preliminary artillery bombardment killed Major-General M.S. Mercer, a lawyer. The Germans then advanced to seize positions which they settled down to consolidate. A Canadian counterattack failed and another was cancelled on 6 June when the German offensive resumed, to stop within sight of Ypres. Julian Byng, the new corps commander, took advantage of this respite to organize a reprisal. On 13 June the Canadian troops retook almost all the ground lost since 2 June. These hostilities, from beginning to end, however, cost the Canadians 9,383 casualties.

The Terror of the Somme

The extremely costly attacks the British mounted on the Somme would extend from 1 July to the end of September 1916. The Allies would lose 350,000 dead and wounded and the Central Powers would suffer similar casualties. When the Canadians reached this sector, the offensive had been under way for several weeks. When the "bloodbath," as the Germans described this whole business, was over, the attackers would have conquered a few miserable square kilometres of terrain.

Up to this point in the war the Canadians had more or less done what was expected of them. On 4 September 1916 they took up position in front of the village of Courcelette, and for the next two weeks the mere occupation and defence of the front trenches cost them 2,600 men. Then, on the 15th, the British and Canadians resumed their offensive along the entire front. The objective of the Canadian troops was a sugar refinery in a Courcelette suburb that they took easily. Up to that time, the practice on both sides had been to stop when the objective was taken and strengthen the new forward positions. This time, however, the Canadians decided to keep going. Accordingly the 22nd Battalion from Quebec City and the 25th from Nova Scotia, followed by the 26th from New Brunswick, crossed through the village. When the next day dawned, over 1,000 prisoners had been taken, along with a considerable amount of equipment, and the Canadians had won distinction in this massive Allied troop movement. However, their momentum was soon lost and everyone went back to the old familiar war. Between 15 and 20 September the Canadians took 7,230 casualties in exchange for Flers-Courcelette, Fabeck Graben and Zollern Graben.

From 26 to 28 September the Canadians took part in the capture of Thiepval Ridge. The ensuing local German counterattacks were damaging. In mid-October three of the four Canadian divisions were sent back north, while the 4th suffered the bitter experience of the Somme in frequently unsuccessful attacks that were repeated from 21 October to 11 November 1916, until it finally seized a trench system called Regina. The 4th Division then rejoined the rest of the Canadian Corps to prepare for a battle that is still renowned today.

On the Somme the Canadians earned a reputation, which would endure to the end of the war, as the shock troops of the British Expeditionary Force. With their four divisions under the enlightened and painstaking command of the future governor-general of Canada, Julian Byng, the Canadians, despite their hardships, now seemed destined for greatness.

Vimy Ridge

In 1917 the French had replaced Joseph Joffre with Robert Nivelle, who claimed that the German wall could finally be pierced in the south between Soissons and Reims. To the north of the French armies the British accepted the mission of mounting some powerful diversionary attacks that would pin down dozens of German reserve divisions in that sector. One of these British diversions, assigned to the Canadian Corps, was Vimy Ridge.

This objective, with its peak nearly 120 metres above sea level, stretched for several kilometres from Lens in the north to Arras in the south. Its conquest would not change the face of the war, but it would deprive the Germans of a plateau in the Flanders plain that dominated the neighbouring area for kilometres. After their defeat on the Marne, the Germans had drawn back to this position from which the French had many times attempted to dislodge them. Moroccan colonial troops had climbed the plateau in 1915 but, lacking support, yielded to the German counterattack.

At this stage in the war—spring 1917—the Germans viewed this place as one of the pivots in the defence of their fortress: Trenches, barbed wire, concrete redoubts, dry shelters and railway lines gave the occupying troops the illusion that they were unconquerable. The Canadians had a slope that was fairly easy to climb, while the defenders often had steep cliffs at their backs. The German defensive strategy at that time accepted the loss of advanced trenches all along their front, anticipating their recapture in strong counterattacks by reserves massed behind. However, the tactic could not be applied in this particular sector, which called for maximum defence of the front lines at the risk of losing everything if the battle went badly, since in many spots it would be difficult to attempt a reconquest of recently abandoned cliffs.

The Canadians made painstaking preparations for their great initial attack of 1917, which would, for the first time, involve all four of their divisions at once. This attack would benefit from the lessons learned from the French, who had developed the art of using their infantry in small groups to occupy points of resistance left behind by the first assault waves, especially concreted machine-gun nests that were resistant to shells and surrounded by trenches and barbed wire. From the British they borrowed the judicious use of accurate barrage bombardments to open the way for the infantry. They reinforced these techniques with counterbattery activity that would enable them to target 176 of the 212 German guns that could smash the Canadian offensive. In all these areas, the Canadians readied themselves with precision.

The troops would be "shown" the ground by means of montages prepared in the rear, and they would be trained to recognize and take their assigned objectives. They would draw on all the technical advances the war had spawned since 1914. These would include rifle-launched grenades and combustion-fuse shells (improving on a French invention) that exploded on striking the ground and destroyed barbed wire, not to mention aerial reconnaissance of enemy batteries and the approach and destruction of well-defended positions through tunnels hollowed in the chalk typical of this region. The assault began on 20 March 1917 with a bombardment of the German position that was intensified until 2 April and then stabilized. The Canadians at Vimy had 480 18-pound guns, 138 4.5-inch howitzers and 245 heavy guns and howitzers; they also had all the shells they needed, which had not been the case with the British troops fighting on the Somme a year earlier. The

British also manufactured 234 other guns, including 132 heavy guns available to the Canadians. This gave them a piece of heavy artillery for every 20 metres of front, providing far superior coverage to what they had on the Somme. Trench raids and flights over the German lines now proliferated along a front more than six kilometres long. Before dawn on Easter Sunday, 9 April 1917, under a blizzard blowing in the Germans' eyes, the offensive opened. Given the features of this front, the assailants would have almost four kilometres to cross on the right before reaching their objective but only 650 metres on the left, where the greatest heights were located and where the fighting promised to be the hardest.

The bombardment that had been stationary since 2 April was now succeeded by a rolling barrage supported by steady machine-gun fire into the German lines. The infantry stuck so close to the barrage that they were on top of the first German positions even before the defenders had come out of their shelters. Surviving points of resistance were left to be dealt with by the units trained for this purpose, including the 22nd Battalion. The enemy artillery saw its usual activity largely frustrated by a highly effective Canadian counterbattery. By 8 am the 3rd Division had reached its objective just across from Vimy. The 1st and 2nd divisions would take their positions just as quickly. Only the 4th, across from Hill 145, would be bogged down until 12 April before capturing this high ground. On the night of 12/13 April the remaining Germans finally fell back.

From the top of the ridge, in the morning, the Canadians watched the enemy withdraw across meadows that contrasted with the mud they had been floundering in for weeks on their side of the ridge. They had just won a very important victory. Their

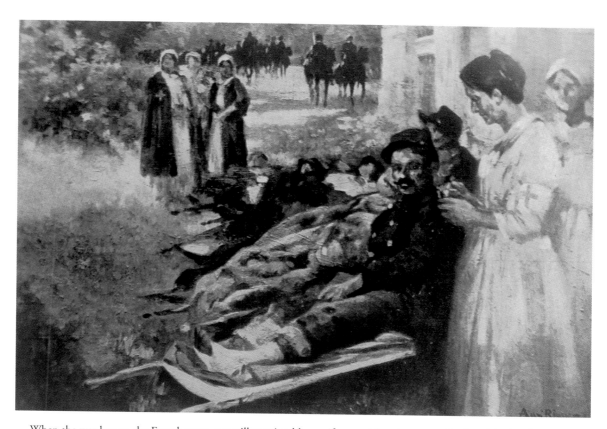

When the war began, the French army was still wearing blue uniforms with red trousers. Deployed in this fashion on the plains of Champagne and Flanders, these soldiers suffered terrible losses from modern machine guns. Since then, all armies have worn drab colours.
(De Riquier, private collection)

trophies: 4,000 prisoners, 54 guns, 104 mortars and 124 machine guns. Four Victoria Crosses were awarded for all this effort. The success of Vimy would prove that gunners, sappers, signalmen and infantry had managed, working very closely together, to solve the numerous tactical problems of the battlefield. Its planning of this action, co-ordination of the arms and many rehearsals conducted in the rear showed the mastery of which the Canadian Corps was now capable. Yet the joys of victory were dampened by its heavy cost: 10,602 casualties, or one man in eight, 3,598 of them dead. Not surprisingly, the most moving of all the Canadian commemorative monuments from the two world wars can be found at Vimy.

Everybody realized that they could not rest on their laurels. Between 16 April and 9 May, Nivelle and the French advanced only six kilometres and the casualties they recorded shattered the calm of the French armies, where certain elements mutinied. These localized spasms would be suppressed by Philippe Pétain, who replaced Nivelle and claimed to be waiting for the Americans who had entered the war that April. While the newcomers gathered their forces and, on the other front, Russia prepared to withdraw from the war, it was virtually left to the British, fairly spread out along the western front if we exclude the Somme, to mount attacks. Over that summer, Canadian brigades took Arleux-en-Gobelle and Fresnoy to the north and south of Arras, at a cost, in the case of Fresnoy, of 1,249 casualties.

Hill 70 and Lens

At the beginning of summer Arthur Currie replaced Julian Byng: The Canadians would henceforth be led by one of their own. The offensives the British now mounted in Flanders included one led by the Canadians on the coal-mining city of Lens. The plan was to attack Lens directly. Currie suggested an alternative, which was accepted: They would take Hill 70, a small feature dominating Lens and one that the Germans would probably attempt to recapture. The Canadian artillery would have to smash these counterattacks, cause serious casualties and force the enemy to abandon the ground.

On 15 August the 1st and 2nd divisions attacked behind a powerful rolling artillery barrage supported by counterbattery activity and a saturation bombardment of the designated positions. The hill was taken and, as predicted, the Germans counterattacked until the 18th, sustaining 20,000 casualties compared to 9,000 for the Canadians. For the first time, a great Canadian victory could be ascribed to the vision of a Canadian.

Passchendaele

Since late July 1917 the Passchendaele sector had been a target of bloody attacks by the British, though little ground had been gained. In the autumn the depressed British troops were still floundering in a foul sea of mud while the heights remained in German hands. It was a matter of urgency to capture the little plateau or fall back to more distant quarters. The Canadians were ordered to return to this sector, where they had been in 1915, and take the hill, by now unrecognizable. The drainage system had been ruined. Guns sank up to their axles in the mud. In the shattered plain, covered with useless weapons, thousands of human and animal corpses were rotting. The air was putrid and steadily falling rains turned the whole area into a nightmare. Veterans of the Somme relived a situation they knew only too well.

Field artillery bound for the front, circa 1916–18.
(Watercolour by Gilbert H. Lindsay, Parks Canada)

Canadian infantry in Valenciennes, 9 November 1918.
(Inglis Sheldon-Williams, DND Library)

Strategically, the conquest of Passchendaele would be insignificant in the Allied drive towards victory, and, although tactically feasible, the mission would be very costly. Currie informed his superiors that the operation could involve more than 16,000 casualties. Was Passchendaele worth this sacrifice? The British answered that it was, since it would enable them to increase pressure in the north of the front and afford the French the break they needed.

The Canadians therefore repeated the painstaking preparations that had earned them the successes recorded since the beginning of the year. To spare the gunners having to constantly readjust their sights, bases were built to support their guns; to ensure that the troops were supplied, the roads were made suitable for motor vehicles over the 15 kilometres of marshland separating Ypres from the front.

On 18 October the Canadian 3rd and 4th divisions moved into position in front of the objective. Under a chilly rain that soaked this nearly three-kilometre-wide quagmire on 26 October, the attack began. Having been unable to surprise the enemy, two battalions launched an assault on Bellevue Peak. The men were decimated by sheltered German machine-gunners. At last a small group from the 43rd Battalion managed to gain a foothold and dig in. The 52nd Battalion, spurred by their comrades' exploit, seized six blockhouses.

The partial victory of that 26 October came at a heavy cost to the Canadians, who counted 2,500 casualties, but Passchendaele was still beyond their reach. On 30 October a new 800-metre advance was won at a cost of 2,300 casualties. There remained 400 metres to cross in order to occupy the remnants of the unfortunate village. Heavy and field artillery were brought up when the 1st and 2nd divisions replaced the 3rd and

4th. On 6 November operations were concluded: They had inflicted 16,041 casualties including 3,042 killed.

All this to advance five kilometres in a salient soaked on three sides. A few months later the British would abandon Passchendaele. The Canadians had already earned eight Victoria Crosses on the Somme; Passchendaele gave them nine. The question of which of these two sectors of operations had been the more terrible remains unanswered by the Canadian participants in both of the battles.

The Final Year

In 1918 the countries that had been fighting in Europe for four years were running short of combatants. Since the Russians had abandoned their siege against the Germans in the east, Germany was able to concentrate its efforts in the west. It had to move fast, for the Americans had been mobilizing since April 1917 and tens of thousands of them were now arriving in Europe. In theory the Germans could marshal 192 divisions to the 173 available to the Allies in the spring of 1918. Division strengths were uneven on both sides. Improvements in technical and tactical resources, combined with the manpower shortage, enabled the British to reduce the number of battalions making up brigades from four to three. With nine battalions instead of 12, the British, Australian and New Zealand divisions increased in number while the strength in each decreased by a quarter.

Taking the same route and bringing its 5th Division on standby in Britain to the front would have given Canada an army comprising two corps. Currie decided instead to keep the structure of his four divisions intact. This amounted to refusing

British and German aircraft in combat. Many Canadians won distinction in the
British Air Force during the Great War. Billy Bishop, a native of Owen Sound,
Ontario, was the British Empire ace with 72 wins. He was followed by a number
of other Canadian fliers, including Raymond Collishaw and Donald MacLaren
from British Columbia, who recorded 60 and 54 victories, respectively.
(Private collection)

a virtually automatic promotion. After Passchendaele, Currie dismantled the 5th Division, which enabled him to reform the officer ranks in the other four and add 100 men to each infantry battalion. He also reinforced the sappers, who would have three battalions of 1,000 men each with their own command and logistics. This last measure would enable the infantry and artillery to focus on combat. In the spring of 1918 each Canadian division boasted its heavy machine-gun battalion with 1,558 men and 96 Vickers, which were added to the increasingly numerous Lewis machine guns in the infantry platoons.

At the end of the war the Canadian Machine Gun Corps comprised 422 officers and 8,349 men, though some still wonder today whether this immense firepower was more effective than the additional infantry brigade these specialists could have formed. Nonetheless, a Canadian infantry division of 24,000 men had 6,000 more than the other imperial formations, though 4,000 fewer than the American ones.

Bristling with confidence, Currie and his men no longer hesitated to openly follow their own convictions. The Canadian Army Corps, like Currie himself, was a self-confident giant among the British formations. Even though Currie was in a defensive position during the spring of 1918, he resisted British pressure to add one or two divisions that would enable them to put an end to some German attacks.

On 21 March 1918, in a last-ditch effort, the Germans attacked right where the British and French armies met. The tactic was quite simple: infiltrate deeply and daringly, disturbing communications centres and deliberately ignoring pockets of resistance that abandoned their ground in the ensuing confusion. The British 5th Army actually withdrew, but managed to re-estab-lish its front. These attacks were repeated in several places in Flanders and Champagne. In a matter of weeks most of the ground regained since 1915 at a cost of hundreds of thousands of casualties fell back into German hands. At this threat, the Allies finally agreed to rally behind a common commander, Marshal Ferdinand Foch.

Fortunately the Canadians had been able to stay clear of these battles, which had reached their limit on 5 July 1918. The Allies were already striking back, their numerical superiority largely assured by massive American arrivals. The Germans suffered a million casualties, the equivalent of the manpower freed from the Russian front. Allied counterattacks had re-established the siege lines by 7 August.

Amiens

The scene was now set for toppling the German militarism that in various forms had kept Europe trembling for more than 50 years. Over the long, painful weeks the Allies lived through in the spring of 1918, the Canadians had learned much. They had also had time to rebuild their strength after the successful but costly attacks of 1917.

The sector now reserved for them was that around Amiens. To give the Canadians the advantage of surprise, they were taken 60 kilometres north of the city. Accustomed to having the Australians opposite Amiens, the Germans also knew the Canadians, whom they had seen spearheading British assaults. Two battalions and two first-aid stations were set up in front of Kemmel, where constant traffic of assorted messages was set in motion and picked up by the Germans. Between 30 July and 4 August, in deepest secrecy, the rest of the Canadian Corps descended to the south. Their discretion was facilitated by the gloomy weather, which reduced German air sorties, and the fact that only the division commanders knew the assault target. This secrecy caused numerous logistical problems—for example, the artillery would have almost no time to prepare. Opposite Amiens, the Canadian officers studying the terrain fooled the Germans by wearing the trademark soft hat of the Australian soldiery.

The noise of preparations for the largest mechanized battle ever seen up to that time revealed nothing to the enemy. In spite of all the precautions, however, some German units were wondering about the movements they had detected. Some 604 tanks of all kinds and thousands of horses would give the battle an aspect that was both ancient and modern.

Just before dawn on 8 August the attack opened with the firing of 2,000 guns. In addition to the tanks, the soldiers could rely on two motorized machine-gun brigades, a battalion of cyclists to serve the Corps and a section of heavy mortars mounted on trucks. A thousand French and 800 British planes took to the air. During this brilliant assault, which would seriously undermine the morale of the German troops, the Canadians advanced 13 kilometres at the head of an immense front more than 30 kilometres wide. Australians, British and French were also in the attack, their role being to keep clear of the advance of the Canadians, who had more ground to cover to reach their objectives. The Canadians lost 1,036 men killed, 2,803 injured and 29 taken prisoner, losses that were largely offset by their remarkable advance, the most impressive on the western front since 1914. The Germans had to accept 27,000 casualties, including 16,000 taken prisoner—5,033 of them taken by the Canadians, who also seized 161 artillery pieces and a large number of machine guns and anti-tank guns. Though the Allies were left with only

132 tanks to start with the next day, the Germans had lost seven divisions. The confidence of their High Command was shaken by the realization that its war machine was no longer effective.

An interesting experiment that day involved the use of 30 Mark V tanks to transport the troops of the 4th Division to the opposing trenches. However, many men were bothered by the heat and by the exhaust fumes that entered the passenger compartment. A few fainted; others got out and walked. The drawbacks associated with the Mark Vs could not be rectified and these tanks were not used again during that war.

During the night of 8/9 August, the British High Command decided to lend its 32nd Division to the Canadians, who wanted to withdraw their 3rd Division from the front. The Canadians of the 3rd Division had already marched about 10 kilometres to the rear when they were recalled, as the British had changed their minds. The men were exhausted on their return. It was therefore decided to use only one of their brigades at the front, which required the 1st and 2nd divisions to expand the sectors they were covering. Under these conditions the attack of 9 August could not get under way until around 11 am, without the element of surprise of the day before. At a cost of 2,574 casualties, the Canadians took 6.5 kilometres of ground.

The pressure continued to mount for several days, but the momentum of 8 and 9 August was indeed lost. The number of available tanks fell to the point where, on the 12th, there were only six left. Despite their 11,725 casualties from 8 to 20 August, the Canadians had sounded the beginning of the end of the German army by advancing nearly 30 kilometres and securing the ground thus taken. In the whole operation, the Germans recorded 75,000 casualties.

A month earlier the French had seized the initiative from the Germans. In this context, the battle of Amiens would have a decisive impact. It shattered the last hopes of the German High Command, along with any confidence they might have had that their troops still wanted to fight. The success of the Canadian troops was based partly on surprise, the concentration of their strength and co-ordination among the various arms (planes, tanks, guns, machine guns).

Code Name: Tank

Throughout the 19th century various inventors had laboured to perfect an endless belt on feet, or a track, for use on vehicles. Around the turn of the century these efforts bore fruit with the invention of the Holt crawler tractor in the United States. Only one more step was required to envisage a tracked vehicle for military purposes, and more than one inventor was thinking about this when the First World War broke out.

Unknown to one another, the British and French both designed and developed an all-terrain armed and armoured vehicle, but the British were the first to use it on the battlefield, in September 1916. The French followed suit in April 1917, the Germans in March 1918.

On 5 January 1915 the First Sea Lord of the Admiralty, Winston Churchill, wrote to Prime Minister Asquith: "It would be very easy to quickly equip a number of steam tractors with small shelters to accommodate men and machine guns safe from bullets.... The track system would make it possible to cross trenches with ease and the weight of the contraption would destroy any tangle of barbed wire."

The job was neither as easy nor as quick to execute as Churchill thought. It would take a year before the prototype was brought out for a demonstration at British army headquarters. Nicknamed "Mother" and shielded by 8-mm armour, the contraption weighed 30 tons. It could cross a trench nearly three metres wide and scale a parapet 135 centimetres high. It was armed with machine guns and two 6-pound guns that could deliver shells accurately at a distance of 1,830 metres. Its 105-horsepower gasoline motor gave it a top speed of 8 kph under optimal conditions. Mass production began in February 1916. For security reasons, it was decided to give it an ambiguous name that would broadly describe its shape when concealed under canvas, and "tank" was finally chosen. From that time until the conflict ended, the British produced two versions of the tank, one termed "male" fitted with 6-pound guns and one termed "female" in the same general style but armed only with machine guns.

A total of 49 tanks saw action for the first time on 15 September 1916 at Flers-Courcelette. Of the eight allotted to the Canadian Army Corps, four got bogged down in the mud, one was destroyed by a shell and one broke down. The other two, dubbed "Cordon rouge" and "Crème de menthe," enabled the Canadians to seize two fortified emplacements and take a number of prisoners. Of the 49 tanks introduced in the battle, 32 managed to reach their line of departure and 10 resisted long enough to provide effective assistance to the infantry. Two days later, despite this mediocre showing, British Field Marshal Douglas Haig commented: "Wherever the tanks advanced, we reached our objectives; where they did not, we did not reach them." The evidence in favour of the tank as a combat weapon could not have been more conclusive.

After this, all major attacks were made with tanks. In the successful offensive of Amiens beginning at dawn on 8 August 1918 the Canadian troops had the support of 420 tanks, 324 male and 96 female. Not only did the tank provide undeniable destructive power, but it also had a significant psychological effect. After the Amiens engagement, the British did not hesitate, whenever they felt that they did not have enough tanks, to deploy fakes—mere tractors camouflaged with painted canvas attached to a wooden frame. A few months later, on 2 October, General Ludendorf advised the Reichstag that it had become impossible to force the enemy to call a truce, primarily due to the power his tanks gave him.

The tanks that supported the Canadian infantry in this conflict were British tanks commanded by Britons. The Canadian army would not acquire its first tanks until 1938, and then only by dint of the determination of Major-General F.F. Worthington, the pioneer of armoured warfare in Canada.

The Citadel Falls

In August of 1918 the German defences had been sorely tested in every sector. In the relatively limited portion of the front it occupied, the strong Canadian Corps had not finished its job. On 26 August it once again spearheaded the 2nd British Army that was launching another attack in the direction of Cambrai. By the 28th the Canadians had advanced eight kilometres, taking 3,000 prisoners and seizing 50 guns and 500 machine guns. This action brought them within reach of the Hindenburg Line.

Although the artillery continued to play its role, the Canadian infantry took a break. On 2 September, tanks and infantrymen resumed their advance behind a rolling artillery barrage. After a difficult 3.5-kilometre advance, the Canadians counted 5,500 casualties. They would have the consolation of being awarded seven Victoria Crosses. Indeed one result of this rather minor engagement was that it enabled the Allies from the western front to get at the Hindenburg Line without resistance. With problems looming, the Germans began to consolidate a new fallback position between Antwerp and the River Maas that was named the Herman Line. With Arras liberated, preparations were made for the next stage, crossing the Canal du Nord to take Cambrai—events that would occur between 27 September and 11 October.

The Canadians' last major fight took place around Valenciennes on 1 and 2 November. The artillery under Brigadier-General A.W.G. McNaughton, who would command the 1st Canadian Army in the Second World War, played a crucial role. Mont-Houy near Valenciennes was successfully taken with 2,140 tons of shells. This was an enormous output when one considers that the Boer War had required only 2,800 tons of shells in all—on both sides. At Valenciennes, 80 Canadians were killed and 300 wounded, compared to 1,000 Germans killed and 2,000 wounded.

At 11 am on 11 November, when the Armistice was struck, the Canadians had entered Mons, Belgium, where the Germans and British had faced off in 1914.

Other Canadian Participants

Tens of thousands of other Canadians served outside the Canadian Army Corps. The Canadian Cavalry Brigade, for example, worked as part of the British Cavalry Division. It had to wait for the spring of 1918 and the beginning of a war of movement to enter the scene and perform acts of bravery that would, in a very short space of time, earn two Victoria Crosses.

Elsewhere behind the front, thousands of men were fighting in the railway troops, and in 1918 a large number of these men would become infantrymen. Nearly 2,000 dead would decimate their ranks between the assault on Vimy Ridge and Armistice. There would also be three companies of sappers with the English engineers' units who would return to be with their countrymen at the front when the war ended. The Canadian Forestry Corps would recruit up to 12,000 men in France and 10,000 in Britain. A number of Canadians, including nurses and doctors, would be with service units in Palestine, Egypt and elsewhere against the Turks.

To contain the Bolshevik Revolution, some 5,000 Canadians would spend a few months in Siberia, where the Allies maintained an expeditionary corps. Between October 1918 and June 1919, when they left Russia, the Canadians were not involved in any large-scale fighting. Their casualties then amounted to eight dead and 16 wounded.

Wartime Tactical Developments

Between February 1915 and November 1918 the tactics of warfare were weapons-driven. In 1918 the infantry was engaged in reasonably fluid assaults under an umbrella provided by artillery, heavy machine guns, tanks and planes. Since 1915 the number of guns per trench of 1,000 infantrymen had no less than doubled, and munitions rationing, strictly applied up to late 1916, had virtually been abolished.

In 1916, tanks appeared on the battlefields. Canadians were
driving the tank in this photo: A maple leaf and the word
"Toronto" can be seen on its front.
(Private collection)

Privates of the 22nd (French-Canadian) Battalion mending trenches in July 1916.
(NAC, PA-253)

Artillery

During the 19th century the artillery piece underwent developments comparable to those of the rifle. At the beginning of the century, the classic bronze, muzzle-loading, smoothbored field gun fired bullets or round shells at a distance varying from 450 to 750 m, depending on the calibre. At that time, calibre was expressed by projectile weight, and the most common guns were the 42-, 32-, 24-, 19-, 9-, 6-, 4- and 3-pounders. Their accuracy left much to be desired, since each shot would send the gun recoiling back a metre or two and sometimes more, depending on ground conditions, which meant the gunners had to put it back in position and re-aim. This operation negatively affected the rate of fire, as did the necessity of cleaning the powder and priming fuse residues in the barrel with a brush after each shot.

In the 1850s, just as with the rifle, came the development of the rifled breech-loading gun that marked the start of a series of technological innovations. The bronze gun gave way to the iron one, and the bullet yielded to the cylindro-ogival shell; new chemical products made it possible for the explosive charge to ignite after percussion; the invention of cartridge ammunition—a single piece containing the shell, thruster, cartridge and primer—increased the firing rate; the invention of cordite produced a greatly improved range; and the appearance of the hydraulic and then the hydropneumatic brake appreciably reduced the recoil effect. The same period saw significant improvement in ammunition: a considerable increase in shell weight, which enhanced the destructive effect, and the introduction of new types of projectiles like the segment shell, the common or explosive shell, the canister shell and the armour-piercing shell.

Until the end of the 19th century, however, field guns were still fired "by sight." They therefore had to be deployed on cleared ground, usually in front of the infantry. Yet the more powerful rifles now made field guns and gunners increasingly vulnerable. In the Boer War it was noted that sight firing had become almost suicidal, and this resulted in the development of indirect or concealed fire. To hit a concealed target, the gunner aimed his gun according to instructions provided by an observer far away with a clear view of the target.

In Canada, the year 1871 marked an important stage in artillery history as the first two permanent batteries were founded, at Kingston and Quebec City. Before the end of the decade all the recently estab-

lished batteries of the permanent force, along with all the militia bat-
teries, were equipped with a new 9-pound gun developed by a British
officer, William Palliser. With a range of 3,300 m, this muzzle-loader
threw a shell fitted with bolts that held and slid along the grooves in
the gun's bore. These 9-pounders were used by Canadian gunners for
over 25 years, and six of them saw action at Fish Creek and Batoche
in the North-West Campaign.

As of 1897 the 9-pound gun began to be supplanted by a new
artillery piece, a breech-loading 12-pounder. Using cordite, this new
gun could throw a forged steel shell a distance of 5,120 m. At the same
time a new dual-purpose fuse (air and ground burst) made it possible
to explode a shell at a predetermined time or on ground impact.
During the Boer War, Canada sent three batteries to South Africa, each
equipped with six of these new guns.

Progress continued, however, and at the turn of the century British
artificers developed a new 18-pound gun with a maximum range of
5,670 m and a firing rate that could reach 20 rounds a minute with
the use of cartridge ammunition. This gun also included an aiming
device that permitted indirect fire. The first 18-pound guns reached
Canada in 1906, and during the 1914–18 war they spearheaded the
Canadian field artillery. They would not be withdrawn from service
until 1941, though by then they had seen a number of improvements.

At the beginning of the 1914–18 war Canadians also had a heavy
artillery piece in a highly accurate 60-pounder that threw shrapnel and
explosive shells approximately 9,150 m, a range that was later extend-
ed by munitions development. This was the Canadian army's main
heavy gun throughout that conflict.

The First World War spurred accelerated development in munitions
and artillery, especially in terms of range. In a few short years the range
of the 18-pound field gun increased from 5,670 m to 8,685 m, and
the range of the 60-pounder was extended from 9,150 m to 13,715 m.
Trench warfare also restored to honour an artillery piece that had fall-
en into disuse for over a century after widespread use in sieges of
fortresses and cities: the mortar. In contrast to the field gun, which had
an angle of departure no greater than 45°, the mortar, like its cousin
the howitzer, fired at angles greater than 45°. This meant that a pro-
jectile's angle of fall could be almost vertical and thus strike targets
behind a ridge or fortified wall. The howitzer differed from the mor-
tar only in that it had more power and a longer range. During the war
the British developed new artillery pieces that benefited the Canadians
as well, including two new howitzers with 6-inch and 9-inch bores.
The latter became the largest weapon in the Canadian army's arsenal.

New Ordnance Developed by the British between 1914 and 1918

Type	Projectile Weight (in pounds)	Range (in km)
8-inch howitzer	200	11.25
9.2-inch howitzer	290	12.05
12-inch howitzer	750	12.85
15-inch howitzer	1,400	9.65
6-inch gun	100	17.70
9.2-inch gun	380	20.90
12-inch gun	850	27.35
14-inch gun	1,586	32.20

In just three years, warfare had changed greatly. In 1918 the artillery played a larger role, but so did motorized transport companies, battalions of engineers and an anti-aircraft company equipped with searchlights. Although the army was still dependent on transmission lines that were frequently cut in combat, communications systems were renewed.

The engineers, for example, had become highly mobile and active under fire. For the crossing of the Canal du Nord on 27 September 1918 they arrived just behind the first troops to cross the obstacle. Under fire from leftover enemy machine-gun nests, they built light bridges to ensure that the bridgehead received fresh supplies of troops and ammunition. At the same time, bigger bridges were built to enable the tanks to join in the battle and enable artillery to cover the troops that had advanced the farthest. For the engineers, this war of movement already greatly resembled what their successors would see in Italy beginning in 1943.

Canadian Aviators

In the First World War, Canada had no military air arm of its own, but this did not stop some 24,000 Canadians from serving in the Royal Flying Corps and the Royal Naval Air Service before these were merged as the Royal Air Force in April 1918. Here, Canada would suffer 1,500 casualties. A quarter of the British flying officers—and some of the best—were Canadians.

Pressure to create a military air arm had been applied to the military authorities in 1911 and 1912, but they had learned only that the contraptions were expensive, dangerous and of dubious usefulness. In this strategic vacuum Canada was not as isolated as one might think. Indeed no one could foresee that, only 11 years after the first "heavier than air" flight, significant technical breakthroughs would result in the airplane's emergence as a formidable weapon of war. Nor could anyone foresee that Canada was on the verge of becoming involved in a war like that of 1914–18.

In Canada, Alexander Graham Bell was a pioneer of aviation. One of his associates, J.A.D. McCurdy, later made an unsuccessful attempt to sell his planes to the Canadian government. McCurdy went on to achieve some success in the United States. Returning to Canada with his flying school

Marrying Combatants

Love and romance were not utter strangers at the front. On 19 March 1915 Blanche Lavallée enlisted in the Medical Corps of the Canadian Expeditionary Force. She was 23 years old and had received her nursing certificate from Montreal's Hôtel-Dieu hospital a few weeks earlier. Lavallée would serve in a number of locations and have ample opportunity to see first-hand the worst of human suffering. In the spring of 1916 she met Lieutenant G.-A. Henri Trudeau, an officer in the Royal Canadian Regiment who had moved over to the Royal Flying Corps. The correspondence that followed their separation due to their many postings would lead Blanche and Henri to the altar in 1924. In order to marry in those days, officers were required to have accrued savings and to obtain the permission of their commanding officer.

Henri Trudeau would become a brigadier and command the 12th Military District in Regina for part of the Second World War. Blanche Lavallée-Trudeau would be a pillar of the local Red Cross branch wherever her husband was posted. In 1918 she was one of two Canadian military nurses sent as delegates to Washington to persuade Congress that American war nurses merited officer rank.

Henri Trudeau and Blanche Lavallée-Trudeau had four daughters.[71]

during the war, in Toronto he founded Canadian Aeroplanes, which would become involved in the mass production and mass export of aircraft—a first in the history of aeronautics.

A young Canadian aspiring to be a military aviator had to pay for his own training, whether in Canada or in the United States. Then, if the British recruited the novice into the air corps, whether attached to the navy or the army, they would reimburse him for the courses. As the war went on, a number of volunteers from the Canadian Army Corps would request or be offered a transfer to the air arm.

The actual birth of the air arm occurred on the Somme. In that sector, as the British began attacking in July 1916, some 240 Canadian aviators were in the front line. At that time the Allies dominated the air. In the early months of 1917 new and more sophisticated German aircraft tipped the balance of air power to the enemy side. By the end of the year, however, the Allies had changed this, with new equipment and a force of thousands of pilots, many of whom had been trained in Canada. Allied air supremacy would continue throughout 1918.

Pilot Training on Canadian Soil

On the Somme, imperial air casualties had been significant. To meet increasing demand for trained aviators, Britain proposed that a structured training programme for the Royal Flying Corps be established in Canada. The timing was right: The exploits of Canadian pilots like Billy Bishop were already being celebrated. Enthusiasm was running so high that the government rethought its air policy and considered building a Canadian air corps, though this would not occur until the 1920s. At the end of 1916 the Royal Flying Corps proposal was accepted. One of the advantages of the project, from the standpoint of the government, was that it allowed Canada to serve the Empire without over-committing itself to air issues that it viewed with some suspicion. In 1917 the British pilot training in Canada began. Thousands of Canadian specialists, pilots and technicians would be trained under this programme. In those days the pilot also had to be a mechanic, in order to repair his plane. Between the wars these men trained in Canada would help to arouse public interest in aviation and aeronautics. Although the new pilots answered to British leaders and British standards, they would soon evoke true Canadian pride and the public would begin to call, albeit rather timidly, for a Canadian air force.

Fleet Air Arm

During the First World War naval aircraft were used for bombing enemy submarines—at which they proved ineffectual—and carrying out surveillance of coastal military activity. On the coasts of France some naval aircraft would on occasion work for the armies. The first aircraft carriers consisted of barges towed by ships. Platforms would soon be constructed on existing vessels. Various kinds of tackle were used for stopping planes on landing but their safety left much to be desired: There would be complaints about the many incidents of men falling into the sea. An Allied fleet air arm formation would be the first to conduct strategic bombing—that is, the flight of a number of planes in formation carrying bombs to an objective to be destroyed.

Air Force Roles

On both sides of the conflict, cities would eventually be bombed. Bombs would rain on London and Paris as well as on the German cities of the Ruhr and in other French and Belgian areas occupied by the Germans. In 1918 aerial night bombing was tested out. Its effectiveness would influence the course of the Second World War.

The bombing raids would foster the illusion that, in a future war, aircraft could play a more important part than land battles. Since a number of aviators had experienced the terrible conditions in the trenches, it was natural for them to desperately seek a less messy way—though unfortunately more deadly for the populations affected—to make and win any potential war.

However, aircraft performed other services as well, such as keeping watch over the enemy, protecting observation balloons, and seeking and destroying enemy submarines, ships and balloons.

In the course of the war, combat aviation tactics and techniques would evolve. For example, machine-gun fire would be synchronized with the rotations per second of the propeller blades in the bullet's trajectories. At war's end, aviators would know how to attack enemy troops on the ground with fighters or modified bombers.

Canadian fliers with their aircraft, British Sopwith Camels. More than 8,000
Canadians served in Britain's Royal Flying Corps during the Great War.

The Great War saw the first flying machines used in battle. The Germans often used Zeppelins
for long-distance night bombing.
(Malfroy, private collection)

Effectiveness of the Air Arm

In the Battle of Amiens on 8 August 1918, the Canadian Army Corps excelled. How did the Allied air corps do? The morning fog prevented take-off before 9 o'clock. Some planes then began laying down smoke screens between tanks and certain German resistance points. Others provided highly ineffectual cover for the Canadian troops by machine-gunning and bombing the Germans. Repeatedly, large numbers of planes tried in vain to blow up bridges on the Somme, especially at Péronne and Python, being used (both then and at night) by numerous German reinforcements, which would slow the Canadian push the following day. Lastly, the air corps would be especially useful during this attack because of its ability to observe enemy positions.[72]

Canadians in Imperial Air Forces

The airmen would not be assembled in Canadian flights or in a national air corps, and they would not be commanded by their own officers. In short, the conditions that underlay Canadian national pride in the army did not exist for the air corps: These were colonial recruits in an imperial force.

Although thousands of Canadians had served in the British air force, no Canadian would rise above the rank of group captain (colonel). These men, who would form the basis of the Royal Canadian Air Force, were deployed everywhere. On the Franco-Belgian front and in Britain they faced off against the best of Germany's aircraft and pilots. They could also be found in less active air sectors: in Italy, in Macedonia where the Bulgarians and Turks were the main enemies, in Egypt and, later, in Russia. Some great names stand out: Billy Bishop, A.A. McLeod and Billy Barker would each

earn a Victoria Cross. Raymond Collishaw recorded 66 kills and D.R. MacLaren 54 in just eight months of fighting. The 10 top aces of all the belligerent nations would include four Canadians: Bishop, Barker, Collishaw and MacLaren.

Canada's Military Effort: Summing Up

Compared with the total industrial and military effort made by the major belligerents, Canada's contribution might seem paltry. However, considering its population (under eight million) and its military experience (virtually nil in 1914), Canada's effort was substantial. The human cost was also very high: 212,688 casualties as of 11 November 1918, with 53,216 dead and dying in the army alone. These figures speak of the immensity of the effort, but they cannot express the courage and selflessness of the volunteers, whether they were to return home or remain in Europe for all eternity. One small example will suffice. In the alumni magazine of Montreal's Loyola College, Gilbert Drolet recalls that of the slightly under 300 young men from that institution who went off to Europe, 37, or 12 percent, lost their lives. The story was repeated from sea to sea.

Canadian sacrifices on French soil are commemorated in a number of places. There is the melancholy soldier near St Julien, site of the first German gas attack. At Vimy, Canada maintains a magnificent monument fraught with significance. Lastly, at Beaumont-Hamel an impressive bronze caribou dominates the battlefield where the Royal Newfoundland Regiment (that dominion was not yet part of the Canadian Confederation) was annihilated on 1 July 1916, in the initial half hour of the first major attack on the Somme.

The Colours of the 38th Battalion, Canadian Expeditionary Force, 1914–18. Except for their distinctive insignia, the Colours of Canadian units were similar to those of the British until 1968. (Watercolour by Thornhill, MCG, K-73-137)

Assertion of Canadian Identity

During the war, the army shaped and moulded the Canadian identity as envisaged by the politicians. In Britain, Canada organized its own supply system, schools and hospitals, which were placed under the command of Major-General Turner, a Victoria Cross recipient in South Africa. In 1916 the Canadian government established the Ministry of Overseas Military Forces in the United Kingdom to deal on the spot with all matters relating to the Canadian forces in Europe. In 1918 the Canadian Corps in combat refused to copy the new British corps. Even in 1915 the Canadians had refused to break up their single division in order to serve short-term British interests.

These hundreds of thousands of Canadians helped to get their country recognized by its allies. Their glorious deeds and their determination to be different would influence the government in its policy of disengagement from imperial ascendancy. Military independence on the battlefield would be succeeded, over the decades, by gradual political independence. In the months and years immediately after the end of the war Canada would participate in peace negotiations, sign peace treaties and become a full member of the League of Nations.

Canadian POWs

During the First World War nearly 3,000 Canadians, including several dozen officers, were taken prisoner of war. The officers' daily routine, though not inspiring, seems not to have been too difficult:

Wakeup	*0800 hrs*
Breakfast	*0830 hrs*
Reading and/or exercise	*until 1300 hrs*
Lunch	*1300 hrs*
Reading and/or exercise	*until 1830 hrs*
Supper	*1830 hrs*
Roll call	*2030-2100 hrs*
Fires out	*2200 hrs*

These officers had to pay for their meals (about 8 Marks a day, or £5 a month). They were entitled to write two letters and four postcards a month.[73]

The "Military" Photographers of the Canadian Expeditionary Force

When the conflict began, Canada still did not have a photographic service. It used commercial photographers, who naturally stayed far behind the front. This situation was rectified on 28 April 1916 when Captain Harry Knobel became official photographer to the Canadians in France. Before falling ill and leaving the front the following August, Knobel took 650 photographs. He was succeeded by Ivor Castle, a photographer from the Daily Mirror, who was given the rank of lieutenant and subsequently snapped 800 photographs. On 4 June 1917 Castle was replaced by Honorary Lieutenant William Rider-Rider, who would soon be known for his daring. Although not obeying any specific order, Rider-Rider seemed to know where attacks would occur and would arrange to be on the spot. His daring cost him an injury. He took 2,800 negatives and would receive an MBE on the recommendation of Sir Arthur Currie.[74]

French Canadians and the French Language in the Canadian Expeditionary Force

The initial call-up of volunteers obliterated the existing militia units and the country's linguistic identities. Pressure from a number of quarters prompted the government to establish the 22nd (French-Canadian) Battalion, forerunner of the Royal 22e Régiment. However, decades of ignoring the Francophone fact in the Canadian military would have repercussions. The historian J.L. Granatstein reckons that a maximum of 50,000 Francophones came forward as volunteers—less than eight percent of all recruits. Conscription would cause serious disturbances in Quebec in 1917–18, in addition to destroying the Conservative party in Quebec for generations to come.

At the outset of the war, however, enthusiasm reigned throughout the country. On 1 August 1914 the 6th Canadian Artillery Regiment from Quebec City and Lévis offered to join in. The authorities, however, were not inclined to mobilize the units. In the event, given the submarine threat, the 6th Regiment was ordered to take coastal defensive positions at Fort de la Martinière and Île d'Orléans below Quebec City. The 6th would be confined to this role for each shipping season until the end of the war. During these periods of service, the officers and men lived in tents and served two batteries. Volunteers from the regiment would also sail to the island of St Lucia where they remained until war's end. Several men from the regiment would volunteer to be sent overseas. Some would be stationed in Bermuda as members of a replacement garrison for the British.

Elsewhere in the country, the Winnipeg Libre Parole reported on 20 April 1916 that 30 descendants of the Métis of 1870 and 1885—19 of them apparently Francophones—had just enlisted at

Qu'Appelle. At the same time, the Winnipeg Free Press *published an article by Captain M.A. Fiset of the 36th Field Battery describing the exploits of Private P. Riel, a nephew of Louis Riel, who between March 1915 and January 1916 had killed 30 Germans as a sniper. When Pte Riel was himself mortally wounded by a shell-burst on 13 January 1916 his rifle was prominently displayed in the window of a London building.*[75]

Given these two examples, one may wonder how many Francophones across the country would have willingly gone overseas had there been a welcome for them before and after the outbreak of war. The insensitivity to the Francophone fact in the Canadian military of the day had repercussions, though not all officers were anti-French. Lieutenant-Colonel Francis Farquhar, the governor-general's military secretary until placed in command of the PPCLI, told his officers he wanted them to be able to read and send a simple message in French. Farquhar believed that officers should know 500 basic French words before reaching France. Courses were given during the Atlantic crossing, though most of the men would gladly have done without them.[76]

Rejection of Volunteers

In Canada there was open talk of a war between white men, meaning that the sport of killing an enemy of the white race should be reserved for whites. The local commanding officers were given the responsibility of accepting or rejecting volunteers. Initially only Aboriginals were explicitly excluded, under the pretext that in the heat of battle the Germans might refuse them the treatment usually reserved for "civilized" combatants. This did not stop a number of commanders, whether or not they were aware of the directive, from accepting Aboriginals, some of whom would later earn sterling reputations, especially as snipers.

However, members of more visible groups such as the blacks in the Maritime provinces or the Asians and Aboriginals in British Columbia, who turned up in the hundreds at various recruiting centres, were barred from participating in this white man's war. In 1915 suggestions for a battalion of Canadians of Japanese origin and a battalion of black Canadians were sidelined, even though the pool of white volunteers was already running low.

Although there was no discriminatory directive as such, it was clear that a discriminatory policy was being applied. But while the idea of companies of blacks or of Asians came to naught, two Aboriginal com-

panies were integrated with a battalion recruiting mainly in Ontario. Finally, in 1916 a black workers' battalion was formed, No. 2 Construction Battalion (Coloured). It would be commanded by whites, with its sole black officer, the chaplain, given the rank of honorary captain.

Beginning in the summer of 1916, with recruiting problems worsening, the defence department finally advocated an open policy. However, as racism was not exclusively a white man's prerogative, problems continued to arise. For example, the Aboriginals made it clear they did not want to serve in No. 2 Construction Battalion, which was short of men. They refused to associate with black men in war. Then, two years after the outbreak of war, the fervour subsided. None of the battalions raised from 1916 on, including No. 2 Construction Battalion, would manage to fill its ranks. That battalion would never be more than a big, 500-man company commanded by a major instead of a lieutenant-colonel.

When conscription came in 1917, it applied to everyone except Aboriginals, who did not fail to point out that they still did not have the right to vote. Japanese Canadians, who were no closer to full-citizenship status, claimed the same exemption. The Indian Act would be used to spare the Aboriginals, and an order in council of 17 January 1918 would exempt both Japanese and Aboriginal Canadians.

Despite these obstacles, the participation of these groups in the First World War has been established as follows: 3,500 Aboriginals, 1,000 blacks and 600 Japanese Canadians.

Special Canadian Souls

In preparing to transport the 1st Canadian Division to the European continent, the senior Canadian chaplain, Richard Steacy, attempted to secure passage for his 33 chaplains, approximately one for every 1,000 men. The British then had five chaplains per infantry division, or one for every 4,000 men. Lord Kitchener asked Sam Hughes to send fewer pastors in future and refused to allow the 33 who were in England to go to France. Steacy then proposed that he take 25 chaplains, only to be refused again by the British, who stuck to the magic number of five. The Canadians were furious.

A delegation made up of a United Church minister and a Catholic priest went to the War Office. The British maintained their resistance until the delegates stated the obvious: Canada was paying its own way and would do what it wanted. The War Office reminded them that *despite the large number of chaplains accompanying the Canadian troops, their conduct on English soil was not the most refined. The response was swift: The situation would be much worse if they were not there, claimed Pastor Frederick George Scott. Finally, the British Chaplain-General promised to intervene on behalf of the Canadian clergymen. On 2 February 1915 the British agreed to 11 chaplains for each Canadian division, a ratio that would later be applied for all British divisions.*

Had the Canadians shown the way in this sector? One thing is certain: They had announced their distinct Canadian status, just as their political minister, Sam Hughes, had wished.[77]

Chapter V

FROM ONE WORLD WAR TO ANOTHER (1919–43)

A Return to Civilian Life

The war would never be completely over for those who lived it. A number of veterans would be haunted by old physical or psychological wounds for the rest of their lives. Many of them would die prematurely, some by their own hand.

The country wanted only to forget the war and those who had fought it. Returning soldiers, who did not always understand or appreciate what was happening on the home front, often refused to talk about their experiences, whether of mass casualties or courageous deeds. At the same time, however, they would come to idealize the comradeship of the trenches and to support civic virtues. Pacifism would find a ready home with these veterans. It is not difficult to understand why.

Substantial pensions—the best in the world—were among the benefits available to war widows and orphans as well as seriously disabled soldiers, and veterans' hospitals sprang up. To the other veterans, however, the Union government was anything but generous. They received a small lump sum reflecting their length of service, $35 to purchase civilian clothing and a year of free medical care.

Political leaders were haunted by deficits as the country came out of the ordeal with a mountain of debt. They declared they were opposed to encouraging dependency and lack of initiative. Veterans seeking to establish themselves as farmers, however,

Sergeant and fighter pilot, Royal Canadian Air Force, circa 1941–43. (Re-creation by Ronald B. Volstad, DND)

were granted land and low-interest loans. By 1930, half of the men choosing this option had lost everything.

Few people had foreseen what would follow the cessation of hostilities. A Presbyterian army padre, Edmund Oliver, wrote in *Social Welfare* in the fall of 1918 that the men returning from the front would not be satisfied with the old order: "We are blind if we do not see profound social upheavals and political adjustment ahead."[78] Oliver advocated for Canadian churches to support veterans' rights, by demanding, for example, that they be offered education and professional training.

The veterans did seek change, yet they were divided on all of the great social, political and economic debates of the day. The spirit of the Canadian Army Corps foundered on the harsh reality of the home front: inflation and unemployment. Growing increasingly more urban, with a working class that had swelled enormously between 1914 and 1919, the country was ill-prepared for the required conversion of its war industries. Many armaments factories simply closed their doors. In economic circumstances that would persist until the period 1924–30, and in a society that was becoming increasingly hardened, only the most desperate of the demobilized men would be helped to find work.

A political fissure had appeared with the Conscription Act of 1917, followed by a rigged election that left the Union government on its last legs. Many political administrations would not survive the war. Military management, never the strong point of post-Confederation Canada, was not going to suddenly improve with the return of the troops. When Arthur Meighen replaced Robert Borden as prime minister, he merely took up the problems where Borden had left off. Mackenzie King would

take the same route. The veterans, however, through demonstrations and other means of applying pressure, would slowly see their lot improve. Their demands would serve their successors well.

Independence and Isolationism

The colony that went to war came out of it virtually an independent partner of Great Britain. Yet when, after 1917, Canada began to take part in the great strategic imperial decision-making, its foreign policy remained that of the Empire. In 1922, however, an incident between Turkey and Greece threatened to erupt into a major conflict. When Britain asked Canada if it would provide military support against the Turks should things take a turn for the worse, Canada declared that it would not. Common imperial doings had reached their limit. The 1931 Statute of Westminster would make Canada officially independent and the equal of the United Kingdom.

In Canada pacifism was in fashion and voices denouncing militarism could be heard daily. William Lyon Mackenzie King, prime minister from 1921 to 1930 and again from 1935 to 1948, would play peace and isolationism as his trump cards until the late 1930s, announcing that in the event of another European war Canada's participation would not be a foregone conclusion: Parliament would decide. In any case, on a visit to Germany in 1937 he gave Adolf Hitler to understand that Canada would not sit idly by if London were bombed. His threat seems not to have made much of an impression on the German Chancellor.

Canada's isolationist determination prompted it to fight Article X of the Geneva Convention, which embodied the principle of mandatory action by members of the League of Nations against belligerent coun-

Corporal of the Princess Patricia's Canadian Light Infantry in winter dress, 1938. (Watercolour by Derek FitzJames, Anne A.K. Brown Military Collection, Brown University)

Sergeant of the Toronto Regiment. Raised in 1920, this regiment was merged with the Royal Grenadier Regiment in December 1936. (Re-creation by Derek FitzJames, Anne A.K. Brown Military Collection, Brown University)

Officer of the Victoria Rifles of Canada, 1933. (Re-creation by Derek FitzJames, Anne A.K. Brown Military Collection, Brown University)

Privates of the Royal 22e Régiment in service dress from a sketch by F.P. Todd, Quebec City, 11 September 1931. (Anne A.K. Brown Military Collection, Brown University)

Private of the 1st Hussars, 1934. (Re-creation by Derek FitzJames, Anne A.K. Brown Military Collection, Brown University)

Private of the Irish Regiment of Canada, 1934. The volunteer militiamen of Irish origin wore the saffron kilt with parade dress. Raised within the Toronto Irish community, this regiment was disbanded in 1965. (Re-creation by Derek FitzJames, Anne A.K. Brown Military Collection, Brown University)

tries. When it came time for the League to consider taking measures against Japan for invading Manchuria and Italy for invading Abyssinia, the Canadian prime minister, who was also undersecretary for external affairs, would draw back from imposing sanctions. However, Canada did sign the high-minded, toothless Kellogg-Briand Pact for peace and became an ardent partisan of compulsory arbitration on the international scene.

Mackenzie King had learned an essential lesson from the experience of 1914–18: Another war, however distant from Canada's shores, might tear the country apart. His objective was to keep the international situation from developing into armed conflict. But King had no leverage with European fascism or the rise of the dictators of the right and the left around the world. Nor could he do anything about the international crisis that, beginning with the stockmarket crash of 1929, would grow more generally financial and economic. The Depression of the 1930s would help trigger the conflict of 1939–45.

Canada's Military Between the Wars

Canada was caught in an almost humorous dichotomy. In the 1920s the United States was basically correct in perceiving Canada as still a British colony. Accordingly, its war plans included an attack on Canada in the event of an armed conflict with Britain. On the other hand, Canada's primary defence plan stated that in the event of an Anglo-American war Canada would seize certain areas of the United States. This secret Plan No. 1 would be set aside in 1926.

From the standpoint of Canadian defence, the years 1919–39 were a period of restructuring. Canada's defence forces reverted to their prewar role. They were small, with a ceiling of 10,000 men for the three arms—a figure that would not be reached until the country entered the Second World War. In the period 1922–35, one of galloping inflation followed by crisis, Canada's financial situation called for military changes.

In 1918, Canada had a ministry of defence and militia, a ministry of marine and an aviation commission. The National Defence Act, which came into force in early 1923, merged the three services as a cost-cutting measure. The Chief of the General Staff became the Chief of Staff of the Department of National Defence and thus responsible for all three arms. The navy opposed the order in council as unenforceable. In 1927 the head of the Naval Service, a member of the Defence Council (which had replaced the Militia Council of 1904), became the Chief of Naval Staff, and the Chief of Staff reverted to his former title. The Council also included the head of the Royal Canadian Air Force.

The budget of this reorganized department was not particularly impressive. It rose from $13.5 million in 1924–25 to $23.7 million in 1930–31, but the economic crisis brought cuts, and in 1932–33 the figure fell to $14 million. Later on, some unemployment funding covered military construction, but this did nothing for the effectiveness of the institution. Beginning in 1936 a much belated rearmament programme got under way. Priority was given to the defence of the national territory, especially its coasts. Accordingly projects were undertaken on the west coast in 1936–37, though these were still not completed in September 1939 and what *was* finished proved useless: Weapons placed in batteries were frequently outmoded or poorly sited; units were under strength; and scout and attack aircraft were virtually nonexistent.

Royal Canadian Regiment bandsman, 1938.
In full dress, regular infantry bands wore red.
(Watercolour by Derek FitzJames,
Anne A.K. Brown Military Collection,
Brown University)

Bugler of the Mississauga Horse in full dress,
1935. After the First World War, the khaki
uniform was the only one issued to
volunteers. However, a few officers and
musicians such as the members of this
cavalry regiment paid for their own
ceremonial red outfits and white helmets.
(Watercolour by Derek FitzJames,
Anne A.K. Brown Military Collection,
Brown University)

Private of the Royal 22e Régiment wearing the full dress adopted in 1928.
(O'Keefe)

Canada decided to retain a navy and accordingly purchased from Britain a light cruiser, two destroyers and two submarines. *Niobe* and *Rainbow* were sent to the scrap heap. With this move, the Union government, which included a number of the Conservatives of 1913, returned to the national naval strategy advocated by Wilfrid Laurier. The leaders of this navy sought a solution, in terms of personnel and equipment, that would enable them to be more active than they had been since 1910. In 1939 the navy would have more than 1,800 professional seamen. It had also created, in 1923, the Royal Canadian Naval Reserve with a maximum strength of 500 and, later, the Royal Canadian Naval Volunteer Reserve, which would not exceed a strength of 1,500 until 1939. Beginning in the 1930s, the navy embarked, little by little, on a rearmament programme. In 1931 it acquired two modern Royal Navy destroyers, HMCS *Saguenay* and *Skeena*. These 1,360-ton vessels had a top speed of 31 knots, a main armament of four 4.7-inch guns and a crew of 181. In the late 1930s four similar destroyers, *Fraser, Saint-Laurent, Restigouche* and *Ottawa,* were added, along with a slightly larger vessel, *Assiniboine.*

To elicit recommendations on what the aftermath of war would hold for the army, the general staff struck a commission for militia reorganization headed by Major-General Otter. As for the professional force, two of the new regiments that had emerged during the First World War, Princess Patricia's Canadian Light Infantry (PPCLI) and the Royal 22nd, would be retained. Thus the Canadian Army Corps would be perpetuated, and for the first time Francophones would have access to a permanent French-language infantry unit. The RCR and the other prewar Permanent

Militia units also survived. In most of them, however, actual strength was less than the authorized maximum. Between 1919 and 1939 Canada would never have a combat-ready infantry brigade, and these regular-force units would not be officially attached to Non-Permanent Militia brigades or the forces planned for overseas in the event of war. The first postwar mass exercise for the permanent force took place in 1936.

As for the Non-Permanent Militia, it was decided that defence of the country would involve 15 divisions (11 infantry and four cavalry). One of the debates making the rounds was whether to keep the numbered battalions of the Canadian Expeditionary Force or to submerge these battle units within the pre-1914 militia formations. The veterans favoured retention of the 1914–18 units in order to preserve the old ties with the Army Corps commanded by Sir Arthur Currie and provide a spur to recruitment. Strongly supported by a panoply of politicians, however, the militia regiments survived. They would, nonetheless, receive the battle honours and recent traditions of those numbered battalions to which each militia unit had contributed the most.

After the disappearance of Defence Plan No. 1, the 15 divisions of the early 1920s were considered too expensive and had to make way for six infantry divisions and one cavalry division, which more or less corresponded to the maximum overseas force Canada could provide in the event of war. The service and artillery units and sub-units were not assigned to any of the brigades in these formations. Going into the 1930s, the Chief of the General Staff tried to sell this revised plan by claiming that a smaller number of units (most of the existing ones being unable to fill their ranks, recalling the pre-1914 situation) could be better trained and equipped. He would not succeed until

A member of the Royal Canadian Air Force Women's Division, which was formed in 1941 and eventually recruited more than 16,000 volunteers. Beginning in September 1942, many of these women served in Britain; by 1945 more than 1,300 of them were serving there. The young woman shown here was a clerk at an air force command post in the south of England. Canadian women serving outside Canada wore the "CANADA" badge on the upper sleeve. (Re-creation by Ronald B. Volstad, DND)

1933, and then only by employing a trick: The reduction became politically acceptable in the context of Canada's contribution to the Geneva disarmament talks. In any case, the 15 divisions were paper tigers.

In 1936, then, the Militia's order of battle as it had existed in 1920 had dropped by more than half and a number of regiments had disappeared for good or been merged with others. Some regiments were also changing their roles to reflect technological progress. Some infantrymen were becoming gunners or members of so-called armoured units, though the Armoured Corps would not appear until 1940. The 1936 reorganization occurred largely without bitterness or protest, as the champions of the Non-Permanent Militia had been assured that the surviving units would have genuine roles to play in any mobilization. In fact the general staff would keep this promise: In the mobilization of 1939, contrary to what had happened in 1914, the Non-Permanent Militia would be the basis for the recruitment of volunteers for overseas and conscripts for territorial defence. In 1939, however, units would still be waiting for the new equipment promised in the reorganization. The horses had gone, but cavalry units had virtually no tanks. The so-called motorized units of the Non-Permanent Active Militia had no vehicles.

A Very British Canadian Navy

At 8:16 pm on 22 January 1932 the commander in chief of Britain's North America and West Indies Squadron, in which Canada's rare destroyers had become accustomed to train, sent a telegram to Canadian Admiral Walter Hose, the Chief of Naval Staff. Briefly, a popular uprising in El Salvador was endangering the lives of British residents and the first British warship would not be able to reach the scene before the 27th. He suggested that the Canadian vessels Skeena *and* Vancouver, *then cruising in the vicinity, be despatched to El Salvador at once. The same telegram was sent to Captain (N) V.G. Brodeur, the senior Canadian officer at sea.*

On receiving the message, Brodeur headed for Acajutla in El Salvador, where the British subjects were located. He telegraphed his decision to Hose some 15 minutes after changing course, expecting to reach Acajutla by dawn on the 23rd. Hose gave his permission at approximately 1:30 pm on the 23rd.

On arrival, the naval force limited its intervention to an embarrassing presence at dockside in Acajutla, where it took on board the wives of five British dignitaries fearing for their safety. Brodeur also met the new president of El Salvador. Altogether it was an uneventful visit that afforded the navy some wonderful media coverage at a time when its allocations for 1932–33 were being debated: The navy could be useful, even to foreigners.

A member of the Women's Royal Canadian Naval Service, which was formed in 1942 and attracted some 4,300 volunteers. The elegant sky-blue summer uniform pictured here distinguished the Canadians from the British and Americans, who wore white. The dark-blue winter uniform was identical to that worn by female members of the British Royal Navy.
(Re-creation by Ronald B. Volstad, DND)

Canadian air force pilot, 1920–24. The first uniform of the new Canadian air force was dark blue.
(Re-creation by Ronald B. Volstad, DND)

Royal Canadian Navy officer, 1940–45.
(Re-creation by Ronald B. Volstad, DND)

The Canadian navy as organized in 1910 was intended to replace a Royal Navy less and less present in North American waters. Since that time, the navy's general staff had taken pains to give as Canadian an image as possible to a force that still considered itself an integral part of the North America and West Indies Squadron.

This process of Canadianization took a step backward with the El Salvador affair. Brodeur had taken the initiative without waiting for orders. It also seems that Hose and defence minister Sutherland acceded to the British request without obtaining the government's consent. Prime Minister R.B. Bennett could only bow to a fait accompli.[79]

The Canadian Air Force was established in 1920 and redesignated the Royal Canadian Air Force in 1924, with Permanent, Non-Permanent and Reserve elements. Until 1938 this force was under the general command of the Army Chief of Staff. At its inception it was given 140 obsolete British aircraft from the First World War, contraptions that were used almost exclusively for civilian operations on behalf of the federal government. The mid-1930s saw the first preparations for a war that by then seemed inevitable. In 1939 Canada acquired and built some British Hurricane fighters, not up to the latest model of the German Me109s but able to play an important operational role. When war broke out, the Royal Canadian Air Force could marshal 53 aircraft, most of them obsolete. The country's only real military arm was a squadron of seven Hurricanes.

Apart from its few ships, Canada was basically without modern weaponry. For example, the militia had four late-model anti-aircraft guns, four anti-tank guns and 14 light tanks barely out of the factory. Its total strength was ridiculously low, and none of the three arms, except for a part of the little navy, was ready to carry out basic operational duties when called upon.

However, the world continued its inexorable journey to catastrophe. On 25 August 1939, Germany and Russia signed a non-aggression pact. Canada proceeded to take immediate pre-mobilization measures, including protection for strategic sites, with two partial divisions of auxiliary troops. On 1 September, Germany invaded Poland. On the 3rd, Britain and France declared war on Germany, followed on the 10th by Canada—though 303 Germans on Canadian soil had already been arrested, on 4 September. The country's glaring unpreparedness, however, would not prevent it from playing a major role in crushing the Axis forces.

The national census of June 1941 counted 11,506,655 Canadians, approximately one quarter and one twelfth of the populations of, respectively, the United Kingdom and the United States. In 1939, after a few years of very slow recovery from the Great Depression, Canada had 530,000 jobless. Two years later, the figure had dropped to 200,000, GDP had risen 47 percent, iron and steel production had doubled, and Canada had resumed its march on the road to industrialization. In 1941 military manufacture occupied a prominent place: light armoured vehicles and airframes (in both

A Sunderland float plane, 1942. This big "flying boat" was used by
the RCAF's 422 and 423 squadrons against German submarines.
(Private collection)

Motor torpedo boat used by the Canadian and British navies,
large numbers of which were built in Canada.
(Private collection)

Canadian Defence Between the Wars

	1923	1933	1936	1939 (prewar)
Budgets	$12,242,930	$14,145,000	$29,986,749	$64,666,875 (forecast)
Total Defence Forces	4,270 professionals 51,375 reservists (estimated)	5,123 professionals 53,072 reservists	5,959 professionals 50,342 reservists	7,945 professionals 54,055 reservists
Army/ Militia	3,554 professionals 50,000 reservists (estimated)	3,570 professionals 51,873 reservists	4,002 professionals 48,761 reservists	4,169 professionals 51,418 reservists
Navy	405 professionals 1,000 reservists	859 professionals 1,100 reservists	931 professionals 1,149 reservists	1,585 professionals 1,671 reservists
Air Force	311 professionals 375 reservists	694 professionals	1,026 professionals 341 reservists	2,191 professionals 966 reservists
Ships	2 destroyers, 4 trawlers (1 cruiser and 2 submarines in reserve)	4 destroyers, 2 minesweepers + 1 in reserve	4 destroyers, 1 minesweeper	6 destroyers, 5 minesweepers, 1 training ship (sail) + 1 motorized, 1 ketch
Aircraft	approx. 140 (gifts: 10 types)	185 (15 types)	166 (13 types) (1935 figure)	53 (for active service)

cases without motors), munitions, corvettes and frigates. Having increased its cash inflow sixfold in under two years, Canada was able to cover 70 percent of its wartime spending from its current account. This was made possible to a large extent by increases in personal and corporate taxes under an agreement with the provinces that was to end one year after the end of the war. This federal tax bite had other effects: It lowered purchasing power and partly controlled competition and runaway prices, two areas that were also regulated by the Wartime Trade and Price Commission. Canada's significant financial effort would take various forms: interest-free loans and large gifts to Britain as well as war expenditures that by 1945 would total $21,786,077,519, over and above the medical services and disability pensions provided to veterans.

On the international stage Canada played a very modest part. It did not have a place on the Allied Chiefs of Staff Committee and was forgotten when the United Nations Declaration was proclaimed. And although Quebec City was the site for two major strategic meetings attended by U.S. President Franklin Delano Roosevelt and British Prime Minister Winston Churchill, in August 1943 and September 1944, the prime minister of Canada stayed away. However, Canadians would sit on Allied committees for munitions, transportation and natural resources.

It should be mentioned that in the period 1939–45 the basis of Canada's current social-welfare system was broadened by the institution of unemployment insurance and family allowances. Many Canadians are unaware of the fact that the society they live in today was substantially shaped in the years of the Second World War.

Having declared war on Germany, Canada joined in "the phoney war." Camp Valcartier was reactivated and, unlike the situation in 1914–18, would operate year-round as the mobilization and training centre for the units of the 5th Military District and as a training centre for infantry generally. Between 1933 and 1936, through a relief programme for the jobless, its infrastructures had been greatly improved. Between 1939 and 1946 numerous "temporary" buildings would be erected—many of them to last more than 30 years.

With the disaster of Dunkirk in June 1940, Canada passed the National Resources Mobilization Act, which, among other things, called for 98,000 conscripts for territorial defence. On the overseas front, the 1939 decision to use only volunteers was upheld, but it must be stressed that 64,000 of those conscripts would volunteer for combat, more than 58,000 of them in the army.

Between 1939 and 1945 more than a million Canadian men and women, or one adult in 12, would don a uniform. During the six years of war 41 percent of men aged 18 to 45 served in the Canadian armed forces in some capacity. Germany's defeat left Canada the world's fourth military power, after the United States, the Soviet Union and the United Kingdom. In some fields, such as various types of merchant vessels and synthetic rubber, Canadian production was proportionately greater than that of the U.S. This large-scale military commitment resonates to this day. Canada still has approximately 400,000 living veterans, the vast majority of them, including tens of thousands of disabled, having served in the Second World War. In 1994 one Canadian in three over the age of 65 was a war veteran.

The Army to 1942

At top combat strength in 1943, the army had five divisions: three infantry and two armoured, plus two armoured brigades. The 1st Division reached England in December 1939 under the command of Major-General A.W.G. McNaughton, who would later be promoted to commander of the 1st Canadian Army. In May 1940 the 2nd Division, initially planned for territorial defence, left for the U.K. and the formation of the 3rd Division was announced. The danger had become very real.

Those who lived through this early period of the war remember that the volunteers would often have no uniforms, boots or winter coats and little or no field equipment. And because her armament was deficient, Canada would once again have to rely on the mother country, at least for the time being.

In theory, a Second World War Canadian infantry division had 18,376 men. The core of this formation comprised 8,148 infantrymen, representing 44.3 percent of its strength—the lowest percentage in this category of all Allied and enemy infantry divisions. The other members of this division could be found in its field artillery (2,122), quartermaster and service corps (1,296), engineers (959), medical service (945), electrical and mechanical technicians and craftsmen (784), signalmen (743), antitank group (721) and a plethora of other small, specialized groups. When the first 7,400 men of the 1st Division arrived in England in December 1939 they discovered the cold and rain of Salisbury Plain that their predecessors had known so well in 1914. The division would not reach full strength until February 1940. The leaders, who genuinely sought to make a contribution to victory, would be well served. However, their desire to see their country acknowledged as an Allied military power would be denied by the politicians at home, who refused to participate in meetings at the strategic level.

Prior to 1943 the Canadian army was involved in a number of actions, not all successful. On 12 and 13 June 1940 elements of the 1st Brigade (artillery and logistics) penetrated Brittany and advanced towards Laval and Le Mans. Before the irresistible German advance, they were ordered to fall back. On 17 June they re-embarked with their guns and some of their equipment, having destroyed the rest. The Breton enclave would not be defended; on British soil, only the 1st Canadian Division, during the long months after Dunkirk, would have enough equipment to defend the beaches of southeast England against a potential German invasion—this would be its mission.

In June 1940, 2,500 men of the 2nd Division were sent to Iceland, an important control point for the North Atlantic. The soldiers' lives there were tough and boring, but no fighting occurred. The following October they rejoined their comrades in Britain, except for the Cameron Highlanders, who would stay in Iceland until the spring of 1941.

In September 1940, Germany, Italy and Japan signed a pact. Then on 7 December 1941 Japan attacked the United States at Pearl Harbor. In the hours and days that followed, a series of objectives were targeted in the Pacific, including the British colony of Hong Kong where two Canadian battalions and a brigade headquarters had just arrived with 1,973 men and two nurses under the command of Brigadier J.K. Lawson.

Since the early 1920s, Canada's Defence Plan No. 2 had spelled out what had to be done in the event of an attack by Japan. In 1930 this became the plan for the protection of Canadian territory in case of a war between Japan and the United States. Once Pearl Harbor was attacked, Canada immediately went to war against Japan—24 hours before the U.S. and the U.K. As we have

Canadian infantryman in Hong Kong, December 1941. The two Canadian
regiments served with the garrison that resisted the Japanese attack.
The Winnipeg Grenadiers from Manitoba and the Royal Rifles of Canada
from Quebec were equipped for the tropics.
(Re-creation by Ronald B. Volstad, DND)

seen, the Pacific coast was ill-prepared. In 1939 Canada had eight aircraft there, all obsolete and unarmed, some without radio and with a dubious flying range. In 1941 this state of affairs was basically unchanged. The anti-aircraft and coastal artillery units were also inadequate. In the latter case the possible gun elevation limited the range of fire. Some 10,000 army troops were deployed along the coast. No doubt some of them would have found consolation in the fact that at this point the northwest coast of the United States was more poorly defended than the Canadian coast. In 1942 radar began to be installed.

Nonetheless, Canada's Pacific interests, though subordinated to Britain's interests, triggered a promise, in the fall of 1941, of two battalions to reinforce the Hong Kong garrison. This force left Vancouver on 27 October 1941 aboard *Awatea* and *Prince Robert* and arrived in Hong Kong at the end of November. Largely untrained, these volunteers scarcely had time to take their positions before Japan moved to the attack. The battle was lost in advance. Brigadier Lawson was killed on 19 December defending his headquarters. This veteran of the First World War thus had the sombre distinction of being the first Canadian officer of his rank to die in combat during the Second World War. By 25 December it was all over. A total of 557 men would perish, nearly half of them in the Japanese camps. Sergeant John Osborne of the Winnipeg Grenadiers would receive a posthumous Victoria Cross for saving the lives of his comrades by throwing himself on top of a grenade.

Things did not stop there. The Japanese were approaching the North American continent by way of the Aleutian Islands. On 6 and 7 June 1942 the islands of Attu and Kiska fell to Japan. Later a Japanese submarine fired on the telegraph station and lighthouse at Estevan Point, British Columbia, but without causing serious damage.

Canadian reaction was immediate. The army on the Pacific coast swelled along with its budget. The air force raised the number of its squadrons to 36, with more modern aircraft. Up to a point the politicians gave in to the demands of the people of British Columbia, who feared an invasion; however, the threat was not very plausible considering that Japanese military commitments were spread throughout a vast sphere of influence.

The situation of Japanese Canadians had been precarious since the beginning of the conflict. They were not well integrated or accepted by the local population. The army had decided not to accept recruits of Japanese or Chinese origin. After Pearl Harbor, anti-Japanese demonstrations were threatened in British Columbia. To avoid provocation, Japanese-language schools and newspapers voluntarily shut down. After the defeat in Hong Kong public opinion exploded, demanding the internment of these Japanese Canadians who might form a fifth column. Journalists and politicos in British Columbia outdid one another in proclaiming the danger and consequences of lack of action on this matter. After a few weeks the federal government gave in and, on 27 February, announced the evacuation of all west-coast residents of Japanese origin. The 22,000 people concerned were uprooted and their property was sold. This flagrant act of discrimination—unjustified on the basis of military intelligence, which saw no danger—did nothing for Canada's moral reputation as an enemy of injustice.

And Canada's descent into Hell was not over. In August 1942 came the disaster of Dieppe. In this enormous ill-conceived raid that should never have taken place, the

A private equipped for Alpine winter combat training,
1943. This specialized training was given in Yoho
National Park, British Columbia.
(DND, ZK-330).

Pieces of a German torpedo run aground on the beach at St Yvon near Gaspé in 1942.
(Musée de la Gaspésie, Gaspé, Quebec)

Canadians, in less than five hours of combat, suffered 68 percent casualties, including 907 dead.

At the time a number of Canadian volunteers, politicians and journalists were complaining about the fact that Canada's overseas formations remained in England while the British, Australians, New Zealanders, Americans and a host of other Allies were fighting all over the world. Although the Japanese navy had experienced significant setbacks, the situation was not particularly rosy for the countries fighting the Axis. Meanwhile the Americans and Soviets were pushing to open a second front on the European continent, where the Soviets were then fighting alone. A number of factors, including a shortage of men and equipment, militated against this plan. However, raids, some substantial, were in fashion. One was planned on Dieppe for June 1942 with the equivalent of two brigades of the 2nd Canadian Division. For various reasons this plan was abandoned and the units involved returned to their barracks in disappointment.

Approximately two months later this plan was abruptly reactivated. The raid would take place on 19 August 1942. The plan was highly complex and relied on precise timing in all its phases. Unfortunately, however, intelligence was poor, the inevitable potential problems had not been taken into account, and naval and air support to the ground troops was highly deficient. There was no element of surprise virtually anywhere on the various landing beaches. By chance, a German coastal defence unit was on an exercise that particular night and able to sound the alarm very early on.

Although the planning was British, the Canadian subordinates, partly carried away by enthusiasm for combat at last, did not subject it to serious criticism. Nothing but gross incompetence from the Germans could have changed the course of events. Some 4,963 Canadians were involved in the raid, which began badly when very few of the planned landings took place at the appointed time and place. Of the 2,210 Canadians who would return to England, only 336 came out of it unscathed. All units—six infantry regiments and one armoured regiment plus hundreds of engineers, medics, gunners and a medium machine-gun regiment—sustained casualties. Blocked virtually everywhere by impregnable cliffs and lacking massive artillery and well-deployed air support, the men were killed (907, over 18 percent of strength), injured (2,460, or about 50 percent) or taken prisoner (1,874, or 37 percent, including 568 wounded). In all, the Allies (Canadian, British and a few Americans) suffered 4,350 casualties: 3,610 army, 550 navy, 190 air force. The Germans got away with 591 casualties: 316 army, 113 navy, 162 air force.

Nor was the suffering over for the Canadians taken prisoner in the raid. From papers seized from the enemy, the Germans discovered that the Canadians had been planning to shackle their prisoners to make them easier to control, which was in contravention of the laws of war. They therefore immediately clapped shackles on their Canadian prisoners, and for some this humiliation would continue for 18 months. Canada would do the same for a few months with its German prisoners of war. In December 1942, however, they abandoned this practice, which was taking them much too close to the monster they were trying to defeat.

The Air Force to 1942

After June 1940 the British air force played an essential wartime role. Before the

A Westland Lysander reconnaissance aircraft. Built in Canada from 1938 on, this airplane equipped the first Royal Canadian Air Force squadron sent to Britain in early 1940. (DND, PCN-5244)

A Bolingbroke bomber, circa 1940–44. This was the Canadian version of the British Blenheim. About 600 were made in Canada, and were used mainly for coastal patrols. In July 1942, a Bolingbroke helped sink a Japanese submarine off British Columbia.
(DND, PCN-5234)

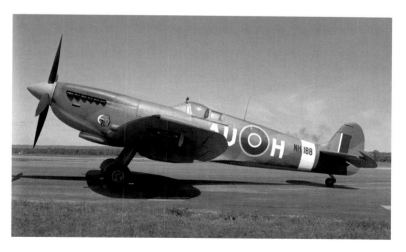

Supermarine Spitfire. Beginning in 1941, this fighter aircraft equipped several Canadian air force squadrons in Europe.
(DND, PCN-5234)

autumn of 1940, Canada did not attempt to obtain special identification for its thousands of aviators serving in the Royal Air Force. After that time, dozens of squadrons would display Canadian colours. Yet outward appearances could not conceal certain realities: 60 percent of Canada's fliers served in the RAF, and they made up 25 percent of the strength of its Bomber Command. The activities of the few Canadian air units were also controlled by the British, who supplied most of their ground crew and even some of their flight personnel. This account of the Canadian air effort would be incomplete if we failed to mention the British Commonwealth Air Training Plan, which was conducted in Canada and prepared 131,000 Allied air crew, including 73,000 Canadians, for action. During the summer of 1939, in anticipation of war, Britain had attempted to revive and expand on the pilot training plan that had been so successful in Canada during the First World War. Mackenzie King rejected the idea. When hostilities broke out, however, the project resurfaced and the prime minister began to see its advantages: It would represent a significant contribution to the war effort without being costly in terms of human lives. The spectre for Mackenzie King was seeing this war result in conscription, to divide the country once again.

In December 1939 the British Commonwealth Air Training Plan was drawn up, with Canada agreeing to cover a large part of its cost. The first trainees would complete their instruction towards the end of 1940, and the Canadian crews trained under the programme would serve in Britain. In 1940 discussions took place concerning implementation of one of the clauses of the Plan, which stated that overseas squadrons would be clearly identified as Canadian. By late 1942 there were 107 schools in Canada,

most having required the construction of infrastructures that would spawn the large airports of today.

During this war, however, Canada would still not control its own squadrons, which did not have majority Canadian ground crews. Eight Canadian fighter squadrons were involved in the air battle over Dieppe on 19 August 1942—which was virtually separate from what was taking place on the ground—without even the support or knowledge of the senior Canadian air force officers posted to Britain. It is often forgotten that the RAF used the Dieppe raid to provoke the biggest air battle over the European continent. Although aircraft losses were two to one in Germany's favour, the Germans could no longer manage to build as many planes as they were losing, whereas the Allies could easily make up their losses.

Throughout the war Canada was seeking its identity in the air, and its significant contribution in this area would become more or less watered down in the context of the overall Commonwealth effort.

As we have seen, Canada sent its entire air fleet, minimal though it was, to England in 1939. But it was not until June 1940 that the well-equipped No. 1 Canadian Squadron went overseas. It became operational on 24 August and inadvertently brought down two British Blenheims. That autumn it would make a more productive contribution to the great Battle of Britain and suffer casualties. Many Canadian pilots were already serving in the RAF as well.

In March 1941 there were still only three Canadian squadrons in Britain, all fighter squadrons. As of that time, all existing or future Canadian squadrons would get a 400 serial number. No. 425 Squadron (June 1942) would be Francophone, as the air force copied the army's effort of 1914. Some squadrons would be stationed as far from England as Burma (Myanmar), Ceylon (Sri Lanka) and Egypt. In January 1942, Canada had 32 squadrons, including 11 bomber squadrons and approximately 10 for coastal defence. Ultimately there would be 48, including those forming the 6th Canadian Bomber Group. No. 423 Squadron would be fortunate enough to destroy two German submarines in May 1942.

At this stage Canada was still in the process of organizing its air effort, despite the fact that nearly three years had elapsed since the beginning of the war. The British Commonwealth Air Training Plan, however, was functioning well. In May and June 1942 representatives of 14 countries met in Ottawa to review its performance. Canada used the occasion to request its own bomber group within British Bomber Command, countering British reluctance by offering to defray all the costs of its overseas air force. Although Britain agreed in principle, it would do nothing to effect its implementation.

The Navy to 1942

The navy was the smallest of Canada's armed forces but certainly not the least significant in terms of services rendered. During the First World War submarines had threatened Canadian coasts and maritime trade, and the British navy, stationed in European waters, could do nothing about it. On 11 November 1916 the Admiralty made it clear that Canada would have to increase its own coastal naval patrols; it could no longer rely on the British for its sea defence.

The First World War had brought some points of view closer together. For French Canadians, a completely Canadian navy held more attraction than the purely financial contributions sought by the pre-1914 Conservatives. English Canadians had

developed their identity and the idea of a national navy had become a necessity. The small Canadian navy of the 1920s recalled Laurier's navy of 1910 and the many earlier plans we have discussed. In 1939 the Canadian navy had four operational destroyers that went to Britain. With the Anglo-American agreement of 1940, which gave the British 50 old U.S. destroyers in exchange for bases to be built in Newfoundland and the West Indies, six more destroyers came into Canadian hands. These dated from the First World War and were more or less reliable. One of them, rechristened HMCS *St Croix*, had to return to Halifax from its initial sortie in British waters: The sea was too rough for *St Croix*, which was extremely heavy above the water line.

In June 1941 the 10 destroyers returned to Canada and joined the corvettes built domestically to escort supply convoys between North America and England. The navy, which is to this day undoubtedly the most British of Canada's three military arms, is also the only one—in spite of its vicissitudes—to obtain an independent command during the war. Ill-equipped and lacking experienced crews, the navy was thrown into an anti-submarine war in which it would initially find little success.

The Germans had begun to increase their submarine fleet a year before the outbreak of war. When hostilities began, neither Britain nor Canada was ready to deal with this threat. In fact the day after Britain declared war, the liner *Athenia*, out of Liverpool bound for Montreal, was sunk without warning by a German submarine 400 kilometres west of Ireland, recalling the sad fate of *Lusitania* in the First World War. It seemed obvious, especially after June 1940, that the reconquest of the European continent would largely depend on the vital transatlantic connection through which Britain would amass the men and equipment needed for eventual landings.

Although preparations had been made for a surface war, the convoy experience acquired some 25 years earlier had not been lost. In the meantime the Germans had improved their submarines, and with the conquest of France's Atlantic coast they became very dangerous. These submarines had a long range (over 10,000 kilometres even for the less sophisticated ones), had a surface speed of 17 to 19 knots (when convoys would do eight to 12 knots), could submerge for as long as 24 hours and had good communications with their European headquarters. Bit by bit the Germans developed their pack approach: One submarine located a convoy and rounded up his neighbouring wolves before moving to the attack, generally in a sector of the North Atlantic that no air patrol could cover in the early years of the war. The build-up of strategic stocks in Britain was in jeopardy.

Things were not going well for Canadian seamen. On 25 June 1940, HMCS *Fraser* was cut in half by the British ship *Calcutta* in the Gironde estuary, resulting in 47 dead. Later, HMCS *Margaree,* on patrol west of Ireland, suffered the same fate at the hands of a merchant ship, with 142 dead. On 6 November 1940, however, HMCS *Ottawa* helped to destroy an Italian submarine.

Early in the war the Germans would seek their targets in European waters, very rarely coming to the Newfoundland waters that fell under Canada's responsibility. Between September 1939 and October 1941 they sank 164 merchant ships in the service of the Allies, but only seven of these ships had been part of convoys.

In August 1941, at a meeting held in Placentia Bay, Newfoundland, between Prime Minister Churchill and President Roosevelt, the United States agreed to help protect the merchant vessels plying the western Atlantic. Up to that time the Americans had patrolled the coasts, the Canadians the sea east of Newfoundland; the two other segments of the convoy route were Newfoundland–Iceland and Iceland–Britain. Suddenly the small Canadian navy came under U.S. command. When the Americans took to the high seas, they escorted the fastest convoys that were less susceptible to attack.

When war was declared on Japan the United States transferred a large part of its fleet from the Atlantic to the Pacific. By the fall of 1942 the Americans were providing only two percent of the protection units for transatlantic convoys, although the area command remained in their hands.

In June 1942 approximately half of the escort vessels and a quarter of the air coastal patrols north of New York were Canadian. Since the U.S. had virtually stopped protecting its Atlantic coast, the Germans hit their seaborne trade head-on. Canada had to send corvettes south, thus weakening its northern escort groups. Just as the Germans were settling in solidly in the rough north Atlantic, the Canadians were left more or less alone, with a growing fleet of small escort vessels, ill-trained crews and outmoded equipment.

In 1940 the Canadians began building corvettes, small vessels some 60 metres long based on the design of the British whaling ships of the late 1930s. Very skittish at sea, they had a top speed of 16 knots and were equipped with a four-inch gun, outdated ASDIC (the British version of SONAR) and an anti-aircraft machine gun. Although they could survive the heavy weather of the North Atlantic and were excellent for manoeuvring, corvettes were very uncomfortable. What is more, most of the professional officers were posted to the larger ships—destroyers, cruisers and, later, aircraft carriers—preparing for the Nelson-style warfare their British colleagues longed for and leaving convoy duty and the corvettes to the Naval Reserve and Naval Volunteer Reserve.

As the domestic naval dockyards produced these corvettes, those intended for Canadian crews were thrown into battle with more or less raw volunteers. In Canada there was no time to train groups of escort crews in working as a team. Rest periods were rare, and the equipment—radar, ASDIC and the sensors for the high frequencies sent by enemy submarine radio—was out of date, often received six months to a year after it had been installed on the British ships. In 1941 some corvettes did not even have radar. The obvious enthusiasm of the Canadian volunteers could not completely make up for the heritage of an inadequate industrial infrastructure and lack of an experienced and sufficiently large navy to take on these duties. At the top of this weak structure sat Admiral Percy W. Nelles, who had reigned since 1934. Competent in his own way, Nelles was uninspired and dwarfed by a situation he had not foreseen and to which he was unable to adjust.

In the summer of 1941 the newly created Newfoundland Escort Force would have some traumatic experiences. One of its greatest problems was lack of air cover on certain parts of the route. Convoy SC-42, leaving Sydney, Nova Scotia, for Britain on 30 August 1941, lost 16 merchant vessels and one of its escorts on 9 and 10 September. Convoy SC-44 lost only four merchant vessels and a corvette, while SC-48 was heavily hit though not as hard as SC-42, and SC-52 about turned and made for port in raging seas. Then things appeared to subside in the

Atlantic as the German submarines shifted their priority to attacking southern traffic out of New York State. When German attention swung back to the North Atlantic in the late summer and fall of 1942 the situation soon became untenable. Convoy ON-127 left England for Canada with 32 merchant ships on 5 September 1942, escorted by two Canadian destroyers and three corvettes—one of them British and the only ship with radar that worked, albeit intermittently. Nine merchant ships were sunk, plus the destroyer *Ottawa*, which lost 114 crew members. On 30 October, SC-107 left Canada for Britain and lost 15 merchant ships. In neither case was an enemy submarine destroyed. The British and Americans wondered about the effectiveness of the Canadian escort when in mid-Atlantic. Between 26 and 28 December 1942, ONS-154, bound for Canada, lost 14 merchant vessels and a British warship. This time, however, the escorts, equipped with up-to-date radar and high-frequency (HF/DF) sensors—though the crews had no experience operating them—managed to sink a German submarine.

On 9 January 1943, under pressure from its allies, Canada decided to momentarily abandon its mid-Atlantic escort role. It would make use of the next few months to fit its escorts with new equipment and train their crews in its use. The Royal Canadian Navy had reached its nadir—yet just a few months earlier the St Lawrence River had had to be closed to all commercial traffic.

Indeed in May 1942 German submarines had cruised the St Lawrence estuary, after which—from August to November—they settled in on a fairly steady basis. Eight submarines were involved at various times, with no losses and a productive hunt that destroyed a corvette, an armed yacht and 19 merchant or passenger vessels, damaging two more. Given the panic gripping the local population, the government had to send some of its escort vessels from the Atlantic, where they were still required, to the Gulf of St Lawrence. In October, finally, this shipping route was closed. All Atlantic trade would now sail directly from the coast. Canada would thus be able to detach escort vessels for the Mediterranean, where preparations were afoot for landings in North Africa (Operation TORCH).

In early November 1942 a German submarine landed a spy on Quebec's Gaspé peninsula, but he was arrested almost immediately. A month earlier, on 14 October, SS *Caribou,* a ferry running between North Sydney, Nova Scotia, and Port aux Basques, Newfoundland, had been sunk by a submarine: 136 of its 237 passengers and crew had perished. Up to 1943 the Royal Canadian Navy had destroyed only four enemy submarines.

After more than three years of war, Canada had managed to mobilize completely but had not been able to get going in the strictly military sense. New opportunities looming on the horizon would enable Canadians to find better expression for their qualities as fighters on the sea, in the air and on the ground.

Chapter VI

TURNING POINT — 1943

The Navy

A host of factors would transform a disastrous naval situation into a resounding success before the year 1943 came to a close. These factors were: the cessation of operations by part of the navy in early 1943, the installation of more sophisticated sensing devices, more extensive training, the addition of more escort vessels and the arrival of long-range aircraft that made it possible to cover the whole North Atlantic.

When the RCAF acquired American Liberators with enough range to cover the entire Atlantic from bases along North American coasts, in conjunction with Allied aircraft operating from Europe, the German submarines began to have less freedom of the seas, especially in daylight.

Having regained control of the situation, Canada, with Britain's support, would finally get what it had been seeking since 1942—a command of its own. The Americans, although virtually vacating the North Atlantic, had wanted to retain control over the entire North American coastline. In March 1943 the Canadian North-West Atlantic Command was formed at an Allied conference on con-

Corporal of the Royal 22e Régiment, Italy, 1943. In southern Italy during the summer, Canadians wore the tropical dress used by the British 8th Army of which they formed a part.
(Re-creation by Ronald B. Volstad, DND)

voys held in Washington. The Royal Canadian Navy was thereafter responsible for all convoys travelling north of New York City and west of the 47th Meridian, some 1,000 kilometres from Halifax. The reorganized RCN that resumed responsibility for convoys in the spring of 1943 was more effective, and in the next two years it destroyed 17 of the 27 submarines it would be credited with sinking between 1939 and 1945. From late 1942 on, the German navy, like the German air force, could no longer replace all of its losses.

The submarine threat to the trade lanes thus slowly subsided, though it did not cease to exist. The snorkel would enable submarines to stay submerged much longer, and the acoustic torpedoes they carried would wreak havoc. *St Croix,* on convoy duty with the Royal Navy's 9th Escort Group, was sunk by two acoustic torpedoes on 20 September 1943. Its 81 survivors from a complement of 147 were taken on board the British vessel *Itchen,* which itself went down the next day. Only one *St Croix* crew member survived this second sinking. Other ships were lost as well. On 17 March 1945 the minesweeper *Guysborough* was sunk near Halifax, taking 44 of its 70 crew members to their deaths. A month later, on 16 April, *Esquimalt* suffered the same fate. On 29 April 1944 the destroyer *Athabascan* was sunk, leaving 128 dead and 83 taken prisoner. On 8 June 1944, however, just off the coast of Europe, the Canadians sank two German destroyers that had sailed too far from their base.

Canada came out of the war with some 400 warships of various tonnages over and above landing craft. A number of them would play roles unconnected with what is now termed the Battle of the Atlantic, but once this sea victory was won the backs of the Allied troops fighting in North Africa

and Europe were safe: 2,024 men and one woman, who was on board the ferry *Caribou* when it sank, gave their lives in the Canadian navy.

Canada also played a major role in seaborne trade. The country is reckoned to have provided 15,000 men to the Allied merchant navy either on Canadian vessels or on ships flying other flags: 1,465 died, including 295 Newfoundlanders, who were not Canadians at that time; nearly 1,250 of these deaths occurred in the Battle of the Atlantic. Canada was also active in shipbuilding. At its wartime peak in 1943, this industry employed 107,900 people.

The Canadian naval effort would be based in large part on the men of the Royal Canadian Naval Volunteer Reserve, formed in the 1920s specifically to receive all Canadians, from sea to sea, interested in joining the navy. The navy thus built up a powerful lobby that would see to its survival, and to its revival in the 1930s.

The Air Force

No. 6 Bomber Group, which became operational as part of Bomber Command on 1 January 1943, was certainly the best-known Canadian air formation of the Second World War. In theory, ground crews as well as flight crews were to be Canadian, but this laudable objective would never quite be achieved, especially as regards the technicians.

Aerial bombing had made its debut in the First World War. The Germans used this tactic before the Allies did, causing 1,414 civilian and military deaths and 3,500 injuries. Though these operations forced their enemies to form batteries of anti-aircraft guns equipped with powerful searchlights and special squadrons of fighters, the Germans decided that they were

Female member of the Canadian army, Italy, 1943–44.
More than 2,000 servicewomen served overseas.
(Re-creation by Ronald B. Volstad, DND)

Infantryman from the Hull Regiment at Kiska
in Alaska's Aleutian Islands, August 1943. For this
joint operation with the American forces, the
Canadians used U.S. headdress and equipment.
(Re-creation by Ronald B. Volstad, DND)

ineffective. On 5 June 1918 the British launched their first big bombers, which would rain 543 tons of bombs on the German cities of the Rhineland. They were after military targets, but a heavy price was paid by civilians on both sides. By 11 November 1918, Allied aerial bombing had killed 746 Germans and injured another 800.

In the 1920s and 1930s theoreticians in a number of nations predicted that the air force would be the decisive arm in the next conflict. To some degree the two atomic bombs dropped on Japan in August 1945 would prove them right. But neither the German experiments in Spain or over England nor the Allies' offensives against Germany using ever greater numbers of heavy bombers succeeded in persuading the enemy to stop fighting.

No. 6 (RCAF) Bomber Group would eventually provide 16 squadrons (up to 20 aircraft each) for numerous strategic raids on specific targets that sometimes involved 1,000 or more planes. Its casualties, including aircraft having to turn back before reaching the objective, would be very high in number in the first few months. By 1945, however, 6 Group had become one of the most illustrious in Bomber Command.

On 17 and 18 August 1943, Peenemünde, on the Baltic coast, was bombed by 541 aircraft including 57 from the RCAF Group. Total casualties were 6.7 percent, but for the Canadian aircraft—the last to arrive over Peenemünde—the casualty rate was 19.7 percent. The Battle of Berlin raged from mid-November 1943 to the end of March 1944. Canadian bombers, which made 1,086 of the 10,813 recorded sorties, suffered 6-percent casualties, compared to 5.8 percent for Bomber Command as a whole. Over Nuremberg during the night of 30/31 March 1944, Bomber Command

suffered 12-percent casualties, 6 Group 11 percent.

Some raids would still be deadly, however experienced the group might be. Bombing Magdeburg on the night of 21/22 January 1944, the Canadians recorded a disastrous 12.3-percent casualty rate, when the total—considered high in itself—was 9 percent. A raid on Ruhr dams by the "Dam Busters" using special bombs involved 30 Canadians among the 133 crew members of the 19 bombers in the heart of the action. Fourteen Canadians died out of a raid total of 56.

Strategic bombing techniques evolved rapidly. Navigation instruments provided more and more accuracy in pinpointing targets, even at night. In time, a specialist Pathfinder group, which also included Canadians, was formed. Its aircraft would arrive above the target area earlier than the main force waves of bombers and drop coloured flares in parachutes as objectives for the bomb-aimers. For even greater accuracy, they added a "master bomber" who could contact aircraft and redirect their fire when necessary and possible. All in all, strategic bombing would remain a facet of war where accuracy remained elusive. More than 50 years later we know that "surgical bombing" still has something of the chimera about it.

Ways of improving crews' chances included using radar to locate enemy fighters, placing machine-gun turrets in the tail and nose of bombers, and interfering with enemy radar—for example, by stimulating multiple targets by dropping long strips of aluminium foil away from objectives.

On balance, strategic bombing would remain a hazardous undertaking to the very end of the war. The morale of crews leaving night after night to fly the 30 missions that would free them from this dirty work would

Canadian navy commando, 1944–45, armed with a Lanchester machine gun and wearing 1942-issue British battle dress and the new MK III helmet. (Re-creation by Ronald B. Volstad, DND)

Crew member of an armoured regiment in northwest Europe, 1944–45, wearing a non-flammable overgarment. (Re-creation by Ronald B. Volstad, DND)

Sniper from the Calgary Highlanders, northwest Europe, 1944–45. (Re-creation by Ronald B. Volstad, DND)

often flag in the face of severe casualties suffered on every sortie, but it did not break.

Canadian aviators would also serve in other sectors and fly other missions. We will have occasion to meet them again.

The Army
Sicily and Italy

From 1942 on, the Germans were on the retreat in North Africa. In 1943 the Allies scored points everywhere. The Canadian army took part in the landing in Sicily in July 1943 and throughout the Italian campaign until February 1945. Curiously, this effort, which in terms of the quantity of troops is almost comparable to the campaign in France after 6 June 1944, has gone virtually unnoticed. Fifty years later, on 1 June 1994, *Le Figaro* would refer to the French, American and British presence in Italy but completely overlook the Canadian Army Corps. Yet many a Franco-Canadian military link was forged on this Mediterranean battleground.

The Canadians who had remained in England were unhappy with the army's long wait there. They were jealous of the success and publicity surrounding the efforts of other Commonwealth troops. The Canadian government, meanwhile, was sensitive to public opinion and to charges that it feared the political consequences of too much bloodletting among its soldiery. In 1914–18 volunteers had been thrown into the fray barely six months after reaching England, and a number of officers in the 1st Canadian Army, remembering battles fought a quarter of a century earlier, keenly resented their lengthy guard duty in the United Kingdom. The critics would not let up, even when told that many battles remained to be fought before war's end and that the morale of the troops was good, or

that the commander in chief was going easy on the Canadian soldiers so that they could lead an Allied offensive across the Channel. It would be logical, the critics retorted, to have the Canadians who would eventually be opening the second front in France acquire some combat experience. In the end, it was probably less for military than political reasons that the government insisted on the 1st Canadian Infantry Division participating in the attack on Sicily in July 1943.

Sicily thus became the first important Canadian battleground in the Second World War. On 8 July 1943 the news release announcing the Allied landing did not mention Canada's participation, but the oversight was rectified the next day. The Canadian campaign under Major-General G.G. Simonds was not a massive one compared to those that would follow in Italy and France, but the terrain was hilly and the resistance sometimes stubborn. The Canadians, flanked by British and American troops on their right and left, respectively, advanced in the dust on twisting, mineladen roads. At Grammichele they encountered some weak resistance. After mid-July, and despite the defensive advantages the mountains provided to the towns of Leonforte and Assoro, they fell too. Around Agira the Germans fought fiercely and had to be driven out of their positions. By early August it could be said that the way was open to wind up the Sicilian campaign. On the 6th the Canadians were placed in reserve. They took no part in the final battles culminating in the 16 August capture of Catania that put an end to enemy resistance on the island.

The attack on the Italian mainland was launched from Sicily across the Strait of Messina on 3 September, the anniversary of Britain's declaration of war. As the Italian troops had no wish to fight and the Germans no intention of defending Calabria, the Canadians were able to advance rapidly in that mountainous region. When Italy officially signed an armistice, the Germans, reinforced by some Italian fascist troops, continued to fight, though this did not help them. Rain and the poor condition of the roads gave the Canadians more problems than the enemy did. In 17 days they were 735 kilometres from their landing point. On 14 October the 1st Brigade occupied Campobasso; the next day the 2nd Brigade took Vinchiaturo. On the Adriatic coast Canadian tanks joined with British units in the attack on Termoli. When the first snow fell, General Montgomery mounted a solid attack on the German line along the Sangro. The left flank of the Allied offensive had gotten bogged down north of Naples after its dramatic landing at Salerno. It was believed essential, to keep the momentum, to advance up the Adriatic. The coastal plain was narrow, however, and intersected at right angles by a series of deep valleys, so that the Britons and Canadians had barely managed to drive the Germans out of the Sangro before they were facing a similar situation on the River Moro, where some of the toughest fighting of the entire war took place. The Germans constantly counterattacked, even hand to hand, while the Canadians cut a path through San Leonardo and crossed the Berardi junction where Captain Paul Triquet of the Royal 22e Régiment earned the first Victoria Cross awarded to a Canadian in the war. The way was now open to Ortona on the coast.

Ortona is a story of seven painful days of close combat conducted with uncommon courage and heroism in cold, wet, snowy conditions. The town sits on a cliff overlooking the Adriatic. The Germans decided to fall back on it. The harbour was blocked by wrecks, many buildings had been razed and the narrow streets of the medieval town were full of debris. The enemy were well aware that artillery and armour would not be very effective against them and that this was going to be an infantry battle fought with rifles, mortars, machine guns, grenades and mines; they also had some of their best troops in the men of the 1st German Parachute Division. Facing them was the 1st Canadian Infantry Division made up of three infantry regiments of the Permanent Force as well as militia regiments from across the country.

On 20 December the Canadian infantrymen left the Berardi junction to advance slowly towards the outskirts of Ortona, where the next day they began the fight to capture the town. The Germans took advantage of their position and attempted to draw the Canadians towards the central Piazza Municipale, where they hoped to slaughter them. Cutting a path through the rubble-filled streets would simply mean fighting as the enemy wanted. Instead the Canadians used their guns to shoot "mouse holes" through walls and buildings. For days and nights, field guns and tanks played an essential role in the infantry advance, when possible bombarding the upper storeys of buildings occupied by enemy parachutists. However, the battle ended as it had begun, in a fight between infantrymen. Strategically the town was unimportant, but the two camps would fight for it with dogged determination.

The experts debate it to this day: Should the town have been attacked head-on, as it was, or passed by and forced to give up? At any rate, on 22 December, the third day of fighting, the Canadian commander decided to take the key to the German position, a coastal road going northwest used by the enemy to relieve and reinforce the defenders of the town itself. An auxiliary attack was launched in the west towards the village of San Tommaso. The Germans seemed surprised, and the men of the 48th Highlanders succeeded in occupying and holding this position northwest of the town against violent German counterattacks. Unable to infiltrate the position, the Germans realized that their men were in danger in Ortona, the centre of which was already in Canadian hands. During the night of 27/28 December the enemy parachutists withdrew. In the morning a Canadian reconnaissance patrol advanced cautiously into Ortona and found only the enemy dead.

The 1st Division had just won one of the most glorious battles in its history, but at great cost. The Germans also suffered heavy casualties: The battalions of the 1st Parachute Division now had just enough men each to form a company.

December had been painful in more than one respect. General McNaughton, having lost the confidence of his British superiors and having been undermined by ambitious subordinates and abandoned by his minister, was persuaded to resign for health reasons. The prime minister was reserving a political future for him—though one that would never materialize. General Crerar replaced McNaughton at the head of the Canadian army.

Unlike Ortona, Rome held immense moral and political significance. Taking Rome would have more effect on the rest of the world than any Allied victory to date. To keep Rome, the German commander had prepared what may have been the most solid defensive position in all Italy. Two lines of fortifications were built—the Gustav and Hitler lines across the deep gorge that lay between Mount Matese and Mount Aurunci. In January 1944 the Americans

came very close to breaking through the Gustav Line beneath Monte Cassino. The Indians and New Zealanders then took their turn. At last the British 13th Army Corps, made up of British and Indian divisions, managed to open a breach in the defence works. No. I Canadian Corps commanded by Lieutenant-General E.L.M. Burns entered the fray with its infantry and armour. Between Saint'Olivia and Aquino, Canadians beheld the prospect of the Liri Valley, the Hitler Line and the Forme d'Aquino River. On 23 May the attack began as troops cut a path through the dust, smoke and morning mist. Shaken by waves of artillery, mortar and small-arms fire, the battalions of the 2nd Brigade reached the enemy line, broke though, and hung on determinedly and valiantly to the positions they had taken. On the left, the Carleton and York Regiment of the 3rd Brigade made a breach in the line and, with support from the West Nova Scotia Regiment and the tanks of the Three Rivers Regiment, opened the way. In the meantime the 1st Brigade drove the enemy out of Pontecorvo. At this point the Germans still held Aquino on the flank, but as 24 May dawned the tanks of the 5th Armoured Division were able to cross the breaches opened in the Hitler Line to take advantage of the situation beyond the front. The Canadians ran into some problems at the Melfa River, Major John K. Mahoney of the Westminster Regiment earning a Victoria Cross. Once this stream had been crossed, however, the real battle for the Liri Valley was over and the operation became a pursuit. On 31 May the Loyal Edmonton Regiment occupied Frosinone and ended the whole campaign. The Canadian Army Corps was withdrawn from operations, and on 4 June the Americans entered Rome. The Canadian troops who had taken part in the bloody

Canadian infantryman fighting in the town of Campochiaro, Italy, on 23 October 1943. (A.M. Sirton, NAC, PA-136198)

Major-General Guy G. Simonds, Commander 1st Canadian Division in Italy, 1943. (DND, ZK-486)

King George VI awards the Victoria Cross to Major John K. Mahoney of the Westminster Regiment (Motor) for his heroism in the battle of the Melfa River in Italy on 24 May 1944. (DND, ZK-804)

battles of Monte Cassino and Liri Valley were refused the honour of marching in the streets of the Eternal City, unlike many other Canadians serving in the Canadian-American Special Service Force.

The fall and winter of 1944 brought the Canadians back to the Adriatic coast. The enemy had fallen back behind the Gothic Line, which ran roughly from Pisa to Pesaro with its barbed wire, anti-tank ditches, slit trenches and tank turrets set in reinforced concrete blockhouses. Since northern Italy's many factories were supplying the Germans with much of the materiel they needed, a fierce struggle to prevent the Allies from entering the great plain of Lombardy was anticipated.

The Allied plan was to attack on the eastern flank where the terrain was more accessible and then veer left towards Bologna. Since the operation's success relied on the element of surprise, it was deemed essential to make the Germans believe that the bulk of the attack would come from the western slopes of the Apennines. Accordingly the Americans made a show of preparations around Florence. Since the presence of the Canadians usually signalled a major offensive, the British were once again able to employ the ruse that had been so successful at Amiens in 1918: Send the 1st Canadian Division to Florence and then surreptitiously relocate it to another sector of the front. It was harder to maintain secrecy in Italy than in France, and there was no guarantee that this subterfuge had actually succeeded. Certainly the Germans offered stubborn resistance to the Canadians in the hills between the Metauro and Foglia rivers. However, two columns from the 1st and 5th divisions passed through the villages of Borgo San Maria and Montecchio. The Gothic Line, which was to have held for six months, had fallen in 24 hours. The Can-

adians had been lucky—a number of German units had not had time to take up their defensive positions—and audacious, advancing persistently after some shaky initial successes. Even though the line had been broken through in late August, it would take the Canadians three weeks to reach Rimini. Indeed the move from summer heat to autumn rains placed new obstacles in the way of the attackers as they watched dusty roads fill up with potholes and streams turn into rivers. But morale was good and the quality of the enemy troops mediocre, with the exception of the parachutists, whose numbers in any case had been eroded by constant fighting. Advancing relentlessly, the Canadians took Coriano and the ridge commanding it, then the hill of San Fortunato that blocked the way to the broad Po Valley from the direction of the Adriatic coast. The immensity of northern Italy now lay before the Canadians: They had had to defeat 11 German divisions to get there.

There still remained some tough battles to fight along the streams between Rimini and the Savio, then across the Senio and the marshlands of Ravenna. However, the Canadian Army Corps would not be part of them. The Canadian government was anxious to see it back with the 1st Canadian Army in northwest Europe. At Malta in January 1945 the Joint Chiefs of Staff Committee agreed to respect this Canadian priority despite the problems raised by the withdrawal of a large military force in full operation. On 9 February 1945 the 8th Army commander said his goodbyes to his senior Canadian officers, and the move to France began in deepest secrecy. On 15 March, I Canadian Corps assumed responsibility for the district of Nijmegen in the Netherlands. Two weeks later the troops of the 5th Armoured Division and the 1st Infantry Division lined up for the last stage of the offensive against Germany in western Netherlands.

Normandy and Northwest Europe

As the great Canadian military historian Desmond Morton puts it, in June 1944 Canada was conducting total war on its own territory—with the mobilization of its national human, physical, economic and financial resources, and with its propaganda, censorship and so on—while conducting a limited external war based totally on the voluntary sacrifice of hundreds of thousands of its young men and women. From this standpoint, Canada's participation in the Normandy landings and campaign represents the culmination of a colossal effort. As soon as Canada agreed to take part in Operation OVERLORD, the Canadians assumed responsibility for their own landing.

Canada participated in the naval and air preparations for the landing, Operation NEPTUNE. However, the Canadian vessels were generally not used in direct support of Canadian land forces. There was a complete lack of co-ordination among the three Canadian elements, with each operating under a different command. For example, Canada provided 16 of the 247 minesweepers: 10 Canadian minesweepers in the 31st Flotilla opened a channel opposite Omaha Beach in the American sector, with the remaining six dispersed in various other flotillas. Canada also had two infantry landing ships, serving primarily the British Gold Beach and secondarily the Canadian Juno Beach. For weeks on end the 19 Canadian corvettes in the force of 181 Allied escort vessels would protect cross-Channel logistics. Another part of Canada's sea forces, made up of destroyers and coastal aircraft, would patrol the western portion of Neptune Zone and the high seas hunting German ships and submarines. No. 162 Squadron of the Royal Canadian Air Force would thus be credited with destroying five U-boats.

The 260th Flotilla of infantry landing craft, however, would be assigned to Juno Beach. Two Canadian destroyers, *Algonquin* and *Sioux,* would make themselves very useful in the early landing phases, with *Algonquin* shelling and destroying an enemy artillery position. Meanwhile the 29th Canadian Torpedo Boat Flotilla would have the role of intercepting coastal trade and enemy warships operating in the landing zone.

The 2nd Tactical Air Force included a number of Canadian squadrons that were among the first to be based at temporary airfields in Normandy itself. On 10 June, 441, 442 and 443 squadrons of No. 144 (Canadian) Wing landed in Normandy. At the end of the month they were joined by Nos. 126 and 127. The air casualties the Canadians inflicted on the enemy that June amounted to approximately 100 aircraft.

The Typhoon fighter bombers of 438, 439 and 440 squadrons of No. 143 (Canadian) Wing reached the bridgehead towards the middle of June. They would soon be joined by the RCAF's 39 Reconnaissance Wing with 400, 414 and 430 squadrons.

This Canadian naval and air effort is too often written off. Neither of these elements, however, met as fierce an opposition as the army. From the very first day, the army counted more dead than the naval and air units in Normandy would together suffer in the entire campaign.

On 6 June, Canada—the only country to have kept an accurate count—was able to land some 12,000 men of its 3rd Infantry Division and 2nd Armoured Brigade, a considerably smaller number than forecast. This represented about 10 percent of the Allied landing at that time. The first Canadians to land in Normandy were members of the 1st Canadian Parachute Battalion. When the Normandy campaign ended on 21 August more than two million Allied soldiers were on French soil, some 100,000—or 1 in 20—of them Canadian.

Between 6 June and 21 August the Canadians would have 18,444 casualties including 5,021 dead—and they still had not reached Rouen. Although it had been relatively easy for the Canadians the first day, things grew complicated on 7 June. In mid-September it had to be acknowledged that of all the divisions in 21 Army Group the most casualties had been suffered by, respectively, the 3rd and 2nd Canadian Infantry divisions forming II Canadian Corps. The taking of Caen, the fighting on and around Verrières Ridge on 25 July 1944 —which became the Canadian army's second most costly day, after Dieppe, in the Second World War—and the closing of the Falaise Gap would unfortunately give the soldiers a chance to measure themselves against some of the best German troops on the western front. Young and inexperienced men would leave Normandy tempered by the fire of terrible ordeals, including two aerial bombardments by their air force comrades in arms. Major David Currie of the South Alberta Regiment earned a Victoria Cross at Saint-Lambert-sur-Dives, near Falaise.

As of 31 July 1944 the 1st Canadian Army, half made up of British and Polish troops, was operational. Under the command of General H.D.G. Crerar, it would be in charge, after Chambois, of the left flank of the Allied advance in France. Coming in to Rouen the Canadians would be blocked for 48 hours in and around the Londe forest and would sustain a further several hundred casualties after Paris had

been liberated. Although many months of hard fighting still awaited them, the 100,000 Canadians then in France could claim a substantial part of the responsibility for 460,900 German casualties, notably as the hammer that crushed the Germans against the American anvil sitting a few kilometres south of Falaise. The other side of the coin was, as we have seen, that they figured prominently in Allied casualty lists, totalling 206,703.

The trials of the Canadian infantry in Normandy would, a few months later, erupt in political crisis at home. In 1939, Canada had chosen to conduct its overseas military activities on a volunteer basis. The National Resources Mobilization Act of 1940 introduced conscription for territorial defence. The spread of war to the Pacific brought increasing pressure for conscription for overseas service as well. In April 1942, Prime Minister Mackenzie King held a referendum on the possibility of freeing the government from its 1939 promise not to use conscription for this purpose. The result was 64 percent in favour, but the vast majority of Quebec Francophones—the original and primary targets of that promise—voted no.

There things stayed, although since the beginning of the war Canada had extended its "territory" to enable conscripts to defend Newfoundland, Bermuda, British Guiana and even some of the Aleutian Islands in the Pacific. From December 1942 to December 1944 there would always be between 60,000 and 75,000 conscripts for territorial defence.

On the European battlegrounds, however, a critical situation was coming to light. Some 70 percent of the army's casualties were occurring in the infantry, as against a projected level of only 48 percent. Very soon, therefore, the reinforcements recruit-

Anti-aircraft gun set up on Juno Beach, Normandy, 6 June 1944.
The star denoted Allied equipment, particularly for aviators seeking targets.
(DND, ZK-1082)

Canadian reinforcements landing in Normandy, June 1944. (DND, ZK-1083)

ed on the 48-percent model ceased to provide adequate manpower. Having fallen back on a few expedients (such as transferring technicians into infantry), and having relied on a flood of infantry volunteers that did not materialize, in November 1944 the government was obliged to send 16,000 of its territorial-defence conscripts overseas. Prime Minister King had tried to avoid this last-resort measure to the very end.

The costly missions handed to the Canadians would lead to some changes at the political level. The defence minister, J.L. Ralston, had been forced to resign several weeks before the November 1944 decision precisely because he had been strongly advocating the use of conscripts overseas. He was replaced by Andy McNaughton, who was expected to convince the conscripts to sign up as volunteers. The air minister, Charles Power, a Quebec native and First World War veteran, would also resign on principle following the decision to send conscripts overseas.

There were indeed a few problems among the conscripts who were chosen for overseas service, but the general public accepted the situation. In the event, only about 12,000 men would have the time to cross the ocean: 2,463 of them would be sent into battle and 69 would be killed while fighting as courageously as the volunteers. This government decision, unlike the conscription of 1917–18, would not destroy national unity.

After Falaise and Rouen, the Canadians moved quickly, in pursuit of the decimated German armies, across France towards Belgium on the left wing of the Allied forces. Dieppe gave them a joyous welcome at a parade starring the unfortunate 2nd Division that had suffered so greatly in 1942. Boulogne, Calais and Cap Gris-Nez put up some resistance. Nonetheless by the end of September the whole Channel coast except for Dunkirk had been liberated and the German V-1 rocket-launch sites had been put out of service.

Meanwhile the British and Americans continued their advance over a wide front. The failure of the airborne operation at Arnhem committed the Allies to a winter campaign. In these circumstances the large port of Antwerp, already occupied by Allied troops, would be essential as a base for the coming decisive battle against Germany. At this stage the main Allied supply routes still extended to Normandy. Just occupying Antwerp was not enough: The Germans controlled the sea access routes and the long, meandering estuary leading to the port. The task of cleaning out these German positions fell to the Canadians. The plan of attack included several separate but simultaneous operations: sealing off the Zuid-Beveland region by a breakthrough north of the Scheldt, clearing the Breskens "pocket" behind the Leopold Canal south of the Scheldt, taking the Isthmus of Beveland and, lastly, attacking Walcheren Island from the sea.

The operation began on 1 October when the 2nd Canadian Division crossed the Antwerp Canal. At the same time, the 3rd Division, supported by the 4th, started the attack on the other side of the Leopold Canal. This was an extremely laborious business. The terrain was difficult: Dikes and flooded fields made armoured vehicles virtually unusable. The heavily entrenched Germans were prepared to give fierce battle both at the entrance to the Isthmus of Beveland and along the south shore of the River Scheldt. Nevertheless on 16 October the tenacity of the Canadians of the 2nd Division won them Woensdrecht, the entry to Zuid-Beveland, and they set up a bridgehead on the Leopold Canal. At this point Montgomery ordered a halt to all

Ship escorting Canadian troops landing in Normandy, 6 June 1944.
(DND, ZK-1084)

The identical British cruisers *Minotaur* and *Uganda* began
service with the Canadian navy in 1945. Above, *Uganda,*
which served in the Pacific towards the end of the war.
The cruisers were later christened *Ontario* and *Quebec,*
respectively.
(DND, EKS-103)

Nootka, one of eight Tribal-class destroyers that served in
the Canadian navy from 1943 on.
(DND, EKS-141).

During the Second World War, the Canadian navy was nicknamed the "Corvette Navy" because it had more
than 130 of these small vessels escorting convoys and hunting German submarines. The custom of painting
a green maple leaf on the funnel began in 1917 and became general practice during the Second World War.
This photo shows *Sackville,* the only corvette that still survives. Built at Saint John, New Brunswick, in
1941, it was restored in the early 1980s and today is moored at Halifax as a naval museum.
(DND, 85-339)

Allied offensive operations elsewhere on that front in order to focus his forces on the mouth of the Scheldt Estuary. The 4th Armoured Division was given the mission of taking Bergen-op-Zoom. Meanwhile the 2nd Division redoubled its efforts to complete the conquest of Zuid-Beveland before the end of the month. After the 3rd Division had occupied the peninsula and taken the Breskens pocket, British troops under Canadian command proceeded to attack Walcheren Island. On 8 November all resistance ended. The men had begun to clear the river of mines even before that date, so that on 28 November the first Allied convoy sailed up the Scheldt to unload its supplies in the port of Antwerp. The convoy was led by the Canadian-built *Fort Cataraqui*.

In the meantime the 4th Armoured Division advanced eastwards, surviving some tough battles at Bergen-op-Zoom, Steenbergen, Saint-Philipsland and elsewhere. The men of the Lake Superior and British Columbia regiments sank a number of German ships in the port of Zijpe just beyond the narrow channel separating Schouwen Island from the mainland. This "naval" combat wound up a campaign that was fought in flooded polders more often than on dry land. As of 9 November all enemy resistance had ended south of the Maas and the Canadians returned to their winter quarters along the Maas and in the Nijmegen salient. But for the tough assignment of driving the German parachutists out of Kapelsche Veer, and the alarms and movements resulting from the German Ardennes offensive, the winter months passed in the relative peace of raids and patrols.

In February 1945 the Allies launched the big western offensive that was to push the enemy back to the far bank of the Rhine and undermine his will to resist. In the east

the Russians had reached Budapest. Massed on the banks of the Oder, they were preparing to march on Berlin while General Eisenhower continued his methodical advance on a wide front. He had victories, but the Russians were the first to get to Berlin, creating a difficult situation in Europe that would last nearly half a century.

The Canadians got into the game on 8 February when their 1st Army attacked the German positions in the Reichswald. General Crerar's troops included the 30th British Corps and three independent armoured brigades: In other words, at this stage most of the 1st Canadian Army was made up of foreign, mainly British, troops.

The Germans had expected the main offensive to fall on Venlo and to coincide with an American attack on the Ruhr. They were anticipating a mere diversionary attack in the Reichswald, so that the Canadians, as predicted, found a surprised and demoralized enemy. As the fighting continued, however, German resistance hardened, abetted by the spring thaw and torrential rains that churned the countryside into mud. Meanwhile the Americans had been prevented from beginning their attack because the Germans had flooded the ground in front of them. This left the British and Canadian soldiers alone for more than a week, cutting a path through pine forest and waterlogged countryside. When they reached Goch on 21 February after fighting both the mud and the Germans, they had broken through the much-vaunted Siegfried Line. The Canadian infantry had suffered immensely, however, and the worst was yet to come.

It was laborious going for the 7th Brigade in the Moyland forest, and the 4th Brigade had as much trouble along the Goch-Calcar road. Next came the big fight for the ridge that commanded two forests: The Hochwald was earmarked for the

176

Infantrymen with the South Saskatchewan Regiment fighting near
the Orange Canal in Holland on 12 April 1944.
(D. Guvarich, NAC, PA-138284)

Sapper C.W. Stevens of the engineers defusing a German mine in
Normandy, 22 June 1944. He is wearing the new British MK III helmet
adopted by the units of the 3rd Canadian Division in 1944–45.
(Ken Bell, NAC, PA-136278)

2nd Division, the Balbergerwald for the 3rd, while the 4th Armoured Division drove through the narrow gap separating the two to come out in open country. The combat was bitter, dogged and merciless. In many respects it resembled some of the battles of the Great War: The rain, mud, desperate resistance, slow progress, fatigue and exhaustion were the same. Casualties were high. The men of the Lake Superior and Algonquin regiments finally reached the end of the breach.

Some tough fighting still lay ahead before they would set foot on the banks of the Rhine. The 3rd Division seized Sonsbeck, and with this as a base the armoured regiments, supported by their motorized battalion and infantry, could head for Veen, which surrendered on 9 March. After a violent fight at Winnenthal, the Canadians could see the town of Wesel on the far bank of the Rhine. Here their battles ended for the moment. The Germans had entrenched what remained of the divisions of their 1st Parachute Army on the right bank. The big Allied offensive was over, but between 8 February and 10 March the Canadians had suffered 5,304 dead and wounded. General Eisenhower was not exaggerating when he wrote to Crerar: "Probably no attack in the course of this war has taken place in such difficult field conditions. That you have marched to victory says much about your talent and the determination and courage of your men."[80]

The road was now open for the final phase of the northwest European campaign. Some troops from the 9th Canadian Infantry Brigade under British command took part in the Rhine crossing at Rees. The 1st Canadian Parachute Battalion, part of the 6th Airborne Division since its arrival in Normandy, was dropped at the edge of the Diersfordt forest near Wesel. Several days later the 3rd Division crossed to the right bank of the Rhine, and the Allied forces were now able to make use of the big advantage conferred by numbers. During this phase the 1st Canadian Army was assigned the mission of opening the northern supply route passing through Arnhem, then liberating the northeastern Netherlands and seizing the coastal strip eastwards to the Elbe as well as western Netherlands.

Strategically the war was now over. Running out of men, technical resources and defensive lines, the Germans in the west fell back before the victorious Canadian, British and American troops just as in the east they fell back before the Russians. The Canadians crossed the northern Dutch border. On their right flank, the 4th Armoured Division crossed the Twente Canal and took Almelo on 5 April; the 2nd Infantry Division crossed the Schipbeek Canal and advanced northward to Groningen, arriving on 16 April; the 3rd Infantry Division crossed the Ijssel to occupy Zutphen after several days of tough fighting, then moved through Deventer, Zwolle and Leeuwarden to reach the sea on 18 April. On the extreme left flank the 5th Canadian Armoured Division and the British 49th Division commanded by General Foulkes attacked and took Arnhem. Then the 5th Armoured Division hurried north to Hardewijk on the Zuider Zee, cutting off the lines of retreat of the Germans defending Apeldoorn against the 1st Infantry Division. On 28 April in western Netherlands, the Germans had control over a line extending more or less from Wageningen to the sea via Amersfoort. That day marked the beginning of a truce in the sector, followed shortly by the arrival of food supplies for the starving civilian population.

In the meantime II Canadian Corps extended its operations from eastern Netherlands to western Germany. The

Major-General R.F.L. Keller, Commander of the
3rd Canadian Division during the Normandy landing.
(Photo dated 20 June 1944, DND, ZK-540)

Lieutenant-General H.D.G. Crerar, Commander
in Chief of Canadian troops in Europe, 1944–45.
(Photo taken in France, DND, ZK-9)

Canadian Sherman tank near Vancelles,
Normandy, June 1944.
(DND, ZK-849)

Canadian soldiers during winter combat in
Holland, early 1945.
(DND, ZK-958)

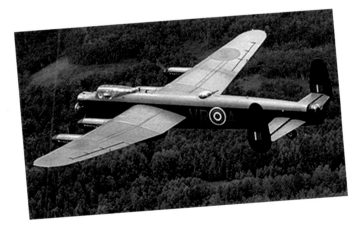

The Avro Lancaster bomber. Starting in 1943, a dozen RCAF
squadrons were at the controls of Lancasters as they took part
in the bombing of Germany. More than 7,300 Lancasters were built
during the war, 430 of them in Canada. This machine was restored
by the Canadian Warplane Heritage Museum and carries the insignia
of the Lancaster in which A.C. Mynarski gave his life to save his
comrades. Mynarski was awarded a posthumous Victoria Cross for
his heroism. (DND, 89-787)

The DeHavilland Mosquito fighter-bomber. A great many
Mosquitoes were made in Canada and, beginning in 1943,
Canadian squadrons in Britain were equipped with them.
418 Squadron used this excellent aircraft to score 103 wins
over the enemy during 1944.
(DND, 75-346)

4th Canadian Armoured Division crossed the River Ems at Meppen and advanced to Friesoythe by way of Sögel, the 2nd Infantry Division moved from Groningen to the Oldenburg area and the 3rd Infantry Division relieved the Poles at the mouth of the Ems. Despite the collapse of the German armies everywhere else, the remnants of its Parachute Corps plus some naval elements continued to resist the Canadians and make the best use they could of the marshy ground to defend themselves. Fighting thus continued west of Oldenburg and north of the Kusten Canal, but the end was only a matter of days. On 4 May the ceasefire order was issued as Canadian troops advanced slowly on the naval base of Wilhelmshaven, Aurich and Emden. The next day the commanders of the two Canadian army corps, Generals Foulkes and Simonds, accepted the surrenders of Generals Blaskowitz and Straube on their respective fronts. The official German surrender was signed on 7 May at Reims, France. Between the Lower Rhine and the German city of Bremen, the Allies had eight divisions, five of them Canadian. The Canadian troops that penetrated the deepest into Germany were those of the 1st Parachute Battalion, who went to Wismar and there met the Soviets on 2 May.

At the end of the 1914–18 war the troops had been eager to return to Canada. In 1945 the feeling was just as strong, and the opinion was that length of service should be the deciding factor for much-desired repatriation. The equivalent of one division would stay on as an occupation force. Comprising volunteers and men who had served only a short time overseas, it was assigned to the British Occupation Zone in northwestern Germany. Its members would spend less than a year in Germany, for in April 1946 the Canadian Occupation Force delegated its responsibilities to the British

52nd Division. By the end of 1946 only a hundred or so Canadian soldiers were still in the United Kingdom.

War in the Pacific

Although five divisions were fighting overseas, three remained in Canada, two of which were stationed on the west coast until the autumn of 1943. After the Japanese had been expelled from the Aleutian Islands, two divisions, the 7th and the 8th, disappeared, and the 6th saw its strength reduced. In autumn 1943, with the Allied victory in the Battle of the Atlantic, all the Axis forces drew back. When that conflict had been at its height, in June 1943, 18 months after the Hong Kong disaster, 34,316 men of all ranks defended the British Columbia coast, compared to some 24,000 on the east coast. It was from among those remaining on the Pacific coast that the 16,000 conscripts for overseas duty were chosen.

In August 1943, one element of this force, the 13th Infantry Brigade Group, plus part of the 1st American Special Service Force made up in part of Canadian volunteers, would gather to attack the Aleutian island of Kiska.

Among the conscript units deployed was the Hull Regiment, which recorded the fewest AWOLs at the time the ships were boarded on 12 August. Of the 34,000 men in the operation, 5,300 were Canadian, including the 500 or so members of the 1st Special Service Force. Despite the American blockade of the island, the Japanese slipped through a few hours before the Canadians and Americans arrived. Some of the Canadians would stay on Kiska until January 1944.

This was not the sole Canadian effort in the Pacific, however. March 1942 would find No. 413 (Reconnaissance) Squadron in

Ceylon (now known as Sri Lanka). On 4 April, Squadron Leader L.S. Birchall spotted the Japanese fleet bound for Ceylon. Before being brought down and taken prisoner, he and his crew were able to send this news to the defence forces, giving them time to prepare. Birchall's feat earned him the title "Saviour of Ceylon."

In October 1944 the light cruiser *Uganda,* given to the Royal Canadian Navy by the Royal Navy, served with the British in the Pacific as part of an anti-aircraft force, a task to which its nine 9-inch guns lent themselves admirably. It would cover, for example, the aircraft carriers *Formidable* and *Victorious* off the Caroline Islands.

Uganda was also to be the scene of a very special event. With the end of the war in Europe, the government announced that Canadian participation in ongoing fighting in the Pacific would be on a voluntary basis. *Uganda* was already active on this naval front, but it was decided that only volunteers would be used in the navy as well. In a vote taken in this ship in July 1945, some two thirds of its crew rejected volunteering to serve in the Pacific. *Uganda* returned to port, and there would be no time to change crews before the war ended. *Uganda* would have been part of a small fleet of some 60 vessels in the Pacific, including two light aircraft carriers, two cruisers and a large number of escort vessels. However, 85 percent of the seamen in HMCS *Prince Robert* would agree to fetch the Canadian prisoners of war who had survived Japanese detention and slavery.

The air war over the Pacific would have been continued by about 15,000 men forming Tiger Force. Lancasters would have been used for strategic bombing. Of the eight squadrons planned, only two served in that sector; they were already there prior to July 1945.

The army was to engage the 6th Division to handle volunteers coming from Europe or directly from Canada. The division was being formed under Major-General Bert Hoffmeister, and it had been decided to equip it U.S.-style when hostilities ended. This brief experience would leave the memory of an army jumping out of British uniforms to leap straight into American ones.

The last significant event of the war occurred on 9 August 1945. Lieutenant Robert Hampton Gray, a Canadian serving in the Royal Navy's Fleet Air Arm, sank the Japanese destroyer *Amokusa* in Onagawa Bay. Gray was killed but was awarded a Victoria Cross posthumously.

Women as War Artists

Sir Max Aitken was a wealthy Canadian who emigrated to England in 1914. In 1917 he was awarded the title Lord Beaverbrook and later became one of Winston Churchill's valued advisors. In 1916, faced with the Canadian government's inertia on some matters connected with the First World War, Aitken saw to the establishment of a Canadian War Records Office, a collection of photographs, maps, and unit and personal war diaries documenting Canada's military participation in the Great War. Sam Hughes, the minister of militia and defence, assumed responsibility for the Office, and Aitken solicited his support for the addition of an artistic dimension to the collection. When Hughes was ousted by Prime Minister Borden, Aitken hastily established the Canadian War Memorial Fund to send artists to the front. The government gave the artists a rank and paid them, but the Fund, a private corporation, managed them, took the credit for their work and assumed ownership of the growing collection.

A.Y. Jackson, David Milne and H.J. Mowatt are unquestionably the best known of the war artists. These men would be joined by female artists, although women were not allowed at the front. Florence Carlyle's portraits, executed mainly in London, include one of Lady Drummond, who headed the Canadian Red Cross there; this picture was funded by the Memorial Fund. In 1914 Caroline Arlington and her husband, architectural engravers living in Paris, offered their services to the Fund, but only Caroline's were used. Two of her etchings were accepted: The British Army *and* Navy Leave Club, Paris, *named for a spot popular with the Canadian troops.*

In 1918 the Fund extended its activities to the home front, and the National Gallery selected 20 artists, including four women— Mabel May, Frances Loring, Florence Wyle and Dorothy Stevens, who would still be painting long after war's end.

At the outbreak of the Second World War a number of artists offered their services to the National Gallery, but the government would not establish the Canadian War Records Program until 1943. Once again the impetus came from London, where the Canadian High Commissioner, Vincent Massey, took a great interest in this project. The artistic portrayal of Canada at war would be conducted both on the battlefield and at home. Among the 33 artists whose works were exhibited were Alex Colville, Willie Ogilvie and Charles Comfort. The work of only one woman was accepted: Molly Lamb. After graduating from the Vancouver School of Art, Lamb entered the Women's Army Corps in 1942, at age 20. She immediately expressed a desire to serve as a war artist but would not join the programme until after the cessation of hostilities in Europe in 1945. The National Gallery accepted nine of her works for its permanent collection. She had painted these in free moments while serving as a private and then corporal in the wartime shows section of the Canadian Auxiliary Services. Lamb went overseas in July 1945 and spent six weeks touring France, the Netherlands and Germany with a car and driver. Two of the results are Wilhelmshaven at Night *and* Ruins of Emmerich. *Apparently Lamb's gender was the main obstacle to her gaining access to battlefields during the fighting.*[81]

Molly Lamb Bobak, 1920–
Captured German Tank
Oil on canvas,
45.2 cm x 60 cm
(MCG 12018)

The National Gallery eventually bought several pictures of Canada at war painted by women. Although they did not go to the front lines, Isabel McLaughlin, Marion Long, Alma Duncan, Dorothy Stevens and several other women made valuable contributions to Canada's heritage of war art.

A Stroke of Luck!

On 6 September 1944 a Royal Canadian Air Force Lancaster was conducting a reconnaissance patrol over the North Sea with six crew members aboard. Suddenly one of its two motors caught fire. They did everything they could to lighten the aircraft, but it lost altitude. The pilot, Gordon Biddle, knew he would never make it to England, so he headed for Norway, a German-occupied country. Not far from Os, on the Norwegian coast, the second motor died and Biddle had to make a landing that in retrospect would seem impossible. The available "airstrip" was at most 25 metres long. The aircraft was heavily damaged but, by a stroke of luck, the crew members suffered no more than a few bruises.

They were close to a school, and in such a remote location few people other than the teacher spoke English. Magness Askvik pointed the Canadians towards the little town of Bjornen. They shed their flying suits and went there on foot. As the Norwegians hid and fed them, the men could look down and see German ships guarding the fjord. Soon the Norwegian secret army, Milorg, took charge of the crew and moved them around the region while some 4,000 Germans searched for them. Times were difficult in Norway and it was no easy matter to feed six young men on wartime rations—to say nothing of concealing them from the occupying force.

The men left the Os area on 1 October 1944 and reached Botnane by boat and on foot. On 9 October, following radio transmissions between Milorg and its British contacts, the Canadians were taken by boat to a rendezvous point on the coast where a submarine was to pick them up. After three days of anxious waiting, they were finally collected.

Eighteen days after their forced landing in enemy territory, the full Lancaster crew returned to Britain without casualties—surely a unique story in the annals of Canadian aviation in the Second World War.[82]

Francophone Servicemen and Their Language During the Second World War

After the First World War the government left its servicemen to their own devices until 1936. Apart from keeping the Royal 22e Régiment in the Permanent Force, virtually nothing was done to advance the presence of Francophones and the French language. Without facilities to accommodate them, and remembering the bitter conscription crisis of 1917–18, Francophones stayed out of the forces. At five percent, their proportion of total strength in 1939 was almost unchanged from what it had been in 1914. The army counted 184 Francophones among a total of 4,169 servicemen of all ranks.

Between 1939 and 1945 the proportion of Francophones in the services, including the conscripts for territorial defence, was estimated at 20 percent. Early in the war serious consideration was given to creating a Francophone army brigade, for which ample strength was available. Ultimately, however, the Francophone units would be dispersed throughout the forces. French was seen in some rare translations of training brochures and heard in conversations among Francophones, but virtually all written material appeared in English, even material written by and for Francophones. However, the air force did establish a Francophone bomber squadron.

The unilingual Francophone wishing to serve his country in battle, but in his own language, would be given no choice but to join the infantry. Indeed many men volunteering for armoured or artillery services were sent to the infantry because of their poor English.

As Jean-Yves Gravel has put it, without basic equality it was hard to exact the equality of sacrifice that was called for in both 1914–18 and 1939–45. In the army, the most advanced of the three services in dealing with Francophones, the Deputy Adjutant-General, Major-General W.H.S. Macklin, wrote on 23 May 1946: "No one has ever explained to me how the Canadian Army could have absorbed a satisfactory proportion of French Canadians if compulsory enlistment had been applied in 1939. There were no duly trained officers to properly accommodate these elements and we would never have been able to resolve the difficulty in the midst of conflict."[83]

The Home Front

The war placed immense power in the hands of a federal government that would be reluctant to relinquish it afterwards. The War Measures Act, invoked once again in 1939, made it possible to govern largely by decree: During the war 6,414 orders in council would be implemented by a public service that grew from 46,000 to 116,000 employees. Nearly everything was controlled, especially after June 1940: rents, labour relations, prices, rationing. Halfway through the war the government began to move towards social democracy—for example, with family allowances.

Externally, Canada was seeing rapid change as well. On 18 August 1940, when all seemed lost in Europe, the American president invited the Canadian prime minister to Ogdensburg, a New York State border town, to discuss the mutual defence of North America. To this end, the still existing Permanent Joint Board on Defence was established. In April 1941 the Board accepted joint decision-making on defence as an operating rule. This political rapprochement had its limits, however: That same month Churchill and Roosevelt held a meeting off the coast of Newfoundland in the absence of Mackenzie King.

In any case, at virtually the same moment Canada and the United States signed the Hyde Park Declaration, whose purpose was to enable Canada to balance its negative wartime accounts with the U.S. Each country would, for their mutual benefit, produce the equipment in which it had manufacturing expertise. Balances and even surpluses quickly developed in Canada's favour. A Crown corporation was formed to accept and negotiate orders for military supplies made in Canada.

The economic dimension of the Canadian effort is striking. An aircraft industry that was virtually nonexistent in 1939 would employ 130,000 in 1945—and would have already produced some 16,400 planes. Shipyards that turned out 16 vessels in 1940 would produce 4,419 before war's end. The manufacture of military vehicles went from 70,000 in 1940 to 147,000 in 1944; the figures for tanks were 100 in 1940 and an average of 1,700 a year thereafter. Farm, forest and fisheries production doubled in the period 1939–45. The debt rose from $3 billion in 1938 to $13 billion in 1946.

The Canadian public has not always appreciated the role played by the Second World War in the country's political, economic and social life. Both the loudly deplored centralization process and the impetus lent to the social programmes that are now being attacked from all sides are substantially rooted in the period of the Second World War.

Wartime Balance Sheet

The Second World War lasted 2,076 days and caused some 40 million deaths world-wide, mostly civilian. On 8 May 1945 newspapers across Canada announced the end of war in Europe and published a list of the latest Canadian military casualties: 76 dead and 169 wounded. Between 1 January and 8 May 1945 some 8,000 Canadians perished in a war that everyone thought was all but over.

War has its very personal dramas. Cabinet minister Ernest Lapointe saw his son, Hugues, for the last time when they said their goodbyes in Halifax on 21 July 1941; Hugues would die before the end of the year. Family stories like that of the Lapointes were told tens of thousands of times. Canada's three services suffered overwhelming losses between 1939 and 1945: The navy sustained 2,343 casualties including 2,024 deaths; the air force 21,000 casualties including 13,589 deaths; the army 75,596 casualties including 22,917 deaths. The dead included a nurse and three members of the Women's Division of the Royal Canadian Air Force. A total of 45,423 women served in the three arms, and another 4,518 in the Medical Corps. Most were in junior positions far from the front, as it was believed women had no place in or near combat units.

These armed forces began from nothing, as we have seen. For example, in 1939 the Permanent Militia had some 4,000 men and 500 officers; by June 1944 it had 450,000 non-commissioned men and women and 50,000 officers. This sharp increase could not have occurred without the conflicts and mistakes that arise in all armies, at all levels. The British Commonwealth Air Training Plan is a case in point. In 1939, to save money, Canada abandoned its aviation manpower to British control. When Canada later wanted to make full use of an article in the agreement to establish Canadian squadrons, it would encounter

Lieutenant-General Charles Foulkes, Commander 1st Canadian Corps, accepts the surrender of
the German army from General Johannes Blaskowitz at Wageningen, Netherlands, on 5 May 1945.
(A.M. Sirton, NAC, PA-116811)

reluctance among both its English allies and the Canadian crews, who were by then used to the existing esprit de corps. The Canadianization of the air force would actually be a qualified failure.

The general rejoicing at the end of the conflict in Europe, then in the Pacific, was shared by 8,995 Canadian prisoners of war. During the final weeks of military operations in Europe, the prisoners of the Germans would frequently have to march under guards who believed Germany would make a comeback. Still, their fate would be enviable to the survivors of German concentration camps, who had lived under conditions of total horror and humiliation day after day. The 1,500 prisoners of war who were subjected to inhumane treatment by the Japanese were treated to a fairly pleasant few weeks after their liberation. This would not entirely heal the evidence of their ill treatment, but it would help to make them presentable for their loved ones.

The 33,843 German prisoners of war in Canada would see their daily rations somewhat reduced between 8 May 1945 and their departure for home, as the end of the state of war also marked the end of the application of the Geneva Convention.

Among those returning to or arriving in Canada beginning in the summer of 1945 were the spouses of 44,886 service personnel who had married in Europe. These were mainly English women, but there were also 1,886 Dutch, 649 Belgian, 100 French, 26 Italian, seven Danish and, despite the rules against fraternization, six German women. Between August 1944 and December 1946 a total of 61,088 dependents, including 358 children, came to Canada.[84] Left behind in Europe were another several hundred illegitimate children and women abandoned by their lovers.

To these new Canadians can be added some 5,000 Polish servicemen who had fought alongside the Canadians and, often, under their command, especially after Normandy.

But first and foremost were the volunteers returning home. Those wanting to go on to the war in the Pacific were the first to depart from Europe, with 30 days' leave. In the end they were fortunate, as they would not be leaving to fight Japan. The basic principle governing repatriation was that the first to go overseas, regardless of rank, would be the first to return. A point system for months of service in Canada and overseas would, for example, give 180 points to a private in the 1st Division enlisted in 1939 and 60 points to an officer enlisted in 1943 and lent to the British under the code name CANLOAN. Before the end of 1945, 184,000 servicemen were already home.

The 3rd Division selected as the occupation force had been reorganized with 10,000 volunteers and 8,000 servicemen who had accumulated fewer than 50 repatriation points. Commanded by Major-General Chris Vokes, it reached Germany in June and July 1945 to relieve the 2nd Division. Within this division and the 11 air force squadrons that had stayed on the scene after 8 May, there were soon "strikes," prompting Canada to cancel everything and bring home its young men, who were eager to rediscover their country and, especially, to take advantage of the generous veterans' plans available to them.

Making use of the experience built up in the First World War, the 1939–45 planners, many of them veterans, launched a series of reforms well before the end of the war. The ministers of veterans affairs (Ian Mackenzie), reconstruction (C.D. Howe) and health and social welfare (Brooke Claxton) were the chief architects. Canada already had a network of military hospitals and had more experience with disability rehabilitation than the United States, while the Canadian Pensions Commission had existed since 1933.

The legislation on reintegration of veterans gave service people the right to resume their prewar employment with—unlike the situation in 1919—the seniority and pay they would have enjoyed had they stayed home. Indeed the Canadian Veterans Charter was more generous than its American counterpart. Every veteran received a $100 allowance to purchase civilian clothing, and a premium of $7.50 for every 30 days served in the western hemisphere plus 25 cents for every day served elsewhere. Those who had remained overseas received seven days' pay for every six months spent outside the country. Thus a private with three years' service including two years overseas would receive $512. He could buy $10,000 of life insurance, generally without a medical examination; if he wanted to settle on a farm, low-interest, 3.5-percent, loans were available. University education or occupational training would be paid for a period of time equal to that spent in uniform. If none of this was acceptable to the young man, he would be paid a premium to buy and maintain a house. Veterans had access to full unemployment insurance benefits (introduced in 1941) after only 15 weeks of work. No other belligerent nation had such an attractive demobilization plan. It was as if the government was trying to redeem itself for the dreadful situation into which it had sent many of its volunteers.

During the war the 45,000 female volunteers were generally paid 20 percent less than men of the same rank. On their return, however, they were entitled to the same benefits. In 1946, 16,000 of these women would be married and 20,000 working. In general, the women would opt for occupational training much more than the men, most often in traditional women's trades like nursing, hairdressing and dressmaking.[85]

In many ways the Second World War continues to this day. Veterans' hospitals still contain too many bodies and souls forever broken. The Canadian Hong Kong veterans have gone before the United Nations Human Rights Commission to obtain reparation for their ill treatment at the hands of the Japanese. The Merchant Marine Coalition of Canada is demanding veteran status for its members, 40 percent of whom came from Quebec in 1939–45, as C.D. Howe once pointed out. The median age of all these surviving veterans is approximately 80 years.

Canadians on the Côte d'Azur, 1944

In August 1939 a young Montreal lawyer, Ralph Wilson Becket, was sent to Prince Edward Island to manage a trust for one of his firm's senior partners. The 31-year-old Becket enlisted as a second lieutenant in the Prince Edward Island Highlanders and on 1 August 1940 his regiment, headquartered in Dartmouth, Nova Scotia, was mobilized. Its first assignment was to defend the east coast. On a train journey that November he read in Liberty *magazine that Americans were receiving parachute training at Fort Benning, Georgia. Becket draughted a memorandum on the value of a parachute unit for combatting enemy landings on the Canadian coast. Since Canada could hardly be expected to launch its own training programme, he wrote, Canadian parachutists could be trained in the United States—although, he added, it was unlikely that such a unit would remain long in Canada if the conflict continued.*

In 1942, when he was a staff officer in the 18th Brigade just formed at Prince George, British Columbia, Becket saw a Top Secret message announcing the formation of the volunteer 2nd Parachute Battalion to be trained at Helena, Montana. The unit would be part of a Canadian-American venture named the 1st Special Service Force. Surmounting some difficulties (he was short-sighted), Becket managed to get accepted.

The disciplined arrival of the first detachment of Canadians, each in the uniform of his home regiment, behind a bagpiper at Fort William Henry Harrison near Helena caused a stir among the Americans present, though not as great as depicted in the film The Devil's Brigade, *says Becket.*

The Force was organized on American lines with three regiments of two battalions, each with three companies. In August 1944 Becket commanded the Force's 3rd Regiment, whose 2nd Battalion was led by John Bourne of the Royal Highland Regiment of Canada (Black Watch) of Montreal.

The Force was preparing for an amphibious landing in the Toulon area of France. Two Canadian troop transport vessels would be on duty for the occasion. Becket's objective was to take, at H-5, Levant Island, one of the Hyères Islands east of the landing area. A coastal battery had been recorded on Levant Island. The landing took place on the night of 14/15 August 1944, one year to the day after the Kiska landing in which the Force, and Becket, had participated, and its purpose was to protect one flank of the main attack on the continent. Indeed Levant Island turned out to be a Kiska of sorts. Few Germans and a false battery were found. However, one of Becket's battalions met with some resistance and took a few prisoners. After helping the 2nd Regiment secure the hardest positions to take on Port-Cros Island on 15–16 August, Becket was transferred to the mainland, first to Fréjus, where he had to fight, then to the advance towards Grasse. The 3rd Regiment was assigned to cross the Alpes Maritimes during this advance. The fierce fighting on the approaches to the perfume capital of the world, says Becket, bore no resemblance to the chapter entitled "The Champagne Campaign" in the book The Devil's Brigade. *The advance to the Italian border was fairly rapid, as the German divisions were not at their best. However, men were killed, wounded or permanently disabled on the Côte d'Azur, the very name of which evokes the pleasures of life. Becket and his men liberated Biot, the German artillery managing to inflict little damage. Here they encountered female collaborators having their heads shaved. Becket put a stop to this practice, to the great displeasure of the women's tormenters, resisters to the end.*

At the end of August, Becket liberated Vence, addressing the mayor and residents in French. Then it was on to L'Escarène, west of Var near the Italian frontier, where they met with violent resistance. They quickly but with great difficulty seized the Nice-Terrin railway tunnel ending at L'Escarène, cutting off the Germans' escape route.

For his heroism here, Sergeant Thomas Prince, the most decorated Aboriginal Canadian of the war, was awarded the American Silver Star on the recommendation of Becket, who had sent Prince on a dangerous but successful reconnaissance mission alone. Next came the capture of Mont-Ours and a fort the French had erected to repel Italian invaders. Becket's regiment, using a heavy machine gun, repelled a counterattack. For taking Mont-Ours, Becket was awarded his own Silver Star, as was Major Hufft commanding the 1st Battalion for going deep into enemy territory on mined roads to carry out a reconnaissance mission. In October a German company would attempt a final counterattack on Mont-Ours before all activities ceased in that sector.

For several weeks the regiment remained in this region, in the vicinity of Fort Castillon not far from the other regiment and near Sospel, site of a German garrison of two companies. Becket suggested they take Sospel from one side and the heights behind Castillon so as to cut off the German garrison without great cost so close to the end of the war. This they did without sustaining Allied casualties, as the Germans defended neither Sospel nor the fort—which was tiny, after all, and just a kilometre from the Italian border. They would not leave until late October, but Becket's patience was finally rewarded.

On 5 December the 1st Special Service Force paraded together. Then the order to disband was read. Becket advanced and gave the order for the Canadians to detach. They left in formation with the Canadian colours, leaving their brethren in arms, with whom, for more than 18 months, they had fought without regard for nationality.[86]

Chapter VII

FROM COLD WAR
TO PRESENT DAY

Canada was transformed by the Second World War. It was a much more centralized country in 1945 than in 1939, and all levels of government were more interventionist. Canada had developed, albeit awkwardly, a better knowledge of its various minorities, which, according to the 1941 census, accounted for some 20 percent of the population. After 1945 the treatment of minorities would be greatly improved. Canada was also more industrialized and more Americanized, and this trend would intensify throughout the second half of the 20th century. Finally, Canada was more aware of its international and continental responsibilities.

The government of 1945 was better prepared than that of 1918 to demobilize its soldiers and secure the future of its military. From the First World War the politicians had learned how to politically manage a conflict in which Canadians participated far from home. From the Second World War they seemed to have learned that good peacetime military organization is essential for a country that expects to be involved militarily abroad, which would be the case from 1945 to the end of the century.

Reorganizing the Military

Canada's defence forces had stagnated in the period between the wars. During the Second World War the committee of senior officials studying the problems that might follow in the wake of the conflict suggested staffing levels that would enable the

A Canadian "Blue Beret" serving with United Nations peacekeeping forces in Cyprus, circa 1975. (Re-creation by Ronald B. Volstad, DND)

military to survive on its own—to adjust and develop.

The post-1945 professional army would reach a strength of 25,000 personnel—the Mobile Striking Force—and the reserve a strength of 180,000. The air force would consist of 16,000 service personnel and 4,500 auxiliary personnel with eight professional and 15 auxiliary squadrons. The navy would have 10,000 personnel with two aircraft carriers, two cruisers and 10 to 12 destroyers.

These professional armed forces totalling some 50,000 personnel had to be ready for any military eventuality—war, support and assistance to the civil authorities, militia training, and the maintenance and operation of communications systems in the Yukon and the Northwest Territories. Above all, they were responsible for the defence of Canadian sovereignty, which included numerous exercises in the north and the development of appropriate equipment.

A lesson the politicians had learned from the 1930s was that international co-operation was of little use in maintaining peace without the means to enforce it. The generation born in the 19th century and then of retirement age knew only too well, as did their successors, that there could be no peace without the forces to safeguard it, withdrawal would not make the problem go away, all peoples were interconnected and Canada had to maintain a presence on the international scene. After 1945, therefore, Canada would have more troops than it did after 1918, and it would revisit the idea of having the three services run by a single minister, whereas during the Second World War each had its own minister. This return to the principle of unification presaged much more radical changes 20 years down the road.

The army would keep its military regions with their headquarters and staffs that in theory could each serve a division. The training sites were still there, along with the administrative staff and militia instructors. The reserve had to have sufficient basic strength to operate six infantry divisions and four armoured brigades. This army, when mobilized, would have two corps plus coastal defence units. However, the armed forces were generally as unattractive after 1945 as they had been before the war. In 1949 the Regular Forces were short several thousand personnel, while the reserves were, as usual, well under strength.

The new National Defence Act somewhat readjusted what had been in existence since 1904 except in wartime. There would henceforth be a Cabinet Defence Committee chaired by the prime minister. Its vice-chairman would be the minister of defence and its other members would be the ministers of finance, industry and trade, and external affairs.

The minister of defence would chair the Defence Council, made up of the minister's parliamentary secretary, deputy minister and assistant deputy ministers, the three chiefs of staff and the chairman of the Defence Research Establishment. A remarkable but often forgotten fact: In 1950, for the first time since passage of the original Militia and Defence Act following Confederation, there was no section providing for compulsory service by men of eligible age. In other words, the law was finally catching up with a practice that had endured since the 1870s.

The substantial defence budgets of the period 1940–46 took a dive: The 1949 budget would be $361 million, compared to $2.9 billion for 1944–45.

However, the forecasts would explode—for two reasons, both based on the government's goal of keeping the peace by preparing for war. The year 1951 would see the passage of a $5-billion, three-year budget that was actually exceeded. In 1952–53 alone Canada would spend more than $2 billion on defence. Strength would be nearly 50,000 men and women in the Regular Army alone as of 31 March 1954, nine years after the end of the Second World War.

This was the first time in peacetime that the total number of professionals exceeded that of the militia, which was established at 46,500. These figures indicate a remarkable change in the public attitude to its armed forces. In 1927, for example, nine years after the end of the First World War, the army had numbered barely 4,000 personnel.

The Army Reserve Since 1945

The Canadian Army Reserve Force had by far the greatest historical resonance of all Canadian forces. Its tradition went back to the French regime—representing, by the end of the Second World War, almost 300 years of officially recorded history. Since Confederation, the reserve had been the backbone of Canada's defence at home and overseas. Its manpower and organization, deeply rooted in both small communities and large cities, had made it indispensable in the two great mobilizations of the 20th century. Beginning in 1945, the professional army that had been so disparaged by the militiamen of the 19th and 20th centuries was supplanted, for the emergence of technologies necessitated a thorough review of army strategies and deployment.

In 1946 the militia was more or less restored to its pre-1939 position. Nuclear weapons existed, but their full potential was largely unknown. Could an army formed in two years virtually from nothing, as was the case in 1914 and 1939, be viable in a con-

flict fought far from its bases? It would quickly be realized that a total war might be terminated before such a "coalescing" army could be deployed.

In 1952 the Chief of the General Staff, Lieutenant-General Guy Simonds, who had just seen to the rapid formation of two infantry brigades, for Korea and the Federal Republic of Germany, concluded that the militia would be incapable of responding to crises. War might be brief and highly technical. In order to wage it, an army required perpetually battle-ready, overtrained professionals. In Western Europe, where after 1951 Canada maintained a brigade, any invasion would have to be stopped within weeks. In such a case, no purpose would be served by organizing six divisions of militia.

In 1953 Simonds, having secured the support of the Conference of Defence Associations, handed the job of studying militia reform to a commission. Its task was to review the rationale and operating budget for the entire reserve. In its report, presented in April 1954 and written by Major-General Kennedy, the commission recommended the elimination of divisions and brigades along with their headquarters and most coastal defences and anti-aircraft batteries. The number of armoured units would rise from 18 to 22, while infantry units would drop from 66 to 54. Training standards would not be reduced, but reservists would be given more time to meet them. Reserve units would be teamed with Regular Force units for a week or two every year.

This much-needed restructuring still came as a shock to some: They were seeing the disappearance of battalions that had attracted excellent recruits in the past—supplying, for example, the Army Corps commander of the First World War and three of the five division commanders of the Second World War. Yet regiments like the Royal 22e absorbed militia units as their 4th and 6th battalions, and the amalgamated Canadian Fusiliers/Oxford Rifles formed the 3rd Battalion of the Royal Canadian Regiment. It was also understood, if not shouted from the rooftops—a number of militiamen were unaware of it—that when two reserve regiments supported one another only the larger of the two would be mobilized in wartime, with the other recruited to offset casualties. The goal was to have the reserve regiments that marched in tandem gradually merge, resulting in 27 reserve regiments or approximately what would be required for two overseas divisions plus territorial defence.

The report also envisaged a Regular Army Reserve made up of persons who had completed their contracts in the Regular Force but were prepared to train for 21 days a year in their former regiments. This highly unpopular system would be abandoned after three years. At this moment of historic fervour, the post-Second World War Reserve became the Canadian Army Militia, restoring continuity with the old French regime.

The reserve was somewhat revived by these changes, but certain facts remained. The proliferation of tactical and strategic nuclear weapons made it highly unlikely that two divisions would be able to reach Europe before the outcome of a conflict was determined. Moreover, the reserve's equipment was getting old and there was no money to replace the Sherman tanks and some of the field guns. Before leaving his job Simonds suggested another review of the reserve, and his successor, Howard Graham, appointed Brigadier W.A.B. Anderson to conduct it. Anderson agreed with past inves-

tigators that the reserve was ill prepared for action. In his view, no unit would be battle-ready within 30 days of a mobilization order and a number of them would need several months to fill their ranks. Anderson's recommendations, which included the elimination of the least productive units, would never be implemented. Under the newly elected Conservative government, the reserve was assigned a new role by defence minister George R. Pearkes, a Victoria Cross recipient from the First World War: organizing survival in the event of an atomic attack. The policy on its use had changed, but the reserve organization recommended in the Kennedy Report had not. In the face of reluctance from Pearkes, who favoured keeping everything, Graham and his successor, Lieutenant-General S.F. Clark, got rid of some 150 ineffective sub-units in particularly remote locations.

The Liberals returned to power in 1963 with a radical programme of change for the Armed Forces, including reduced budgets and strength and a new study of the reserve. On 18 November 1963 the Chiefs of Staff Committee reported to the minister, Paul Hellyer, that the reserve would not be very useful in a major overseas conflict but could always be employed for territorial defence and survival operations following a nuclear attack. However, Lieutenant-General Walsh explained that the militia could have a future if its personnel were cut back from 51,000 to 30,000—the numbers had stood at 180,000 immediately after the Second World War—and given real military tasks in Canada and overseas.

Hence yet another commission was established, this time to see what could be done with 30,000 men and women. The job of this commission was to define the role of a force whose size had been politically determined. As might be expected, large numbers of units were expunged from the order of battle to become mere names on the supplementary list. Also, units were identified as major or minor.

In the 1970s the reserve manpower ceiling would fall to 19,200, then rise again in the 1980s and officially stabilize at around 23,000 after the various cuts beginning in 1993 had been made. Of this total—which could actually be higher—approximately 14,500 are members of the Army Reserve.

A 1987 white paper restored the reserves to a place of importance. NATO's strategy of "proportional" response to attacks implied that the potential of rapid nuclear war as envisaged in the 1950s and 1960s now yielded to a notion of conflict that would turn atomic only after a sequence of conventional battles that would give the belligerents time to mobilize their reserves. The result would be to reduce the Regular Force and to increase the Reserve Force to 40,000, with most of these places going to the militia. Emerging at the same time was the concept of a Total Force in which the Reserve and Regular forces would be more fully bonded and encouraged to interact. Developed in the latter part of the 1980s, this concept would have the professional and the reservist remain under their own service conditions. The reservists are not happy with this plan, but it is in the process of being resolved. Since 1991, thousands of reservists have served in the former Yugoslavia, Haïti and Cambodia.

The end of the Cold War and tough new budgetary imperatives necessitated another white paper, this one (1994) calling for, among other things, a review of the reserve to be conducted between April and October 1995 by the Right Honourable Brian Dickson (Chairman), Lieutenant-General (Retired) Charles H. Belzile and Professor Jack L. Granatstein. The commission focused on the three reserve elements with their total personnel of 23,000, and concluded that the reserve should reflect the operational requirements of the Canadian Forces, taking into account socio-economic factors and regional circumstances. The commission recommended an overall rationalization of infrastructure (especially for the militia), consolidation of units and elimination of superfluous subcomponents. The overall mandate, it should not be forgotten, was to lower the reserve's operating costs, which after 1996 would still be $895 million annually.

The Naval Reserve has some 4,300 members in 24 divisions across Canada, with headquarters in Quebec City. Its main role is to ensure the country's coastal defence with new vessels, most of them built by the year 2000. This very clear, specific role no doubt explains the absence of major problems.

The Air Reserve has 1,500 reservists out of an authorized strength of 1,800. This reserve is well used despite a lack of consensus on what the proportion of flying personnel should be.

The three reserves are designed to support a potential national mobilization. There are problems, however, in the militia. From sea to sea there are 133 militia units in 125 towns and villages in 14 districts in four regions—Atlantic, Quebec, Ontario and Western. The units are often under-strength yet the number of officers is excessive. In a way, today's militia is reminiscent of that of 1868. In other words, the total number of militiamen in 1995 was about right—18,347 of the 19,957 militia positions were filled, with Quebec the only region to reach (and even exceed) its ceiling—but the large number of units means that many of them have sufficient members for only one company.

The commission recommended that the militia be organized into an army corps of seven militia brigade groups, each responsible for training and administering nine to 11 units. Again, the objective is the amalgamation of numerous existing units. For example, Ontario region, with 43 units, should consolidate its units for a maximum of 22. The commission recommended that the militia participate in the rationalization process and that its allocation of funds be spent on recruiting and maintaining reservists, not on keeping pointless headquarters and officers with no troops.

The commissioners found an army of two "cultures"—a militia distrustful of a Regular Force that it finds condescending, and a Regular Force resentful of militiamen whom they believe have it too easy. This is the basis for the commission's call for a rapprochement in all areas and for similar standards, such as in physical fitness.[87]

Reforms notwithstanding, the reserve, reduced in numbers once again in 1995 by government decree, remains prey to a problem it seems unwilling to solve: Although recruitment for the units functions well, maintaining strength is problematical. As well, the regimental system for militia units continues to survive despite the many attacks against it. Since 1954, the strategic scenario has been thoroughly overhauled so many times that all the recommendations of the commissions of inquiry have been no more than temporary solutions. This structural instability hardly encourages stability in strength.

Like it or not, the militia does not possess the political strength it did a hundred years ago. Even if thousands of reservists are given a more realistic role to play, they will not necessarily stay in the reserve after an operational tour.[88] Here again, the recommendations of the recent commission of inquiry included the following: a guaranteed number of monthly training days from September to May, over and above the two weeks of camp; equal pension and other benefits for professionals and reservists; and job protection for a reservist who leaves on a tour of duty. Recruitment for the Regular Force and the Reserve Force is already conducted jointly.

Changes

The Permanent Forces would also be caught between domestic political imperatives and external strategic change. Canada was drawn into the Cold War very early on, if only through the atomic research conducted on its soil during the Second World War and, only weeks after the end of the war in the Pacific, the defection of Igor Gouzenko, a Soviet Embassy cypher clerk who put Canada in the centre of a Soviet spy network. A February 1948 pro-Soviet coup d'état in Czechoslovakia was followed in March by the blockade of Berlin. The Western European reaction to the threat from the East would be followed by a North American rally to the defence of the European democracies.

Canada had been out of Europe militarily since the spring of 1946. Its troops stationed at home—those who survived demobilization—were few in number. The navy had requested 20,000 men and a fleet that would include two aircraft carriers and four cruisers; the government gave it half of what it wanted. The army asked for 55,788 regular soldiers, 155,396 reservists and 48,500 conscripts; it did not get conscription and was allocated a strength of 25,000. The air force got 16,000 of the 30,000 personnel it requested.

It was understood that these forces would ensure national security while preparing for potential conflicts overseas. The navy, however, had an immediate problem—keeping personnel—which it addressed in 1947 and 1948 by increasing both salaries and the ratio of non-commissioned officers to seamen. On the high seas in February 1949, when the latter reform came into effect, some ships found themselves with more NCOs than seamen, even though those tasks reserved for seamen had not been reduced. What is more, since seniority prevailed for these promotions, some of the new NCOs were not necessarily the best. There resulted some incidents that were too easily labelled as mutinies. In the aftermath of these "work stoppages," much was made of the fact that Canadian naval officers were cut off from their men by their British training. Discipline as learned in Britain should not be applied in Canada, concluded a commission, presided over by Rear Admiral Rollo Mainguy, appointed to investigate the incidents. While their recommendations were valid, the commissioners made much of the short-term reaction to reforms in personnel management that would prove to be highly positive in the medium and long terms.

The army established the Mobile Striking Force that Lieutenant-Colonel Ralph Wilson Becket and others had advocated during the war. Soldiers were trained as parachutists, and the force, transported by the Royal Canadian Air Force, could be rapidly deployed on any point of the territory susceptible to attack. As the acknowledged enemy quickly became the USSR, which might strike from the north, arctic exercises with special equipment and materiel were the order of the day.

The Korean War and the founding of the North Atlantic Treaty Organization would soon change this perspective. Between 1950 and 1953, the strength of the Regular Force increased from 47,000 to 104,000. The 1947 budget was multiplied tenfold, reaching $1.9 billion in 1953.

The navy, which needed good technicians, would not reach its newly authorized strength until the late 1950s. The air force would also take a few years to reach strength, since it was once again starting with phased-out combat equipment. In 1952 the army revived the historic red rectangle of the 1st Division, worn high on the sleeve near the shoulder. This patch would disappear a few years later to return once more in the 1980s.

As we have seen, several militia regiments would be transferred to the Regular Force, including the Queen's Own Rifles of Canada and the Black Watch. There would be an attempt to rewrite history by creating the Regiment of Canadian Guards with four battalions, a unit with no historical basis in Canada. From 1955 on, exercises at the divisional level would be held at Gagetown, New Brunswick, a newly acquired camp with an area of 440 square miles.

With the Conservatives' return to office in 1957, national defence budgets began to shrink again, from $1.8 billion that year to $1.5 billion in 1960. In 1963, however, the Regular Force still had 120,871 personnel, a peacetime record. In 1967 this figure was cut to 110,000. The following year, all the new battalions added to the order of battle in 1953, except for the 2nd and 3rd battalions of the Royal 22e Régiment, the Princess Patricia's Canadian Light Infantry and the Royal Canadian Regiment, were returned to the reserve. In the 1970s the military membership of the Regular Force fell to approximately 80,000 before rising to 88,000 in the 1980s. In 1999 this figure would fall to 60,000. Budgets would be frozen in the 1960s at around $1.5 billion before increasing to more or less parallel the rate of inflation. They levelled off at $12 billion in the early 1990s before falling towards $9 billion at century's end.

Unification

One of the most striking changes to affect the armed forces since the end of the Second World War was the integration and unification of the Canadian Armed Forces during the 1960s.

These changes did not come about as abruptly as we are often given to believe. The first step towards integration had actually taken place in 1923, when, to increase both savings and effectiveness in national defence, the department of militia and defence was merged with the Naval Service, to which was added the newly created air ministry. As we have seen, the same period saw an unsuccessful attempt at limited integration of the main headquarters. The senior officers resisted this move. The Chiefs of Staff Committee was formed in 1939 but would not acquire a chairman until 1951. This position would survive, though with no real power or staff of its own, until it was replaced in 1964 by the new position of Chief of the Defence Staff. Also in 1939, a bill to unify the Armed Forces was draughted, though it was never introduced in Parliament: First it met with powerful domestic resistance; then the war in Europe put it in mothballs.

Impetus for unification resumed in 1947 when Brooke Claxton was minister. He presented his department's long-term objectives to Parliament under 14 points, the first of which set out the need for tighter coordination between the military and the unification of the department in order to create a single defence force, within which the three services would function. Claxton immediately ordered the establishment of a single headquarters to bring the three under one roof, with the three civilian administrators united in one position, Deputy Minister of Defence. He then ordered each service to adopt a similar organizational structure made up of three main divisions, namely planning and operations, personnel and payroll, and supply and equipment. In the face of inertia on the part of the services, the Korean War and the establishment of NATO, Claxton was unable to pursue this ambitious plan.

In the period 1947–51, however, some advances were made. Dental services were integrated in 1947, though it would be another 11 years before the process was complete, and in 1951 the medical service began making the move towards eventual consolidation (1959). The Defence Research Council was also created. The Royal Military College in Kingston was reopened to serve all three forces. Royal Roads Military College in Victoria and the bilingual Collège militaire royal in St Jean, Quebec, would later be founded and, from the beginning, receive officer cadets and officers from all three forces. The legal and chaplaincy services were also integrated in the main headquarters, along with functions like payroll and catering. The position of Chairman of the Chiefs of Staff Committee finally materialized in 1951, in response to needs created by the Korean War and the organizational requirements of NATO, which held regular conferences of member countries' chiefs of staff or their committee chairmen.

The Avro CF-100 fighter-interceptor. First seeing service in 1953, the Canadian-designed
CF-100 had a very large range for its day and could reach speeds of 660 mph (960 kph).
Its role was to attack enemy bombers detected by DEW Line radar stations in the
Canadian Arctic.
(Avro Aircraft Ltd. advertisement, private collection)

First seeing service in 1952, the Fairchild C-119 "flying boxcar" was the main transport plane used by the Canadian forces until the early 1960s. (DND, PCN-2838)

The CF-104 Starfighter. This U.S.-designed aircraft had a top speed of 1,450 mph (2,320 kph) and served in the Canadian air force from 1961 to the mid-1980s. It equipped squadrons based in Germany. (DND, 83-943)

A CF-101 Voodoo fighter intercepting an old Soviet Bear bomber used for reconnaissance in Canadian air space. This type of incident was frequent during the Cold War. Made in the U.S., the Voodoo was the Canadian Forces' main fighter from 1961 to 1984. With a top speed of only 1,220 mph (1,952 kph), the Voodoo was definitely inferior to the CF-105 Avro Arrow. (DND, 84-940)

The Yukon four-engine transport built by Canadair in Montreal, the largest Canadian aircraft built at the time, was used by the air force for transporting personnel until it was replaced by the Boeing 707 in 1981. Following the adoption of the red and white national flag, the external rondels on some Yukons were painted red, as shown in this photo. (DND, 67-723)

The DeHavilland Chipmunk trainer used to train pilots during the 1950s and 1960s. (DND, PCN-5597)

A Labrador helicopter in the early 1980s. (DND, 82-694)

The Albatross float plane conducted sea rescue operations during the 1960s.
(DND, 66-44-5)

The U.S. Liberator B-24 bomber was assigned to transport duty between England and India by 426 Squadron in 1945. These aircraft were later used for coastal surveillance.
(DND, 68-1276)

A DeHavilland T-64 Caribou light transport during the 1960s.
(DND, 67-962)

A McDonnell-Douglas CF-18 fighter aircraft during an attack exercise in 1985. This aircraft came into service in the early 1980s.
(DND, 85-921)

The CF-140 Aurora reconnaissance aircraft, used for submarine detection since 1981.
(DND, 85-150)

The Avro Arrow CF-105 in 1958. This Canadian-designed aircraft was the most advanced fighter in the world at that time, with a top speed of 1,650 mph (2,640 kph). It was expensive, however, and the government halted production. The five existing examples of this triumph of Canadian engineering were destroyed. All this stirred up such controversy that it remains a subject of passionate debate in the country more than 40 years later. (DND, 82-384)

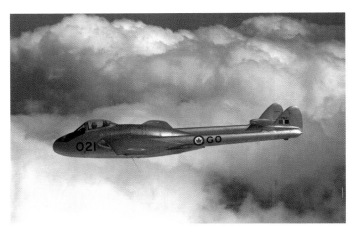

The DeHavilland Vampire became the first jet fighter to serve in the Canadian Air Force after 86 of them were received in 1946. Designed in Britain during the Second World War, the Vampire could reach speeds of 548 mph (876 kph). It was taken out of service in 1958. (DND, PC-251)

A Grumman Avenger AS 3 of the Royal Canadian Naval Air Arm, circa 1952. In 1946, the red maple leaf replaced the circle. (DND, CT-825)

A North American F-86 Sabre fighter aircraft. This excellent American fighter was the main combat aircraft of the Canadian air force during the 1950s, capable of reaching speeds of 700 mph (1,120 kph). Canadair made large numbers of F-86s in Montreal, using Canadian Orenda engines that were more powerful than the American engines. The Canadian flag replaced the tricolour strip on the rear aileron in 1954. (DCN, PCN-2664)

The Canadair CF-5A, the Canadian version of the American F-5 Freedom Fighter, in service beginning in 1968. (MDN, 89-1048)

Lancaster bombers were converted into reconnaissance aircraft after the Second World War and remained in service until 1956. Starting in 1947, Lancasters photographed 3.5 million sq. mi. (5.6 million sq. km.) in the Canadian North and Arctic and established the first accurate maps of these immense areas. (DND, PCN-2950)

In the years 1951–61 the integrating impetus subsided. This could be called a period of digestion or consolidation. Numerous joint committees functioned in the main headquarters, but they remained centres for information rather than for co-ordination or unification. A Royal Commission on Government Organization was established in 1961, chaired by J. Grant Glassco. Its report, submitted in 1962, provided solid reasons for greater integration of functions common to the three forces but avoided making specific recommendations.

The Pearson government came to power in 1963 and ordered a review of Canada's entire defence policy, whose weak links had contributed to the fall of the Diefenbaker government. Questions concerned the cost of military equipment, the Canada-U.S. defence relationship, especially the issue of air defence, and, finally, the nuclear issue (having opted out of the nuclear club, was Canada still obliged to accept or use American nuclear weapons?). The need to economize was also being made painfully clear, yet the forces had to be re-equipped. The proportion of the military budget used for equipment procurement had plummeted from 42.9 percent in 1954 to 13.3 percent in 1963. At this rate, by 1966 other defence expenditures would absorb all the funds available for new acquisitions.

The Glassco Commission had indicated the need to rationalize not only departmental spending but also duplication, even triplication, in the services. It noted the weak role played by civilians, especially the deputy minister, at national headquarters, and argued the need to review regulations that were impeding the transfer of skilled personnel from one force to another.

The new defence minister, Paul Hellyer, therefore decided it was time for another white paper (the previous one dated from 1959), which was tabled in Parliament on 26 March 1964. This white paper argued that for all practical purposes Canada was unlikely to undergo direct attack and that its defence policy should maintain a focus on collective security through a system of alliances and participation in peacekeeping operations. It concluded that well-equipped, mobile troops under a single, unified command would better serve Canadian interests.

Taking as essential an effective system of operational control and the need to simplify administrative procedures and cut general administration costs, the white paper held that there was only one satisfactory solution: the integration of Canada's Armed Forces under a single Chief of Defence Staff and a single Defence Headquarters. This decision would mark the first stage in the creation of a unified defence force for Canada.[89]

Shortly after tabling the white paper, the minister submitted Bill C-90, which was passed on 7 July and came into force on 1 August 1964. As of June 1965 a new Chief of Staff would head all of Canada's military forces, backed by a general headquarters that was integrated and restructured to reflect six so-called functional commands—replacing the 11 previous ones. "Functional" described a command that was non-geographic, beyond any particular element or traditional arm. The "military base" became the focus of administrative support at the local level, providing all necessary services to "lodger" units—including those that came under a command other than the one governing the base. In addition, regional responsibilities were assigned to the main functional commands, especially with regard to civilian personnel, cadets and the control of civil disturbances.

This 1964–67 integration phase caused little controversy. It was viewed primarily as administrative reorganizing that would not affect units directly. The Forces, although losing their chiefs and privileged direct access to the minister, legally survived the change. This top-down integration was more complete and effective than the attempts made at the lower levels between 1947 and 1964.

The restructuring of the military headquarters had little impact on the Deputy Minister's Division. Although the deputy minister's responsibilities remained the same, the role was slightly changed: The deputy minister would henceforth be one of two advisors to the minister, the other being the Chief of Staff.

The 1964 defence white paper and Bill C-90 carried the seeds of unification. With the abolition of the chief of staff position in each of the three arms, the creation of a general chief of staff position and the consolidation in one headquarters of planning, personnel, administration, training, logistical support, and command and control, the notion of the three arms as separate entities became outdated.

In May 1967, Parliament passed Bill C-243, thus completing the process of reorganizing the national headquarters and commands. The three forces were dissolved and all military ranks had to comply with the new terminology of a single command. A common system was devised for personnel evaluation, selection and promotion. Committees began the search for a common uniform and the traditions to be observed by a unified force. The old names of army, navy and air force were abandoned in favour of the designations land, sea and air elements. A single command and a single force became the watchwords.

Most servicemen and civilians had envisaged unification as a possibility consigned to a distant future somewhere in the 1970s that might as well have been never. But the minister insisted: For Hellyer, 1968 represented the "few years later" he had spoken of in 1964 when announcing unification. The champion of change against the forces of inertia, he succeeded in getting Bill C-243 passed. To ensure its application, the minister gave the four maple leaves to the only general he considered worthy of the job. In his memoirs, Jean V. Allard, the only French-Canadian lieutenant-general up to that time, recalls his appointment as Chief of the Defence Staff—the man who would, when Bill C-243 came into force on 1 February 1968, guide the destiny of the unified force into uncharted and highly troubled waters.

In 1964 neither the minister nor the chairman of the Chiefs of Staff Committee could rely on the services of independent personnel to assess the demands from each of the old forces or plan for the armed forces as a whole. No precise plan or timetable had been drawn up for the stages of unification; thus they would occur somewhat randomly. This approach stirred up concerns among parliamentarians and the public. There was even greater confusion among members of the military, who, whether at National Headquarters or in the commands, were getting little in the way of specific orders. The entire period 1964–72 was dominated by a single ever-present constant: change. Although all the convulsions took place in the military, they had been prescribed by civilians, primarily the minister and his circle.

Canadian Forces unification was not copied elsewhere. Yet this is less a judgement on the value of the product than on Canada's unique circumstances and quali-

HMCS *Protector* resupplying the battleship USS *Wisconsin* in the Persian Gulf. Canadian ships and aircraft participated in the Gulf War against Iraq. (DND, 90-4030)

Formed in 1945, the Royal Canadian Naval Air Arm began operations in 1946 with the aircraft carrier *Warrior,* soon to be replaced by HMCS *Magnificent,* which served from 1948 to 1957 and is shown here at Port Said, Egypt, in 1957. (DND, CT-457)

The submarine *Onondaga,* one of three of this class that first saw service in 1965. (DND, 87-567)

The icebreaker *Labrador,* which served from 1954 to 1957. (DND, CT-553)

The carrier *Bonaventure,* which served from 1957 to 1969. (DND, EKS-203)

ties: a huge territory, a small population (and thus a limited number of combatants), a weak military tradition based on voluntarism, the object of none but indirect threats to national security, neighbour to an allied superpower.

Although unification did succeed in reducing, by however little, the staff at National Headquarters in Ottawa—this is hard to calculate, given the changes in the responsibilities of other headquarters and the creation of new ones—the anticipated savings never materialized. Here again, unification is hardly responsible for the meagreness of this result. As of 1968, galloping inflation ate up much of the savings that might have accrued.

In the end, the land and air elements accepted integration and unification fairly well. The first Chief of the Defence Staff of these integrated forces was an aviator, Air Marshal F.R. Miller, and the air force administrative model was chosen for functional commands and military bases. Succeeding him, in the heat of the unification debate (1967–69), was General Allard with his charismatic personality and firm grip on the "former" army. It was the navy that would lead the campaign against unification and feel its effects the most. Far from being bilingual, it had remained the most British of the three forces in its traditions and practices. Naval bases were situated far from the capital, and from 1964 to 1966 the senior naval officers were located on the coasts, away from National Headquarters and—they felt—shielded from the unifying tidal wave that was about to wash over the department. Clearly, its preoccupation with the intrinsic "difference" of seamen isolated the navy. Already a numerical minority, it would suffer the effects of the "admirals' revolt" against unification. Not until 1977

would an admiral occupy the position of Chief of the Defence Staff, and then for only three years. The next admiral, appointed in the early 1990s, would hold the position for just a single year.

For some, the most serious change in functions, responsibilities and chain of command since 1947, despite integration and unification, was the restructuring of 1972 that attempted to productively blend the military and civilian streams within the department of national defence.

The responsibilities of the Deputy Minister's Division, representing the civil authority with respect to the functions of economy and effectiveness, had not been defined in the framework of unification. Yet despite all the upheavals in the military structure between 1964 and 1968, the defence department was still wrestling with management problems. The ship replacement programme was making little headway and was being hit by frequent cost hikes. There was concern over the planning process, the sharing of responsibilities and the control of fixed assets. In 1971 a task force was appointed to examine the ship acquisition programme and, more generally, relations between civilian and military organizations including the Defence Research Council. Its report, completed in 1972, recommended the creation of a new National Defence Headquarters (NDHQ) that would merge the duties of the deputy minister with those of the Chief of the Defence Staff. This restructuring was implemented that same year, along with a programme management system.

More reorganizing would follow, without unification being called into question, at least initially. Air Command was established in 1975, and certain restrictive practices believed to be demoralizing were abandoned—for example, those preventing the wearing of distinctive badges on uniforms or the use of traditional titles and ranks in the navy, which some felt had mitigated the absolute character of unification. In fact, the unifying suit was beginning to come apart at the seams.

The 1979 election of the Clark government, which would last only six months, provided yet another minister with an opportunity to strike a task force, this time to "study the advantages and drawbacks of the unification of the Canadian Forces and...at the same time provide an opinion on the unified system of command."[90] After many hearings and some highly detailed research, the task force concluded that it was difficult to assess the direct role played by unification in terms of defence savings in the years 1964–80, given the reductions in resources, both personnel and equipment, imposed on the department during the period. The Forces remained generally under-equipped, said the report, and the financial savings that unification would have made possible had been absorbed by inflation, a frenzied rise in the cost of military equipment, the oil crises of 1973 and 1979, and pay equity between military and civilian personnel beginning in 1972. The task force was evasive about the achievement of all the objectives sought by unification: There was no basic plan to facilitate comparison of the goals of 1964 with the outcomes of 1979; nor did the task force have the means of assessing whether unification had made possible a speed-up in decision-making or a cut in response time. Without making any absolute judgements, the task force offered 30 recommendations on particular problems.

The report was, however, submitted to the newly elected Liberal government, which called for an immediate review. On 31 August 1980 the review concluded that the task force had not reached a verdict on unification as such and that its 30 recommendations were based on the principle of improving existing central institutions, inferring that the unification policy should remain in force.[91]

The Conservatives, returning to office in 1984, did nothing about unification, and white papers in 1987 and 1994 would not call centralization into question. Since 1980 the commanders of the commands have been sitting on the Defence Council and the Defence Military Committee, and since 1985 members of the military have once more been wearing three distinctive uniforms. Far from signalling a return to the past or the disunification or disintegration of the Canadian Forces, these changes reflect the flexibility and adaptability the military and civil authorities have been able to find in the face of the problems inherent in creating an organizational structure that is unique in the world.

The long process of integration and unification comprised three phases: the first was administrative, the second had to do with command and control of the armed forces, and the third was bureaucratic amalgamation as a government agency. This centralization is finding a place in the history of a relatively young country at a point when it is defining itself in the context of national unity while at the same time dealing with the problems of acquiring expensive military equipment when not under any external threat.

Francophones in the Military

After 1945, Brigadier J.P.E. Bernatchez was asked to look into the reasons for the shortage of Francophones in the army and to offer solutions. In the prevailing atmosphere of Canadian defence, his recommendations would not go far, except for that advocating the establishment of a school for Francophone recruits to receive instruction in their own language, which would be implemented in 1949. The armed forces had been reorganized after the war in response to political pressures and new realities, and there was little enthusiasm for further reorganization to reflect the French fact, as some would have wished. Changing the ways of a victorious army is not an easy task.

The Francophone presence in the expanding forces of the 1950s was marked by a series of studies involving the three arms. These were the first stirrings of interest in this problem, accompanied by observations that were clear to any Francophone, whether serving in the forces or not. Those who had thus far avoided thinking about the problem now learned that French Canadians perceived the Canadian forces as an English institution. A military career was not an option for Francophones who were unilingual, or even those who were less than completely fluent in English. Transfer to various parts of Canada precluded a French-language education for their children and a full cultural life for their families. Surveys revealed that Francophones were well aware of this reality. It negatively influenced their participation in the military and thus the cohesiveness of Canadian defence activities.

The various surveys conducted in the 1950s revealed that French Canadians, who represented approximately 27 percent of new recruits, were leaving the military at an alarming rate, from their very first year. Those who survived 12 months of adjusting to a new life and a new language would stay as long as Anglophones, but they were very few in number. In 1951, Francophones made up 2.2 percent of naval officers,

11 percent of NCOs and seamen. An average of 38 weeks of training would be required for a Francophone recruit to become functional in a naval environment, as opposed to 21 weeks for an Anglophone recruit. The 17 weeks of English instruction would very often prove inadequate when it came time for technical courses. The message was clear: French Canadians were not wanted in the navy. The initial reaction from the navy came in 1952, with the establishment of an English-language school where Francophones would be able to spend up to six months before tackling instruction in English. In short, they were proposing assimilation. One wonders whether the people who dreamed up this solution suspected just how small the response would be. In the air force things were not much better, with Francophone representation standing at 4.7 percent among officers and 16.3 percent among NCOs and troops. In the army of 1958 the percentages were 14 and 21, respectively.

In the 1950s the army made changes, though partial and sometimes awkward. In 1954 a Francophone artillery sub-unit was formed up and sent to the town of Picton, Ontario, where Francophobia was alive and well. In 1957 a tank squadron was formed. In the early 1960s both of these sub-units would be struck from strength. On the other hand, in 1952 Collège militaire royal de Saint-Jean in Quebec opened for officer cadets from all three forces, and it would remain, until 1995, as a part of the movement for a greater Francophone military presence. It preached functional bilingualism for all officer cadets, Anglophone as well as Francophone, offered university and other courses to each group in its own language and recruited an average of two Francophones for every Anglophone. For nearly two decades, however, if the first three years were spent in St Jean the last two were spent at the Royal Military College in Kingston, and in English only. What is more, the military training—or "summer training"—sessions were frequently held in English. The Francophone attrition rate in this programme would remain very high at the outset.

Thus the situation was slowly improving when, in the late 1950s, Quebec Francophones began making ever stronger demands for formal equality. The department simply continued to conduct studies. In 1960, Marcel Chaput, a future champion of Quebec separatism, produced an analysis of test scores for infantry officers applying for promotion that had resulted in Anglophones receiving higher marks than Francophones: The tests had been prepared in English, then loosely translated; and answers written in French were translated before being marked. Here was the source of many problems, Chaput declared. It should be noted that all of this was transpiring in the army, where French Canadians had the strongest presence and the greatest success. In fact two major-generals from the Royal 22e Régiment in a row, Jean V. Allard and Paul Bernatchez, would occupy the second-highest position in the army headquarters hierarchy.

The 1962 Glassco Report contained the germ of the principle of institutional bilingualism that would take root in the Canadian public service. One commissioner in particular, Eugène Therrien, devoted long paragraphs to the problems encountered by Francophones in the Forces, stressing the impossibility of their feeling comfortable there.

The next year saw the establishment of the Royal Commission on Bilingualism and Biculturalism. In April 1966, Prime Minister Lester B. Pearson announced a series of measures to ensure a degree of Francophone and French-language proportional representation in federal institutions. In 1969, finally, the Official Languages Act supported federal institutional bilingualism: Though not all public servants would have to be bilingual, the system would have to be able to serve both external and internal clients in their own language. Pearson's 1966 statement had excluded the armed forces, but the Act of 1969 did not. Between these two events, however, things had begun to move quickly in the military. Integration and unification had done their job. The two studies calling for the reorganization of the old trades (men) and classifications (officers) included chapters on bilingualism. The trades review committee, chaired by a rear admiral, categorically refused to countenance any more French-language units— the Royal 22e Régiment was enough—or afford French more than a social role. The classifications committee chaired by an army major-general, on the other hand, went so far as to suggest that the full training programme might eventually be available in French. Having gone over the preliminary conclusions of the Royal Commission's report, this review group even hazarded an initial estimate of the number of bilingual officer positions the unified forces would need.

In the mid-1960s, amid preparations for large-scale restructuring, there was a readiness to deal, however imperfectly, with the issue of Francophones and the French language in the Forces. But there was more. The two defence ministers in the years 1964–70, Paul Hellyer and Léo Cadieux (later ambassador to France), were determined to see the situation change, and for the first time a French Canadian landed the top military job. General Jean V. Allard was a Second World War hero who in 1943, when his career appeared to be blocked, had transferred from the armoured division to the infantry. Against all odds, he had managed to preserve his Francophone identity and have his three children schooled in French. Allard devotes an entire chapter of his memoirs, published in 1985, to his efforts on behalf of Francophones in the military, reversing the fortunes that had been theirs for over a century.

In the years 1966–69, General Allard made the Francophone issue a priority, advancing on all fronts and setting some major objectives. Two years after his departure, the 1971 white paper would feature one of his innovations, a commitment to have Francophones represented in all trades, classifications and ranks in proportion to their numbers in Canada. In Allard's three years as Chief of Staff, he increased French-language units (FLUs) in all three forces as well as in the various arms of the army. He launched a programme that would enable Francophones to be recruited and trained in French before serving some career segments in their own language within FLUs.

Having made these major thrusts, Allard would leave the issues to his successors. The course he charted has been continued with varying degrees of felicitousness by his Francophone and Anglophone successors. National defence requires the participation of all Canadians, including the large Francophone minority. They must be treated fairly, and their culture and language must be recognized and respected.

It would be simplistic to conclude that all the traditional anomalies in the Forces have been eliminated. Since 1983, Francophones have accounted for some 27 percent of military personnel—one of Allard's goals. However, they are still over-represented in the lower ranks and under-represented everywhere else. In the military occupations where they had been conspicuously absent up to the 1960s, the shortfall is far from bridged. Instruction in French made impressive gains between 1969 and 1972, then slowly progressed for several years before falling back in some respects in the early 1980s, not to recover momentum for another dozen years.

While bilingualism has been a virtual Francophone monopoly, plans in the late 1960s and early 1970s allowed for Anglophones to receive French-language instruction. Unfortunately few of the objectives in this area have been reached.

In short, much has been done to formally recognize the need for full Francophone integration into the military in the interests of cohesiveness in national defence. A viable framework is in place for anyone to join the military in French and to function in French. However, an impartial observer will readily see that much remains to be done. Without the setbacks of the 1970s, the present situation would be more positive.

Peacekeeping

Canada's window on the world has reflected its role in international life. When the League of Nations failed, the world's leaders attempted to do better with the United Nations Organization. In the 1920s Canadians were able to say they were so far from the source of ignition that they needed no fire insurance. But the years 1939–45 proved, as had the years 1914–18, that what was happening in another part of the world could easily affect Canada.

Canadian foreign policy after 1945 would focus on international security.

Canadian infantryman in Korea, 1951–54.
(Re-creation by Ronald B. Volstad, DND)

On 24 and 25 April 1951 the 2nd Battalion of Princess Patricia's Canadian Light Infantry stationed in Kap'yong, Korea, fought day and night to repel repeated attacks by the Chinese 118th Division. This action stopped the Chinese army advance on Seoul, the Korean capital. Impressed by such gallantry and tenacity, the U.S. president awarded the battalion the American Distinguished Unit Citation, which it has worn ever since. (H. Charles McBarron, United States Army Center of Military History, Washington)

Sherman tanks of Lord Strathcona's Horse in Korea, 1951.
(DND, ZK-2011)

Canada would not hesitate to agree to Chapter VII of the United Nations Charter calling on member nations to act "in case of a threat to peace, a breach of peace or act of aggression." Obviously, in the world of law every word has a meaning. Towards the mid-1970s the U.N. managed to agree on a definition of the word "aggression," but it would not use this word again until the Iraqi invasion of Kuwait.

Part III of the U.N. Charter empowers the Security Council "to undertake by means of [armed] force any action it deems necessary to keep or restore peace and security." The U.N. Secretary General was empowered to investigate situations where peace was being threatened, and was free to send observers. The immediate postwar period was a troubled one, both in the Middle East, with the creation of Israel, and in the world generally, with events surrounding decolonization. It was in an observer role in Kashmir that Canadian soldiers first served the U.N.

Serving in an observer role and peacekeeping were not, however, among the highest defence priorities. Before 1955 one would have had difficulty finding any reference to this function in the official documents of the defence department. All the same, Canadian soldiers would be asked to conduct numerous observer missions, most notably in the Middle East under the U.N. Truce Supervision Organization (UNTSO), which investigated and reported on violations of the 1949 ceasefire between Israel and its neighbours. This mission has involved hundreds of Canadian military personnel right up to the present, some occupying very important positions—for example, Major-General E.L.M. Burns was UNTSO's Chief of Staff in the mid-1950s after commanding a Canadian corps in Italy

during the war. Canadian servicemen would also participate, directly or indirectly, as U.N. observers in the conflict between India and Pakistan, as well as in Yemen and Lebanon. Over the years this work would extend to a host of activities, including helping to organize and supervising elections in various African, Asian, Central American and Caribbean countries.

Canada's actions on behalf of the peace objective have occasionally involved significant resources. This was the case with the first major peace mission under the aegis of the U.N., though commanded by the United States, better known as the Korean War. In 1945 the Japanese occupying northern Korea had surrendered to the Soviets, those in southern Korea to the Americans. The Allied agreement stipulated that Korea-wide elections would be held immediately. A special U.N. commission responsible for supervising the election process came to naught. During the night of 24/25 June 1950, North Korea decided to settle Korean reunification in its own way, launching a massive attack on the southern portion of the peninsula. The Cold War, which had been raging since 1945 but with more bite after 1948, now risked turning into a real war. The empty-chair policy adopted by the USSR on the Security Council at that time enabled that body to resolve on a U.S.-led intervention on behalf of South Korea.

On 30 June, to help restore peace, Canada sent three destroyers that would quickly become involved in convoy escort and bombardment in support of U.N. troop landings and departures and against enemy trains using coastal railways. In July an air transport squadron was also placed under U.N. command to serve between the U.S. and Japan. On 7 August came the announcement that a Canadian Army Special Force

Nurse Gagné caring for injured children in a makeshift dispensary during the genocide in Rwanda, 1994. (DND, 95-1239)

Canadian observers on the roof of the building that served as United Nations Forces HQ in Leopoldville/Kinshasa, Congo/Zaire, 1961. (DND, ZK-1905)

Serving with the United Nations in front of the presidential palace at Port au Prince, Haïti, 1996. (DND, 96-815)

Canadians serving with the United Nations in Cyprus, 1965. (DND, ZK-2049)

Canadian armoured personnel carriers serving with the United Nations at the Sarajevo airport in Bosnia during the 1993 siege of that city. (DND, 93-5381)

Canadian military personnel evacuating a wounded United Nations soldier in Bosnia, 1994. (DND, 94-501A-4)

was being formed. Rather than sending the Regular Force brigade, the volunteer principle was employed, as in 1914 and 1939, to create the 25th Infantry Brigade. The three existing regiments would each form a second volunteer battalion for the occasion.

The honour of being the first to see combat fell to the 2nd Battalion PPCLI. By the summer of 1951, when the Canadian brigade in Korea was complete, it would form part of the 1st Commonwealth Division, which included Australian and British troops as well. An action that was intended to be brief would continue for four years. Canada would ultimately commit, in rotation, its Regular Force battalions as well as the 3rd Battalion that each regiment would add to its 1st and 2nd battalions.

Back in 1945 the planned Canadian division for the war in the Pacific was to have received U.S.-style training and equipment. This is exactly what happened in 1950 with regard to training, although the equipment was a mixture of Canadian, British and American.

Before the arrival of Canadians in the field, the troops supporting South Korea, mainly American, re-established a temporary balance. By November 1950 they had retaken everything that had been lost in the south—actually, most of South Korea—and had made such advances in the north that they were close to the Chinese border.

At this point the Chinese became directly involved, joining their North Korean allies to drive back the U.N., which counterattacked in February 1951. This phase of the fighting engaged the 2nd Battalion PPCLI. By mid-April they were north of the border as it had existed since 1945. On 22 April, however, a South Korean division was routed north of Kap'yong, and the 27th Commonwealth Brigade was brought up from its reserve posi-tion to prevent a breakthrough across the Kap'yong Valley. From dusk on the 22nd until the morning of the 23rd, the PPCLI fought off all attacks with minimal casualties—10 dead and 23 wounded. This feat would earn it a mention in despatches from the U.S. president, a unique event in Canadian military history. It also more or less marked the end of the Chinese-led advance. The front was re-established around the 38th Parallel on the frontier that had separated the two Koreas before hostilities began. The years 1952 and 1953 would see a number of small- and medium-scale defensive battles and actions for control of no man's land until a truce was signed on 27 July 1953. Some of these engagements would be costlier than Kap'yong. In May 1953, for example, the Canadians lost 60 men during an attack on a position held by the 3rd Battalion RCR. In November 1953 the men of the 2nd Battalion Royal 22e Régiment suffered a fierce attack. On 8 November 1954 the Canadian combatants returned home.

Almost 22,000 Canadians served in Korea. With more than 1,500 casualties, including 309 dead, this action became the third most costly of Canada's overseas military commitments.

These would not be Canada's only substantial U.N. commitments. Between 1960 and 1964, for example, more than 400 Canadians served, mainly as signalmen, in the mission to restore and maintain law and order in Congo (Zaire), which required a total of over 20,000 U.N. representatives. In Cyprus, Canada intervened between Turkish and Greek Cypriots from April 1964 to June 1993, with 58 different contingents totalling tens of thousands of men and women, a number of whom served in Cyprus more than once. Since 1993, Canada has maintained only a very small number of service members (one or two at a time) in the headquarters of this international interposition force.

The action most resembling Korea was the Persian Gulf War of 1990–91, which entailed the deployment of three Canadian ships, two fighter squadrons, an infantry company and a field hospital. The Canadians, under the command of an integrated headquarters located at Al-Manāma, Bahrain, served mainly in the naval blockade of Iraq and air reconnaissance or combat patrols. No casualties were suffered. Canada participated in a minor way in the U.N.-mounted anti-Iraqi coalition under American command, an involvement totalling some 1,000 men and women, and played a role in liberating Kuwait after the Iraqi invasion in the summer of 1990.

Since 1991, Canada has contributed to other major U.N. peacekeeping operations such as: in the Red Sea with a ship and 250 men, in the former Yugoslavia (1991–95), Cambodia and Somalia (1992–93), Rwanda (1994–96), Haïti (1995–97) and East Timor (1999–2000).

Canada is valued for its record in various U.N. peacekeeping missions. It also invented a new type of mission. In 1956, Lester B. Pearson, then Secretary of State for External Affairs, proposed stationing U.N. soldiers between Israel and Egypt along the armistice line drawn after several weeks of conflict in which the Israelis had been supported by France and Britain. Pearson made his proposal on 1 November and the U.N. General Assembly approved the plan a few days later. The idea was to separate the belligerents until an agreement could be reached. In this case, fighting that was expected to be over in a few months went on for more than 20 years. Although this new approach to peacekeeping with a U.N. Emergency Force (UNEF) was far from perfect, it would initiate a process that continues, in various forms, to this day.

When the first UNEF was sent in, Canada elected to contribute a battalion of the Queen's Own Rifles of Canada. At that time Canadian soldiers were barely distinguishable from their British brethren who had only just left Egypt, having supported Israel in October and November 1956. The Egyptians let it be understood that this unit, though Canadian, would be less than appreciated in the circumstances. In the end Canada provided the mission with logistical support by more than 1,000 signalmen, engineers, logisticians, pilots and seamen. In UNEF II (1973–79) Canada would provide a similar number of personnel, and their role would approximate that of their predecessors.

Lieutenant-Colonel George Alfred Flint: A Hero Soon Forgotten

When Canada announces that it is sending military observers to foreign countries, the public rarely grasps the complexity of the problems the observers might encounter. In addition to acclimatizing themselves to conditions that often differ markedly from those at home, they might face extremely challenging obstacles in carrying out their duties. The events that led to the premature death of Lieutenant-Colonel George Alfred Flint, in charge of the Israel-Jordan and Mount Scopus

217

Mixed Armistice Commission (IJMAC) under the UNTSO from January 1956 to May 1958, illustrate the type of problems that are encountered by members of the Canadian military.

Born in Outremont, Quebec, on 27 February 1911, Flint joined the army reserve on 19 February 1941, then the active army. A member of Princess Patricia's Canadian Light Infantry as of October 1948, he would serve with its 1st Battalion in Korea. He was named Director of Military Intelligence in November 1952 with the rank of major and, in January 1954, the rank of Brigade Major of the 3rd Canadian Infantry Brigade at Valcartier. Loaned to the department of external affairs in January 1956 to serve in Palestine under the UNTSO, he took over the IJMAC.

Only a few months after arriving in Jerusalem, Flint shared a traumatic experience with another Canadian, Major Marcel Brault, a St Hyacinthe (Quebec) journalist, veteran and militia officer in the St Hyacinthe Regiment, which had become the 4th Battalion of the Royal 22e Régiment. While investigating a conflict in the demilitarized zone, both men were seriously injured by a land-mine from the 1948 war. Fortunately they survived and returned to service. Following a three-month convalescence, Flint resumed his duties, while Brault was transferred to Damascus. The chain of events leading to that incident were, in Flint's view, typical of what was happening around them. Other observers had been killed or seriously injured by mines during that same week.

In May 1957, Israel informed the UNTSO Chief of Staff, in a letter, that it would no longer be co-operating with Flint because of his conduct as chairman of the IJMAC and as UNTSO representative in the affairs of Mount Scopus. Insisting that he be recalled to Canada, Israel declared that it would henceforth be dealing directly with UNTSO headquarters. The letter stated that Jordan had already announced its refusal to have any further dealings with Flint; however, an analysis of various recall cases that UNTSO headquarters investigated in 1963 casts serious doubt on this claim.

As he approached the end of his term as head of the IJMAC, Flint chose not to renew his contract, believing that a replacement would be able to turn around the feelings of those concerned and forge better relations. However, the United Nations did not want to lose a man of his integrity. On receiving a special request from the Secretary General, Flint agreed to stay on until July 1959. He insisted, though, that his wife and two daughters, who had followed him to the Middle East at the beginning of his term, return to Canada.

The efforts of Flint and his UNTSO Chief of Staff, Major-General Carl von Horn, to defuse the situation between the Israelis and Arabs of Mount Scopus had thus far been fruitless. On 26 May 1958, three days after von Horn had paid a visit to Golda Meir, the Israeli minister of foreign affairs, in an attempt to ease tensions, some Israeli police officers were shot in the Gardens of Solomon. Two soldiers died on the spot and the ensuing exchange was fierce and prolonged. Waving a white flag, Flint ran to the victims, who were lying on the ground. Amid the confusion of continuing gunfire from the Israelis and Jordanians, two more Israelis were hit. A few moments later, Flint was felled by a sniper's bullet.

The subsequent inquest was nothing but a farce, according to General von Horn. Two eyewitness accounts and the medical evidence, however, indicated that the bullet had come from the Jordanian side and had been deliberately aimed at Flint—a clear attempt on his life. The U.N. was not prepared to let the matter drop. The Secretary General's claims for reparation from Jordan triggered a copious exchange of correspondence that would come to naught: Jordan steadfastly refused to take responsibility for Flint's death and accused Israel of causing the exchange of gunfire and the fatal shot by the sniper.

In one document the Secretary General returned to the original verdict: "One thing is certain: LCol Flint was not killed accidentally or even amid an exchange of fire between the parties...he was killed deliberately by a single bullet coming from the territory controlled by Jordan after a mutual cease-fire agreement."

The body of George Albert Flint lies in the Moascar military cemetery at Ismailiya, Egypt.[92]

A Canadian Military Cemetery in the Middle East

On the edge of the town of Gaza, in a carefully maintained sanctuary beside the burial grounds of 3,000 Allied soldiers killed in the First World War, 22 Canadians rest in eternal peace. The iron gates at each end of this small haven are decorated with gilded maple leaves. These 22 men died on duty, most in accidents while serving with the UNEF between 1957 and 1967. Some of them were killed by stepping on mines. One, however, Trooper Ronald Allan of Halifax, aged 24, fell under the bullets of an ambush in the early hours of 28 November 1959 while on patrol. Peacekeepers have not only friends.

In all these peacekeeping missions, more than 40 to date—not all under the U.N., as Canadian observers in Vietnam, Laos and Cambodia in 1954–73 came under the four-nation International Commission for Supervision and Control—the Canadian Forces have supplied a total of over 100,000 men and women, more than 100 of whom have been killed in various parts of the world.

NATO

Four years after the end of the Second World War, Canada became a member of a conventional alliance as defined in Article 51, Chapter VIII, of the U.N. Charter, which provides for regional agreements to maintain international peace and security. The 1949 North Atlantic Treaty stands as a significant event in Canada's modern history, because it made Canada part of a vast military alliance: Canada's defence zone now included both coasts of the Atlantic Ocean and part of the Mediterranean Sea.

This treaty cannot be properly understood without focusing on a few significant facts. The Soviet Union had embarked on an immense territorial expansion in the wake of the Second World War, swallowing up small states like Lithuania and seizing parts of Finland. It had already conquered Poland, Hungary and Czechoslovakia. The USSR had grown by hundreds of thousands of square kilometres and scores of millions of individuals had fallen under its yoke. This annexation policy was based on both a dynamic Communist ideology and an army that was not demobilized after 1945. The Soviet army presence was apparent even in central Germany.

On the other hand, American strength in Europe was reduced in 1945–47 from 3.1 million personnel to 154,000. British numbers fell from 1.3 million in 1945 to 500,000 in 1946. Canadian troops were all repatriated by the end of 1946. Canada's contribution to European recovery would take the form of financial credits or shipments of food and supplies of all sorts, including much equipment from demobilized Canadian formations offered to Dutch and Belgian divisions.

At the same time, Western Europe was experiencing a spate of economic reconstruction. Priority was being given to basic needs. Armed forces were poorly equipped or virtually nonexistent. A military force with substantial manpower and powerful weaponry to intimidate potential aggressors, such as the Soviet Union, was a logical step. The Treaty of Brussels, signed on 17 March 1948 by France, Britain, Belgium, the Netherlands and Luxembourg, laid the foundations for this military power.

However, the Europeans were aware that only an American military presence in Europe could protect them from the Soviet Union. Even before the Treaty of Brussels had been signed, Britain sent the United States a proposal for an alliance of countries fronting the North Atlantic, including Canada. From March through June 1948, Canada joined Britain and the United States in negotiations that would later include other interested countries.

Although in these negotiations several of its viewpoints were rejected, Canada did have mitigated success. As soon as the talks began, Canadian negotiators insisted that the Treaty not be limited to the military dimension. This view was accepted after long discussions with incredulous delegates from other countries.

The second of the Treaty's 14 clauses is often described as the Canadian clause.

Many troops were deployed in Montreal during the October Crisis of 1970.
Flags were flown at half-mast following the discovery of the body of Quebec cabinet
minister Pierre Laporte, who was killed by FLQ (Front de libération du Québec) terrorists.
(DND, 70-466)

The Oka Crisis of 1990 was intensively covered by
the mass media, as shown in this photo of a Mohawk
"Warrior" and a soldier surrounded by a group of
journalists and photographers.
(DND, 90-506)

The German Leopard C1 battle tank replaced the
British Centurion in the Canadian Forces in 1978.
(DND, 81-137)

An Inuit volunteer with the Canadian Rangers, who have been active in the Canadian Arctic since 1947.
(DND, 880-367)

Essentially, it encourages economic co-operation among member countries. Strong misgivings stemmed mainly from the opinion that it was pointless to add to the already numerous agencies for international economic co-operation. This opposition to the Canadian proposal was germane up to a point, and it is not surprising that Clause 2 of the North Atlantic Treaty was little used until very recently. Nonetheless some strong political and economic ties have been formed among member countries since 1949.

Today, some 18 countries form an Alliance in which, according to Clause 5 of the Treaty, any attack on one member would be considered an attack on all. Although there have been fluctuations, Canada's naval, land and air contributions to NATO have essentially remained constant over the years. They are seen today in Canada's participation in a mission to support the restructuring of the former Yugoslavia. NATO's role here is closer to the U.N. peacekeeping one the Canadians are accustomed to than to the role for which the NATO armies are trained. When fully analysed, this may turn out to be a sign of NATO's success.

In any case, alliances are based on conglomerations of special interests, and the NATO allies have been far from speaking the same language on some issues. In the Cuban missile crisis of 1962, NATO's numerous advisory systems were sidelined by the United States. Clearly the superpower was prepared to brush its partners aside as it deemed appropriate. Other big powers were capable of similar behaviour, an example being France and Britain in the 1956 Suez crisis.

Initially, in 1949–50, Canada saw its participation in Treaty activities as economically driven, such as through the Marshall Plan. The Korean War accelerated developments, however. Was Korea merely a diversionary attack, it was wondered, with the real thing to come in Western Europe? The establishment of NATO was top priority. General Dwight Eisenhower agreed to leave his gilded retreat to assume supreme command of NATO troops. Even before being installed in this position in the fall of 1950, Eisenhower asked Canada to provide him with troops, and Canada agreed.

Coming so soon after 1945, the Korean affair had a powerful psychological impact. As Brooke Claxton remarked on 18 July 1951 on CBC radio: "The successes in Korea, far from lessening the need for power, have shown that we must never disarm again in the presence of a fully armed potential enemy. This is why we have to continue this combined effort to prevent aggression by building our forces and maintaining them in constant readiness." He went on to say that Korea had underscored our shortcomings and that there were lessons to be learned from the human and financial losses: "The burden of maintaining our armed forces is a heavy one and will continue to be heavy for some years to come. The fact that the current conflict may end in Korea should strengthen our resolve to be strong enough to prevent aggression elsewhere."

In 1951 the government added a new infantry brigade group, the 27th, to be largely recruited from militia units, as the 25th had been for Korea, and to serve in Europe under NATO. For the moment this formation was to be part of the Special Service as distinct from the Regular Force and militia. This brigade group would have its headquarters, field artillery, armoured squadrons (from the Regular Force), sappers, signalmen, and other support units in three infantry battalions. This was in addition to

It is sometimes forgotten that many Canadian soldiers deployed on United Nations missions have young families.
(Photo-composition by Sergeant Attilio Sartori, "Military Life," DND, 94-390)

the Mobile Striking Force (a Regular Force infantry brigade group) and the two militia divisions serving in Canada, as well as the 25th Infantry Brigade Group in Korea.

Canada's longest peacetime troop deployment began with the arrival of the vessel *Fairsen* in Rotterdam on 21 November 1951, carrying the first elements of the 27th Brigade Group. By 1993, when Canada was preparing to end this European presence, more than 100,000 Canadian personnel had served under NATO.

The army was not alone under NATO command. There would be nine fighter squadrons, rising to 11 and then 12 for a full air division in 1953. In the 1950s the RCAF would also train numerous pilots from other NATO countries. The Royal Canadian Navy would participate in the protection of trade lanes between North America and Europe: For years, one of its ships (in rotation) has been a member of NATO's permanent Atlantic fleet made up of units provided by a number of allies.

At the outset Canada believed that its troops could be repatriated once Europe recovered, and in fact their numbers would drop substantially in the early 1970s. However, Canada would maintain a military presence in Europe until the Soviet threat began to wane in 1991. It has never been possible to quantify with any accuracy the economic benefits of this presence, but it is not at all obvious—contrary to what many commentators have argued—that the economic benefits alone would justify the expense.

One thing is certain: NATO made possible the Canadian rearmament drive of the 1950s, a time when Europe was economically weak. Billions of dollars were spent to develop a navy with 100 ships of all tonnages, 40 RCAF squadrons and the equiva-

lent of an infantry division. In the late 1960s, however, the Canadian presence in Europe under NATO would be reduced from some 10,000 army personnel to 2,800, and the number of fighter squadrons would drop to three, using CF-104s instead of the original Sabre F-86s. The aircraft carrier *Bonaventure* would go to the scrapyard and Maritime Command would be reduced to approximately 10,000 personnel. In the 1980s, after years of neglect, the Forces would undergo an expensive rearmament, especially at sea and in the air, with 12 new frigates, 137 new fighter aircraft and 18 Lockheed Aurora scout planes.

All through the years 1951–93, NATO would be one of the government's priorities, sometimes even its main priority.

The Infantry Brigade Group

The militiamen leaving for Europe in 1951 had signed two-year contracts. As soon as Canada realized that its European stay would be longer than expected, the 27th Brigade Group of the Special Force was renamed the 1st Canadian Infantry Brigade Group of the Regular Force, officially established in mid-October 1953. The formations became permanent, and reservists ending their contracts could choose between returning to civilian life and enlisting in the active force. At that time a number of the Regular Force units that had gone to Korea with the 25th Brigade Group were moved to Germany as part of this new Brigade Group that fell under British command in part of the British sector.

In the meantime the 2nd and 3rd Brigade groups formed in the reorganization of 1954 were starting to train. In 1955 the 25th Brigade Group repatriated from Korea became the 4th Infantry Brigade Group.

There would now be a brigade reserved for NATO while the other three remained in Canada—two brigades attached to the 1st Canadian Division and the other forming the Mobile Striking Force. A 2nd division was intended to be battle-ready 30 days after a mobilization order was issued.

In 1967 the parts of the air division stationed in France under American command had to leave. They were installed at Lahr, a few kilometres from Baden-Solingen, where Canadian squadrons had been stationed since the mid-1950s. In 1970 what remained of the 4th Brigade Group left its quarters in northern Germany to move with the air force in southern Germany. This made it possible to unify Canada's participation and place it entirely under American command. However, given the cuts in strength and the disappearance of a tactical nuclear role for the army, the Canadian troops found themselves in reserve with a mission that, though important, reflected their limited potential.

After some brigade changes, Canada adopted the following policy: The army formation in Germany would be named the 4th Mechanized Infantry Brigade Group and rotations within it would henceforth be of individuals, not of units. Over the years, Canada had to try to better the lives of its service members and their dependents—for example, by providing schools. All this became extremely expensive. As soon as the Soviet threat was no more, the Canadian overseas effort followed suit.

Major-General George R. Pearkes

George R. Pearkes was born in 1888 in England, where he received his education and officer training. In Canada when the Great War broke out, he enlisted as a private in the Canadian military and quickly regained his officer status. During the celebrated Battle of Passchendaele, Pearkes earned the Victoria Cross. By war's end he had earned two more coveted decorations. After 1918 he remained in the small Canadian permanent army.

In December 1939 Pearkes sailed to England as a brigadier and in 1940 became a major-general. In September 1942 he returned to Canada to take over Pacific Command. When he left this position in 1945 he joined the Progressive Conservative Party and entered politics. In June 1957 he was named minister of defence and quickly concluded that the NORAD agreement had to be accepted, a decision the outgoing Liberal government would likely have made itself had it remained in power.

In 1960 Pearkes was appointed lieutenant-governor of British Columbia, a position he would occupy until his retirement in 1968.

One of the buildings that house the NDHQ in the Ottawa-Hull region bears his name. George R. Pearkes passed away in 1984.

NORAD (North American Air Defence Command)

The military aspect of Canada-U.S. animosity tended to disappear in the 20th century. During the 1930s, in anticipation of the impending world upheaval, the defence of the western hemisphere became a concept to be reckoned with.

In 1936, President Franklin Delano Roosevelt let it be known that the defence of Canada formed part of United States defence policy. Two years later he stated, this time very clearly, that the United States would not stand by if Canadian territory was threatened with invasion. Prime Minister William Lyon Mackenzie King replied that his country would do everything in its power to shield itself against attack or invasion; Canada would ensure that if such an occasion arose, its enemies would be unable to pursue their route through Canadian territory to the United States, whether by land, sea or air. The two countries then held secret discussions to develop common defence measures in the event of attack.

In August 1940, two months after France's defeat in Europe and while the United States was still neutral, Roosevelt and King met and agreed to an American proposal to establish a Permanent Joint Commission for Military Planning. This advisory body held closed meetings and prepared recommendations for both governments.

A dynamic collaboration began. It dropped off after 1944 to re-emerge in 1946 as the Cold War approached. The technological innovations of the period 1939–45 combined with the appearance of the Soviet enemy to make the whole North American continent highly vulnerable. Common defence measures were now imperative.

Between 1950 and 1954 three radar networks, including the DEW (Distant Early Warning) Line, were built in the northern reaches of the continent largely on Canadian territory. In the event of any threat from that quarter, they would alert the American air forces earmarked for atomic defence and reprisals. In 1956 a Canada-U.S. task force focused on the air defences of the two countries and in December recommended the creation of an integrated binational structure as the most effective method for ensuring this defence.

On 10 June 1957 the Conservatives formed a government after 22 years in opposition. Almost immediately Canada's military leaders submitted to defence minister George Pearkes a draught agreement, already accepted by the Americans, that would establish a Canada-U.S. operational command for continental defence. On 24 July, Pearkes and Prime Minister John Diefenbaker, without consulting any other member of the cabinet, approved the agreement.

On 12 September 1957 an integrated operational command for the air defence of the North American continent began operations on an experimental basis. Its headquarters was set up in Colorado Springs in the United States. Officers from both countries serving there, along with part of each country's air force, came under this command. The commander and his deputy had to be of different nationalities—to date, the first role has always been filled by an American, the second by a Canadian. A common battle plan was drawn up. On 12 May 1958 an exchange of diplomatic notes between Canada and the United States, valid for 10 years, made this command official. Since that time the two countries have renewed the agreement at regular intervals.

An agreement such as that used to create NORAD, involving two neighbour states dramatically imbalanced in their political, economic and military power, might be expected to give rise to numerous disputes. Such disputes have occurred and continue to do so. The most significant ones are political and in one way or another have to do with the sensitive issue of Canadian sovereignty.

The Cuban crisis of autumn 1962 was revealing. The United States, claiming to be threatened by the installation of Soviet missile launchers in Cuba, became involved in some dangerous anti-Soviet manoeuvres that could have resulted in war. Canada was not consulted on the decision, as the Americans expected the Canadians to accept it instantly: This was not the case and it created a great sense of unease.

From the outset NORAD divided North America into regional commands, several of which—including areas on both sides of the Canada-U.S. border—were covered exclusively by the American air force. In 1969, Prime Minister Pierre Elliott Trudeau announced that NORAD activities on Canadian soil would come solely under Canadian jurisdiction as quickly as possible. In 1986 some Canadian regions remained under U.S. protection. The new defence weaponry that Canada has since acquired has at last made it possible to put this policy into effect.

Since 1978, Canada has become involved in an immense rearmament programme that will be useful not only to NORAD but also to NATO. At the same time, Canadians want full control over their civil and military air space. Billions of dollars are being invested and will continue to be invested to back up these decisions: A warning and defence system against air attack is extremely expensive, whatever one's point of view.

Some have claimed that NORAD was absolutely essential to Canada, as it would have been unable to assume the costs of such defence alone. Others have been interested in profiting from it. In 1958 the question was posed: Would Canada have at least its fair share of defence production for NORAD? The affirmative answer would be provided the following year, with the creation of the Joint Military Production Program, under which Canadian industries could bid for U.S. defence contracts. This would lead to a kind of common defence market that very quickly became profitable to Canada. In October 1980 the Standing Committee on External Affairs and National Defence estimated that since 1959 the programme had enabled Canada to achieve an overall positive balance of $1.1 billion. Canada had also been able to stay in the forefront in sectors like electronics and aeronautics.

In NORAD, in contrast to NATO, Canadians and Americans meet head-on. Does Canada really enjoy freedom of choice in its military affairs? Does it or would it have a say about when and how the Americans use nuclear reprisals? In the end, is Canada really running its own show, or is it merely a wagon hitched to the U.S. locomotive? That depends on whether a number of the encroachments on Canadian sovereignty ascribed to NORAD would have occurred in any event.

Conclusion

There have been constants in military life over the years we have been examining. The Canadian military has always been subject to the country's political authority. It is a civilian-military relationship that requires much of both parties and has seen both high and low points. Some soldiers have attempted to disregard the will of the politicians—this was especially the case throughout the 19th century. This has not served their military careers well, and it has harmed the military itself, causing politicians to distrust it. On the other hand, some defence ministers have interfered excessively with the functioning of the military—during the First World War, for example—and damaged their credibility among the troops who were spilling their blood on the battlefields. It must be recognized that the end result of a decision can be a matter of life or death for Canadians serving their country. Errors of judgement remain all too human a reality, unfortunately. They should be acknowledged and corrected, but not thrown needlessly in the faces of those who have made them.

The navy, army and air force of today are, like the forces of 1871, instruments of war, always ready to adapt. One 20-mm M61A1 Vulcan machine gun at the end of the 20th century can provide as much firepower as four battalions of 750 men each in the early 19th century. In fact it is more accurate and has a much longer range and far more impact than the battalions of 1815. The warrior has had to evolve along with the technology, which today ranges from the surgical air strike to the nuclear submarine. We have seen how tactics were modified during the First World War to survive assaults on defensive positions thought to be impregnable. To serve overall strategy, the constantly evolving technology-tactics partnership remains the basis of the warrior's survival.

Nineteenth-century Canadians were eager to go off to fight in foreign lands. By the turn of the 20th century this trend had become irreversible. Anyone wishing to visit a Canadian military cemetery today will have to travel outside the country. The resting places of military heroes, with their monuments of various styles and sizes, are to be found in South Africa, the Middle East, Asia and Europe. The Canadian commitment to the world under the general and evolving concept of peacekeeping is a contemporary extension of a trend that existed under French rule, when young Canadians would enlist in the royal armies. Since 1945 this peacekeeping concept has become an international institution, whose purpose is to make a modest contribution to conflict resolution by peaceful means and thus also to world stability and security. However, the two great wars of the 20th century remain the high points of Canada's military presence outside its borders.

The French and British regimes enabled Canadians to have the burden of their defence largely shouldered by others. At the end of this era Canada went to the aid of its two mother countries. During the period covered in this volume, however, even during the Second World War, Canadians have been inclined to remain subject to Britain. February 1946 saw the establishment of a joint U.S.-Canada committee for military co-operation. Both countries appointed military delegates from all three arms, along with foreign affairs officials. On 12 February 1947 the Canadian prime minister and the American secretary of state issued simultaneous statements on the peacetime defence co-operation agreement they had reached. It provided for: exchanges of servicemen and, on occasion, observers for manoeuvres;

development and trials of new weapons and the standardization of weapons, equipment and organization; mutual sharing of naval and air facilities; and minimal formalities concerning movements in the air above the territory and within the territorial waters of each country. In a way, the Americans had merely taken over the process of unified standards begun by the British before 1914.

Despite this strong thread of dependency, another thread was working its way through the period covered in this volume, just as in the periods covered in the previous two volumes: Canadianization. This has been seen in the attitudes and actions of the military community, on both big issues and small. But we seem unable to take the final and most telling steps. For example, the Canadian system of military honours established in the 1970s has retained, at its apex, the Victoria Cross. This supreme British Empire honour has not been awarded to a Canadian since the Second World War. The question arises: Why not award a "Vimy Cross" in recognition of an exceptional act of valour by a Canadian combatant?

One last factor that deserves mention is the still vital presence of the militia or reserve element in the concept of defence. It was clearly more important in relative numbers and influence in 1871 than it is in 2000. Until 1939 it was officered by a small permanent army. During the Second World War a postwar planning committee of senior officials chaired by Norman Robertson decided to reverse that situation. Hence-forth—though it took a good 30 years to fully establish the new system—the reserves would merely support a larger professional army, better equipped and busier than the prewar model. Perhaps the following historical testimony about the reality of annual militia training is indeed accurate: "Officers and soldiers considered these training camps in Lévis as elsewhere as something pleasant, a recreation or kind of sport, or else a chance to get together with people from the same community that reflected our gregarious mentality, but never could these experiences have been viewed as effective enough in the event war was declared."[93]

When the recommendations of the latest study on the reserves have been fully implemented, the reservists, gathered in a smaller number of units, will have a role equal to their potential and will operate under the conditions they deserve—perhaps even with the reservist/professional relationship rebalanced in their favour. In short, the "contract" in force as these lines are written between the small Canadian population living in an immense territory with no near enemies and its professional and reserve defence forces will hold for several decades, unless the international situation undergoes sudden and drastic changes.

At the heart of our historical considerations are the young Canadians who are ready, now as always, to commit their lives to a great cause. They are respectfully saluted in these pages.

NOTES

[1] Robert Craig Brown and Ramsay Cook, *Canada 1896–1921: A Nation Transformed (2nd ed.)* (Toronto: McClelland & Stewart, 1976), p. 32.

[2] C.P. Stacey, *Introduction to Military History for Canadian Students (6th ed.)* (Ottawa: Canadian Forces Headquarters, n.d.), p. 20.

[3] Jean-Yves Gravel, *Les Voltigeurs de Québec dans la milice canadienne, 1868–1898* (The Quebec Voltigeurs in the Canadian militia, 1868–1898) (PhD thesis, Université Laval, 1970), p. 102.

[4] Ibid., p. 142.

[5] Ibid., p. 180.

[6] Léopold Lamontagne, *Les Archives régimentaires des Fusiliers du Saint-Laurent* (Rimouski, QC: n.p., 1943), p. 85.

[7] Oscar C. Pelletier, *Mémoires, souvenirs de famille et récits* (Memoirs, family recollections and stories) (Quebec: n.p., 1940), pp. 264–67.

[8] Ibid., p. 308.

[9] The figures are from Gravel, op. cit., p. 92.

[10] See especially L.G. D'Odet d'Orsonnens, *Considérations sur l'organisation militaire de la confédération canadienne* (Thoughts on the military organization of the Canadian confederation) (Montreal: Duvernay Frères and Dansereau, 1874).

[11] Ibid., pp. 36–37.

[12] Captain Ernest J. Chambers, *Histoire du 65ᵉ Regiment Carabiniers Mont-Royal* (Montreal: Guertin, 1906), p. 8.

[13] D'Orsonnens, op. cit., p. 38.

[14] Ibid., p. 39.

[15] Chambers, op. cit., p. 80.

[16] D'Orsonnens, op. cit., pp. 35–36.

[17] Lamontagne, op. cit., p. 85.

[18] Gravel, op. cit., p. 111.

[19] Ibid., pp. 25–26.

[20] *Sir Adolphe Caron, C.C.M.G., ministre de la Milice et ses détracteurs ou huit années d'administration militaire* (Sir Adolphe Caron, C.C.M.G., Minister of Militia, and his detractors, or eight years of military administration) (Montreal: Gebhardt-Berthiaume, 1888), p. 6.

[21] Gravel, op. cit., p. 109.

[22] D'Orsonnens, op. cit., p. 31.

[23] Gravel, op. cit., pp. 273–75.

[24] August-Henri De Trémaudan, *Histoire de la nation métisse dans l'Ouest canadien* (History of the Métis Nation of Western Canada) (St Boniface, MN: Éditions du Blé, 1979), p. 406.

[25] Desmond Morton, "Middleton, Sir Frederick Dobson," in *Canadian Dictionary of Biography, 1891 to 1900 (Vol. 12)* (Toronto: University of Toronto Press, 1990), p. 801.

[26] Pelletier, op. cit., pp. 254–55. Short commanded the gun troop to which Pelletier and Edmond Chinic were assigned. Both were included in the deal, which explains the "us" in the quote.

[27] Gravel, op. cit., pp. 279–80.

[28] Georges Beauregard, *Le 9ᵉ Bataillon au Nord-Ouest: Journal d'un militaire* (The 9th Battalion in the North-West: A soldier's journal) (Quebec: Jos. G. Gingras, 1886), p. 14.

[29] Ibid., p. 11.

[30] Pelletier, op. cit., pp. 209–14.

[31] Gravel, op. cit., p. 336.

[32] Peter Robertson, *Irréductible vérité/Relentless Verity: Les Photographes militaires canadiens depuis 1885/ Canadian Military Photographers since 1885* (Quebec: Presses de l'Université Laval/Public Archives of Canada, 1973), p. 11.

[33] Brereton Greenhous (ed.), *Guarding the Goldfields: The Story of the Yukon Field Force* (Ottawa: National Museums of Canada, 1987), p. 8.

[34] Jean Pariseau, *Le maintien de l'ordre au Canada: Perspective historique* (Maintaining order in Canada: A historical perspective), Research Notes #9, Papers in Strategic Studies (St Jean, QC: Collège militaire royal de Saint-Jean, 1994).

[35] Gaston P. Labat, *Les Voyageurs canadiens à l'expédition du Soudan, Ou quatre-vingt-dix jours avec les crocodiles* (Canadian Voyageurs on the Sudan expedition, Or ninety days with the crocodiles) (Quebec: Printer to the *Canadien* and the *Événement* [I.J. Demers & Frère], 1886), pp. 153–54.

[36] Gravel, op. cit., p. 111.

[37] Goldwin Smith, *Devant le tribunal de l'histoire: Un plaidoyer en faveur des Canadiens qui ont condamné la guerre sud-africaine* (Montreal: Beauchemin, 1903), p. 25. Translation by Henri Bourassa of Smith's *At the Bar of History.*

[38] Duguesclin, "Notre marine de guerre: Que fera-t-on de la marine Laurier-Brodeur? Est-il vrai qu'elle ne servira qu'à la défense du Canada?" (Our navy: What will they do with the Laurier-Brodeur navy? Will it really be used only to defend Canada?) (Montreal: *Le Devoir,* 1911), p. 36.

[39] Carman Miller, *Painting the Map Red: Canada and the South African War, 1899–1902* (Montreal and Kingston: Canadian War Museum and McGill-Queen's University Press, 1993), p. 144.

[40] Ibid., p. 218.

[41] Ibid., p. 392.

[42] George F.G. Stanley, *Nos soldats: L'Histoire militaire du Canada de 1604 à nos jours* (Montreal: Éditions de l'Homme, 1980), p. 385. Translation of Stanley's *Canada's Soldiers: A Military History of an Unmilitary People* (Toronto: Macmillan, 1974).

[43] Ibid., p. 387.

[44] Miller, op. cit., p. 335.

[45] Ron Haycock, *Sam Hughes: The Public Career of a Controversial Canadian, 1885–1916.* Canadian War Museum Historical Publication #21 (Waterloo, ON:

Wilfrid Laurier University Press/National Museums of Canada, 1986), pp. 88–90.

46 Miller, op. cit., pp. 238–39.

47 Ibid., p. 429.

48 Stanley, op. cit., p. 408.

49 Thomas Richard Melville, *Canada and Sea Power: Canadian Naval Thought and Policy, 1860–1910* (PhD thesis, Duke University, 1981), pp. 116–19.

50 Ibid., pp. 320–27.

51 Richard Gimblett, *"Tin-Pots" or Dreadnoughts? The Evolution of the Naval Policy of the Laurier Administration, 1896–1911* (MA thesis, Trent University, 1981), pp. 10–12.

52 Richard Gimblett, "Reassessing the Dreadnought Crisis of 1909 and the Origins of the Royal Canadian Navy," in *The Northern Mariner/Le Marin du Nord, 4*(1), Jan. 1994, p. 35.

53 Ibid., p. 41.

54 Melville, op. cit., pp. 2–3.

55 Ibid., p. 50.

56 Henri Bourassa, "Le Projet de loi navale" (The Naval Bill), speech given at the Monument National, Montreal, 20 Jan. 1910 and issued as an off-print by *Le Devoir*, 1910, p. 25.

57 Duguesclin, op. cit., p. 67.

58 Gimblett, *"Tin-Pots" or Dreadnoughts?*, op. cit., p. 209.

59 Ibid., p. 222.

60 Pariseau and Bernier, op. cit., p. 66.

61 Pelletier, op. cit., p. 307.

62 Pariseau and Bernier, op. cit., p. 68.

63 Ibid., p. 69.

64 Lamontagne, op, cit., p. 9.

65 Information from H.M. Cathcart, *L'Histoire du camp Valcartier, P.Q., 1647–1957* (mimeograph, 1957).

66 From Desmond Morton, *When Your Number's Up: The Canadian Soldier in the First World War* (Toronto: Random House, 1992), pp. 17–18, and William Rawling, *Surviving Trench Warfare: Technology and the Canadian Corps, 1914–1918* (Toronto: University of Toronto Press, 1992), pp. 16–18.

67 Rawling, op. cit., p. 221.

68 Jean-Pierre Gagnon, *Le 22ᵉ Bataillon* (Quebec: Presses de l'Université Laval, 1986), p. 139.

69 Morton, *When Your Number's Up*, op. cit., p. 181.

70 Information from Rawling, op. cit., pp. 71, 117, and Brereton Greenhous, *The Battle of Amiens, 8–11 August 1918*. Canadian Battle Series #15 (Toronto: Canadian War Museum and Balmuir Books, 1995), p. 16.

71 Liliane Grantham, "Blanche Olive Lavallée: Military Nurse During the First World War and Philanthropist," in *Canadian Defence Review, 16*(2), Fall 1986, pp. 46–49.

72 Greenhous, *The Battle of Amiens*, op. cit., pp. 24–28.

73 Canadian Field Comforts Commission, *With the First Canadian Contingent* (Toronto and London: Hodder & Stoughton and Musson Book Company, 1915), pp. 71–73.

74 Robertson, *Irréductible vérité/Relentless Verity*, op. cit., p. 11.

75 De Trémaudan, *Histoire de la nation métisse*, op. cit., pp. 338–39.

76 Williams, *First in the Field*, op. cit., p. 70.

77 Duff Crerar, *Padres in No Man's Land* (Montreal and Kingston: McGill-Queen's University Press, 1995), p. 39.

78 Ibid., p. 166.

79 Sylvie C.R. Tremblay, *La Marine royale canadienne, 1919–1936: Une progression relative envers et contre tout* (Royal Canadian Navy, 1919–1936: Relative progress in spite of everything) (MA thesis, University of Ottawa, 1991), pp. 75–79.

80 Stanley, op. cit., p. 505.

81 Teresa McIntosh, *Other Images of Wars: Canadian Women War Artists of the First and Second World War* (MA thesis, Carleton University, 1990), 207 pp.

82 SHist, 96/12.

83 C.P. Stacey, *Armes, hommes et gouvernements : Les politiques de guerre du Canada 1939-1945* (Arms, men and governments: The politics of war in Canada 1939–1945) (Ottawa: Department of National Defence/Information Canada, 1970).

84 Desmond Morton and J.L. Granatstein, *Victory 1945: Canadians from War to Peace* (Toronto: Harper-Collins, 1995), p. 154.

85 Ibid., pp. 170–71.

86 R. Becket, *Memoirs of Ralph Wilson Becket* (working title). Unpublished manuscript deposited with the PHD Archives, National Defence, Ottawa.

87 *Report of the Special Commission on Restructuring the Reserves* (Ottawa: Department of National Defence, 1995), 133 pp.

88 Steve Harris, "Militia Reform, Historical Service," speech delivered at Land Force Headquarters of Canada, 30 Mar. 1995, 19 pp.

89 *Defence White Paper* (Ottawa: Queen's Printer, March 1964), p. 21.

90 *Report of the Task Force on Review of Unification of the Canadian Forces* (Ottawa: Department of National Defence, 1980, 15 Mar.), p. 37.

91 *Report of the Review Group on the Task Force on Unification* (Ottawa: Department of National Defence, 1980, 31 Aug.), p. 5.

92 Vignette prepared by Liliane Grantham of the National Defence Historical Service.

93 G.-E. Marquis, *Le Régiment de Lévis: Historique et Album* (Lévis, QC: n.p., 1952), p. 17.

CHRONOLOGY

1884 – 14 September

Some 396 Canadian "voyageurs" leave Halifax to take part in the British relief expedition to Khartoum; by spring 1885 most of them will have returned to Canada.

1885 – 26 March

Near the Duck Lake depot in present-day Saskatchewan, a party of Métis under Louis Riel and Gabriel Dumont defeat a troop of North-West Mounted Police under Superintendent Lief Newry Fitzroy Crozier; the Métis lose only five men, while the government troop counts 12 dead and 11 wounded.

1885 – 2 April

Kapapamahchakwew, or Wandering Spirit, the chief of a Plains Cree band, attacks the Frog Lake depot in present-day Alberta, pillaging the Hudson's Bay Company stores as well as the police barracks and massacring nine men including two Oblate missionaries.

1885 – 24 April

At the head of 200 Indians and Métis, Gabriel Dumont manages to rout a troop of Canadian soldiers under General Frederick Dobson Middleton at Fish Creek.

1885 – 2 May

At Cut Knife Hill, some 325 to 350 Canadians under Lieutenant-Colonel William Dillon Otter fall back before Cree warriors commanded by Pitikwahanapiwiyin (Poundmaker).

1885 – 12 May

Some 175 to 200 Métis entrenched at Batoche are conquered by Middleton's troops with over 800 men.

1885 – 15 May

Riel surrenders to Middleton.

1885 – 26 May

The Plains Cree chief Pitikwahanapiwiyin and his comrades surrender to Middleton's forces at Battleford.

1885 – 28 May

Led by Chief Kapapamahchakwew, the Cree repel an attack by Major-General Thomas Bland Strange near Frenchman's Butte in present-day Saskatchewan.

1885 – 2 July

The Plains Cree chief Mistahimaskwa, or Big Bear, who has thus far eluded all the soldiers looking for him, surrenders to a policeman at Fort Carlton, ending the Rebellion. Outcome of this military campaign for the Canadian militia: 26 dead, 103 wounded.

1898 – 14 May

Some 200 soldiers leave Vancouver for the Yukon to ensure a Canadian presence and maintain order in the Klondike gold rush.

1899 – 31 October

Approximately 1,061 Canadian volunteers, including four nurses, four reporters and 23 supernumerary officers, board *Sardinia* headed for South Africa.

1900 – 28 February

Conclusion of the Battle of Paardeberg, one of the toughest for the First Canadian Contingent. The engagement lasts 10 days. Under General Piet Cronje, 4,000 well-entrenched Boers stand off 35,000 British before surrendering unconditionally. The Royal Canadian Regiment lose 34 dead and 96 wounded.

1900 – 22 April–17 November

The Second Canadian Contingent takes part in nearly 40 engagements, the main ones being:

22–24 April	Leeuw Kop
3 May	Brandford
4 May	Constantia
5 May	Vett River
7 May	Virginia Siding
10 May	Verdris Vrag
25 May	Viljeons Drift
27–28 May	Klip Riversburg
30 May	Driefontein
3 June	Kalkhenval
11–12 June	Diamond Hills
18–19 June	Loutspans Drifts
6 July	Rietfontein
7 July	Olphansfontein
8–10 July	Rietfontein
12 July	Withooporrt
6–7 November	Komati

1900 – 7 November

Near Leliefontein a rear guard made up of a Canadian artillery battery and some members of the Royal Canadian Dragoons is attacked by 200 mounted Boers. The Dragoons lose three men killed and 12 wounded out of a total of 95 officers and men. Three Canadians are awarded the Victoria Cross.

1910 – 4 May

Royal assent to the Naval Service Act creating the Canadian navy.

1914 – 3–6 August

On 3 August, Berlin breaks off diplomatic relations with France. The next day, German troops invade Belgium and Britain declares war on Germany. Canada is automatically and immediately at war.

1914 – 3 October
The fleet carrying the first Canadian contingent leaves Gaspé, Quebec, for Plymouth, England, where it arrives on the 15th.

1915 – 22 April
Second Battle of Ypres, in which the Germans use asphyxiating gas for the first time. The Allies retain control, thanks to the Canadians, who lose 6,035 men.

1915 – 18 May
At Festubert a Canadian attack aborts, causing the loss of 2,468 men.

1915 – 3 June
At Givenchy a mine intended to devastate German trenches blows up some Canadians; the assault fails.

1916 – 13 June
After losing Mount Sorrel to the Germans on 1 June, the Canadians manage to retake it 12 days later in a battle that costs them 8,000 men.

1916 – 15 September
The Canadians take the village of Courcelette where more than 2,000 Germans are entrenched and then push back seven German counterattacks. It is in this battle that the first tanks see action.

1917 – 9–12 April
The Canadians take Vimy Ridge with 10,602 casualties including 3,598 dead.

1917– 15 August
From Lens, two Canadian divisions successfully attack the well-fortified Hill 70. The Germans then launch 21 unsuccessful counterattacks to drive them out. The confrontation costs the Canadian Expeditionary Force 9,198 men, compared to some 20,000 for the Germans.

1917 – 26 October–6 November
Canadian troops capture Passchendaele (now Passendale) Ridge, which dominates Flanders. This victory concludes the third Battle of Ypres that began on 31 July. In their advance on Passchendaele, the four Canadian divisions cover themselves with glory; 3,042 Canadians lose their lives, a thousand others disappear in lakes of mud, and 12,000 are hospitalized behind the lines.

1918 – 8–9 August
In the Battle of Amiens the Canadians and Australians form the shock troops of the 4th British Army. In a single day the Canadians cover 13 kilometres, at a cost of 1,306 dead and 2,803 wounded, and clear the Amiens–Paris rail line.

1918 – 26 August
Canadian troops take Monchy, one of the best-fortified points in the celebrated Hindenburg Line, along with many prisoners.

1918 – 10 October
The Canadians enter Cambrai; the Hindenburg Line, an exceptionally well-organized German defence system, is finally breached.

1922 – 28 June
Passage of the National Defence Act consolidating the Naval Service, the Department of Militia and Defence and the Air Board into a single department.

1923 – 1 January
The National Defence Act comes into force.

1924 – 1 April
Begun in 1922, the organization of the Royal Canadian Air Force is finally completed.

1939 – 1 September
German troops invade Poland.

1939 – 3 September
France and Britain declare war on Germany.

1939 – 10 September
Canada enters the war.

1939 – 10 December
At Halifax, an initial Canadian contingent of some 7,400 men set sail for England under General A.W.G. McNaughton; they arrive without incident six days later.

1939 – 17 December
The United Kingdom, Canada, Australia and New Zealand conclude an agreement setting up a British Commonwealth Air Training Plan to be managed by the Royal Canadian Air Force.

1940 – 10 May
Germany begins its invasion of the Netherlands, Luxembourg and Belgium.

1940 – 22 June
France capitulates.

1940 – 2 July
The crew of the Canadian destroyer *Saint-Laurent* save hundreds of German and Italian civilians after their ship, *Arandora Star*, en route from England, is torpedoed by a German submarine. This rescue operation by a single ship will be one of the largest of its kind during the war.

1940 – 25 September

In the first significant capture by the Canadian navy, the auxiliary cruiser *Prince Robert* inspects and seizes the German freighter *Weser* in the Pacific Ocean off Mexico.

1941 – 6 April

Germany comes to Italy's assistance in the Balkans; its troops invade Yugoslavia and Greece.

1941 – 15 April

The first Canadian air force attack over enemy territory, near Boulogne, France.

1941 – 22 June

Germany attacks the USSR.

1941 – 29 June

The government announces the creation of the Canadian Women's Army Corps.

1941 – 2 July

An order in council authorizes the establishment of the Women's Division of the Royal Canadian Air Force.

1941 – 7 December

A Japanese air raid on Pearl Harbor brings the United States into the war. Canada declares war on Japan the same day.

1941 – 25 December

In Hong Kong two inexperienced and poorly equipped Canadian battalions share the fate of the entire British garrison and surrender to Japanese troops after 17 days of fighting, resulting in 290 Canadians dead, 493 wounded, 1,682 taken prisoner.

1942 – 11 May

During the night a German submarine torpedoes two freighters off Anticosti Island in the St Lawrence River and slips away with impunity.

1942 – 20 June

On the Pacific coast a Japanese submarine torpedoes an English freighter off Cape Flattery, while another fires on Estevan Point on the west coast of Vancouver Island, where 17 shells explode. These attacks on Canada's Pacific coast will have no sequel.

1942 – 6 July

Three ships in a convoy are torpedoed in the St Lawrence River off Cap Chat.

1942 – 19 August

Some 6,100 men, 4,963 of them Canadians, participate in a failed Allied landing at Dieppe. The Canadians lose 3,369 men, including 907 dead and 1,946 taken prisoner.

1942 – 27 August

The German submarines *U-165* and *U-517* sink three vessels in the Gulf of St Lawrence.

1942 – 6 September

The German submarines *U-165* and *U-517* torpedo five ships in the Gulf of St Lawrence, sinking two.

1942 – 13 September

At approximately midnight the Canadian destroyer *Ottawa*, on escort duty in the North Atlantic, is struck by two torpedoes and sinks rapidly, resulting in the deaths of five officers, including the commander, and 109 crew members.

1942 – 15–16 September

In the Gulf of St Lawrence the German submarines *U-165* and *U-517* sink four freighters in two successive attacks, during the afternoon of 15 September and the early hours of the 16th, on the same Quebec–Sydney convoy.

1942 – 14 October

The passenger vessel *Caribou* is torpedoed in Cabot Strait, resulting in 136 dead. Since May 1942 seven German submarines have sunk no fewer than 23 vessels in the St Lawrence River and Gulf.

1943 – 10 July

Allied troops, including the 1st Canadian Infantry Division, land in Sicily.

1943 – 10 August

The last German units withdraw from Sicily, where 564 Canadian soldiers have been killed and 1,664 wounded since the Allied landing.

1943 – 14 October

Canadian troops take Campobasso, Italy.

1943 – 16 December

Around Casa Berardi, on the crest of a very deep ravine, the 1st Canadian Division concentrates its efforts against German troops for two weeks before it is able to take the house on 16 December. During this engagement Captain Paul Triquet of the Royal 22e Régiment becomes the first Canadian to earn a Victoria Cross in the Mediterranean campaign.

1943 – 27 December

After six days of fierce fighting, Canadians manage to drive German troops out of Ortona, Italy, at a cost of 176 officers and 2,163 men killed.

1944 – 23 May

The 1st Canadian Division manages to breach the Hitler Line in the Liri Valley with heavy casualties: 51 officers,

838 men. Some 700 Germans are taken prisoner and hundreds more are killed.

1944 – 6 June
D-Day: 5,000 Allied vessels invade the Bay of the Seine to land 107,000 troops and 7,000 vehicles in a single day. By nightfall the Canadian infantry have penetrated further inland than any other Allied division. Casualties amount to 1,064 dead, wounded and missing.

1944 – 28 June
In aerial combat over Normandy, 34 enemy aircraft are downed by Allied forces, 26 of them by Canadian pilots.

1944 – 3 July
In the English Channel, four Canadian motor torpedo boats sink two German merchant ships and seriously damage a third as well as two escort vessels.

1944 – 16 August
Falaise falls to Canadian troops after four days of bitter fighting.

1944 – 30 August
After suffering heavy casualties, the 2nd Canadian Division succeeds in liberating Rouen.

1944 – 1 September
In France, the Canadians commanded by General H.D.G. Crerar take Dieppe without opposition: The Germans withdraw before they arrive. In Italy, after a week of fighting, Allied troops, including I Canadian Corps, manage to neutralize the eastern part of the Gothic Line and take the town of Tomba de Pisaro.

1944 – 22 September
In France, Canadian troops take Boulogne after six days of fighting.

1944 – 1 October
At Calais, France, after seven days of confrontation the Germans capitulate: More than 7,000 are taken prisoner by the Canadians, who lose only some 300 dead or wounded.

1944 – 9 November
Walcheren Island capitulates to Canadian forces.

1945 – 27 February
End of the Italian campaign for the Canadian forces. The last men of I Canadian Corps leave Italy to join the 1st Canadian Army on the northwest European front.

1945 – 16 April
The Canadian navy suffers its last disaster of the war when the Bangor minesweeper *Esquimalt* is torpedoed near Halifax, killing 39 men out of a crew of 65.

1945 – 2 May
The 5th Canadian Armoured Division fights its last battle near Delfzijl, taking more than 3,000 prisoners and liberating the northern Netherlands.

1945 – 5 May
At Wageningen, Canadian General Charles Foulkes accepts the surrender of the German armies in the Netherlands; at Bad Zwischenahn, Canadian General G.G. Simonds officiates at a similar ceremony.

1945 – 7 May
The German forces agree to an unconditional surrender, with the ceasefire to be effective the following day at 11 pm.

1945 – 2 September
Japan surrenders unconditionally.

1945 – 6 September
In Ottawa, Igor Gouzenko flees the Soviet Embassy with evidence of the existence of a large-scale Soviet spy ring.

1948–2000 United Nations missions
In Kashmir, Canadian soldiers complete their first tour of duty in the role of U.N. observer. More than 100,000 Canadian military men and women, professionals and reservists, will serve in various capacities as peacekeepers around the world, sometimes for agencies other than the U.N.

1948
U.N. Truce Supervision Organization – UNTSO.

1949
U.N. Military Observer Group India-Pakistan – UNMOGIP.

1953
U.N. Temporary Commission on Korea – UNTCOK. The U.N. General Assembly observes and supervises elections in South Korea.

1954–74
International Commission for Supervision and Control (Vietnam) – ICSC.

1956–67
First U.N. Emergency Force in Sinai – UNEF.

1958
U.N. Observation Group in Lebanon – UNOGIL.

1960–64
U.N. Operation in Congo – UNOC.

1962–63
U.N. Temporary Executive Authority and Security Force (West New Guinea and West Irian) – UNTEA.

1963–64
U.N. Yemen Observation Mission – UNYOM.

1964
U.N. Peacekeeping Force in Cyprus – UNFICYP.

1965–66
Mission of the U.N. Secretary General's Representative in the Dominican Republic – DOMREP.

1965–66
U.N. India-Pakistan Observation Mission – UNIPOM.

1968–69
Observer Team in Nigeria – OTN.

1973
International Commission for Supervision and Control (Vietnam) – ICCS.

1973–79
Second U.N. Emergency Force in Sinai – UNEF II.

1974
U.N. Disengagement Observer Force on the Golan Heights – UNDOF.

1978
U.N. Interim Force in Lebanon – UNIFIL.

1986
Multinational Force and Observers (Sinai) – FMO.

1988–90
U.N. Good Offices Mission in Afghanistan and Pakistan – UNGOMAP.

1988–91
U.N. Iran-Iraq Military Observer Group – UNIIMOG.

1989
U.N. Angola Verification Mission – UNAVEM.

1989–90
U.N. Transition Assistance Group (Namibia) – UNTAG.

1989–92
U.N. Observer Group in Central America – ONUCA.

1990–91
U.N. Observer Group for the Verification of Elections in Haiti – ONUVEH.

1990–91
Op. FRICTION (pre-hostilities), Op. SCIMITAR, Op. FLAG (post-hostilities), Persian Gulf.

1990–92
Office of the Secretary General in Afghanistan and Pakistan – OSGAP.

1991
U.N. Mission for the Referendum in Western Sahara – MINURSO.

1991–92
U.N. Advance Mission in Cambodia – UNAMIC.

1991–93
The U.N. Iraq Kuwait Observation Mission (UNIKOM) supervises the Khawr Abd Allah Channel and the demilitarized zone between Iraq and Kuwait to comply with the delimitation of borders established by the Iraq-Kuwait Border Demarcation Commission in 1993. When UNIKOM is set up, Canada provides a high-ranking officer for the mission headquarters and a regiment of 300 members of all ranks of the Canadian Forces. The commitment is later reduced to four military observers. Two Canadians also serve on the U.N. Special Commission (UNSC) with offices in Iraq and New York.

1992
U.N. Operation in Somalia – UNOSOM (Op. CORDON).

1992–93
U.N. Transitional Authority in Cambodia – UNTAC (Op. MARQUIS).

1992–93
The U.N. Security Council sanctions peace enforcement in Somalia – UNITAF (Op. DELIVRANCE).

1992–94
Support to the U.N. Commission of Experts (former Republic of Yugoslavia) – UNCOE (Op. JUSTICE).

1992–95
U.N. Observer Mission in El Salvador – ONUSAL (Op. MATCH).

1992–95
U.N. Protection Force in ex-Yugoslavia – UNPROFOR (Op. CAVALIER).

1993
Under the authority of U.N. resolutions, the Cambodian Mine Clearance Centre is mandated to conduct major mine clearance projects and train Cambodians so that they

will eventually no longer require international technical support. The CMCC includes 14 clearance sections and 19 international technical military advisors, including some from Canada, provided through the U.N. Development Program – UNDPCMAC.

1993
U.N. Observer Mission Uganda-Rwanda – UNOMUR.

1993–94
U.N. Operation in Somalia II – UNOSOM II (Op. CONSORT)

1993–94
Enforcement of the embargo on Haïti – UNMIHA (Op. FORWARD ACTION).

1993–95
U.N. Operation in Mozambique – ONUMOZ (Op. CONSONANCE).

1993–96
U.N. Operation to Assist Rwanda – MINUAR (Op. LANCE).

1995–96
Organization for Security and Cooperation in Europe – OSCE.
Vienna-Nagorny-Karabakh Peacekeeping Mission (Op. NYLON).

1995–96
NATO Peace Plan Implementation Force (IFOR: Op. ALLIANCE) – Bosnia-Herzegovina.

1996
The SF will contribute to the secure environment needed to consolidate peace in Bosnia-Herzegovina. In December the Canadian government announces that it will provide a well-equipped force of 200 to the NATO-led SF-SFOR.

1997
In November the UN Security Council establishes MIPONUH as the successor to the U.N. Transitional Mission in Haïti (MTNUH). At one point the transitional missions are run by Canada and the U.N. forces include approximately 650 Canadians and 550 Pakistanis. Their mandate is to restore power to the government of Haïtian President Jean-Bertrand Aristide, which has been toppled by a coup d'état.

1997
U.N. Mission Guatemala – MINUGUA.

1999
U.N. Mission in Kosovo (mainly land participation) and in East Timor (naval, land and air)

1949 – 4 April
In Washington, delegates from 10 European states, the United States and Canada sign the North Atlantic Treaty. From 1951 to 1993, Canada will maintain troops in Western Europe (Germany and France) as a contribution to the North Atlantic Treaty Organization stemming from the Treaty. To date, Canada is still participating, with at least one ship in NATO's naval effort.

1950 – 25 June
The North Koreans invade and quickly occupy South Korea, except for a small area called the "Pusan perimeter." U.N. contingents from 16 countries intervene, the Canadian contingent being the third largest.

1951 – 22 April
The 2nd Princess Patricia's Canadian Light Infantry repel a Chinese attack in the Kap'yong Valley at a cost of 10 dead, earning a citation from the U.S. president.

1953 – 27 July
End of fighting in Korea, where some 22,000 Canadians served, more than 300 losing their lives.

1968 – 1 February
Official date for the unification of the Canadian Forces.

August 1990–March 1991
Gulf War
Canada is part of a coalition of countries formed under the aegis of the U.N. to force Iraq out of Kuwait after its invasion of 2 August 1990. On 24 August an operational group of three ships leave Halifax for the Persian Gulf to control seaborne trade there. A fighter squadron is then transferred from Lahr, Germany, to Doha, Qatar, to be responsible for air patrols under the naval force. A Canadian headquarters is also set up, on 6 November 1990, at Al-Manāma, Bahrain.

On 15 January 1991, the day hostilities are declared, Canada also provides a field hospital to the British armoured division. The Canadian air force takes part in the fighting against Iraqi forces with escort and bombing flights. The naval forces play a logistical role in the coalition. Hostilities between the U.N. coalition and Iraq end on 31 March 1991. Canada continues its activities in Saudi Arabia after the Gulf War by providing a contingent for the U.N. Iraq Kuwait Observation Mission (UNIKOM).

1999
Canada is a member (mainly with air and naval participation) of the coalition to stop ethnic cleansing by the Serbs in Kosovo province against inhabitants of Albanian background.

SELECT BIBLIOGRAPHY

Beauregard, Georges. *Le 9e Bataillon au Nord-Ouest: Journal d'un militaire* (The 9th Battalion in the North-West: A soldier's journal). Quebec: Jos. G. Gingras, 1886, 100 pp.

Becket, R. *Memoirs of Ralph Wilson Becket* (working title). Unpublished manuscript deposited with the PHD Archives, National Defence, Ottawa.

Bernier, Robert. *Jacques Chevrier, chef d'escadrille, R.C.A.F., tombé en service au large de Cap-Chat* (Jacques Chevrier, Squadron Leader, R.C.A.F., fallen while in the service of duty off Cap Chat]. Montreal: A.C.J.C., 1943, 95 pp.

Bernier, Serge. *French Canadians and Bilingualism in the Canadian Armed Forces. Vol. II: 1969–1987. Official Languages: National Defence's Response to the Federal Policy*, with Jean Pariseau. Ottawa: Canadian Government Publishing Centre, 1991, 870 pp.

Bernier, Serge. *The Memoirs of General Jean-V. Allard.* Vancouver: UBC Press, 1988, 366 pp.

Blackburn, George G. *The Guns of Normandy: A Soldier's Eye View, France 1944.* Toronto: McClelland & Stewart, 1995, 511 pp.

Boissonnault, Charles-Marie. *Histoire politico-militaire des Canadiens français (1763–1945)* (Political and military history of the French Canadians, 1763–1945). Trois-Rivières, QC: Bien public, 1967, 310 pp.

Brillant, Jean. *Le Capitaine Jean Brillant, C.V., C.M., par ses amis* (Captain Jean Brillant, V.C., M.C., by his friends). Rimouski, QC: Imprimerie Vachon, 1920, 49 pp.

Bruchési, Jean. *Canada: Réalités d'hier et d'aujourd'hui.* Montreal: Variétés, 1948, 406 pp. Translated as *A History of Canada.* Toronto: Clarke Irwin, 1950, 358 pp.

Canadian Field Comforts Commission. *With the First Canadian Contingent.* Toronto and London: Hodder & Stoughton and Musson Book Company, 1915, 119 pp.

Castonguay, Jacques. *Les Voltigeurs de Québec: Premier régiment canadien-français* (The Quebec Voltigeurs: The first French-Canadian regiment). Quebec: Voltigeurs, 1987, 523 pp.

Cathcart, H.M. *L'Histoire du camp Valcartier, P.Q., 1647–1957.* Mimeograph, 1957, 25 pp.

Chambers, Captain Ernest J. *Histoire du 65e Régiment Carabiniers Mont-Royal.* Montreal: Guertin, 1906, 151 pp.

Clint, M.B. *Our Bit: Memories of War Service by a Canadian Nursing-Sister.* Montreal: Barwick, 1934, 177 pp.

Crerar, Duff. *Padres in No Man's Land.* Montreal and Kingston: McGill-Queen's University Press, 1995, 424 pp.

De Malijay, Paul. *Observations critiques sur les considérations sur l'Organisation militaire de la Confédération Canadienne* (Critical comments on "Thoughts on the military organization of the Canadian confederation"). Montreal: Franc Parleur, 1874, 58 pp.

Desjardins, Captain L.G. *Précis historique du 17e Bataillon d'infanterie de Lévis depuis sa formation en 1862 jusqu'en 1872, suivi des ordres permanents du même corps* (Brief history of the 17th Lévis Infantry Battalion from its formation in 1862 to 1872, followed by the standing orders of that corps). Lévis, QC: *Écho de Lévis,* 1872, 89 pp.

De Trémaudan, Auguste-Henri. *Histoire de la nation métisse dans l'Ouest Canadien* (History of the Métis Nation of Western Canada). St Boniface, MN: Éditions du Blé, 1979, 448 pp.

D'Orsonnens, L.G. D'Odet. *Considérations sur l'organisation militaire de la confédération canadienne* (Thoughts on the military organization of the Canadian confederation). Montreal: Duvernay Frères and Dansereau, 1874, 71 pp.

Duguesclin. *Notre marine de guerre : Que fera-t-on de la marine Laurier-Brodeur? Est-il vrai qu'elle ne servira qu'à la défense du Canada?* (Our navy: What will be done with the Laurier- Brodeur navy? Will it really be used only to defend Canada?). Montreal: *Le Devoir,* 1911.

English, J.A. *The Casting of an Army: Being a Treatise on the Bases and Conduct of Canadian Army Operations Beyond the Normandy Bridgehead to the Closure of the Falaise Gap.* PhD thesis, Queen's University, 1987.

Faderowich, Edward Kent. *"Foredoomed to Failure": The Resettlement of British Ex-Servicemen in the Dominions 1914–1930.* PhD thesis, London School of Economics, 1983.

Fenety, D.J. *RCAF Strategic Planning, 1919–1949.* PhD thesis, Carleton University, 1982.

Fortier, Rénald. *Intervention gouvernementale et industrie aéronautique. L'exemple canadien, 1920–1965* (Government intervention and the aircraft industry: The Canadian example, 1920–1965). PhD thesis, Université Laval, 1984.

Gardam, John. *The Canadian Peacekeeper/Le Gardien de la paix canadien.* Burnstown, ON: General Store Publishing, 1992, 70 pp.

Giesler, Patricia. *Souvenirs de vaillance: La Participation du Canada à la Seconde Guerre mondiale/Valour Remembered: Canada and the Second World War.* Ottawa: Veterans Affairs Canada, 1981, 47/45 pp.

Gimblett, Richard. *"Tin-Pots" or Dreadnoughts? The Evolution of the Naval Policy of the Laurier Administration, 1896–1911.* MA thesis, Trent University, 1981.

Gouin, Jacques. *Par la bouche de nos canons: Histoire du 4e Régiment d'artillerie moyenne, 1941–1945* (By the mouths of our cannons: History of the 4th Medium Artillery Regiment, 1941–1945). Montreal: n.p., 1970, 248 pp.

Gouin, Jacques, and Brault, Lucien. *Les Panet de Québec: Histoire d'une lignée militaire* (The Panets of Quebec: Story of a military dynasty). Montreal: Bergeron, 1984, 238 pp.

Granatstein, J.L. *The Generals: The Canadian Army's Senior Commanders in the Second World War.* Toronto: Stoddart, 1993, 369 pp.

Gravel, Jean-Yves. *Les Voltigeurs de Québec dans la Milice canadienne 1862–1898* (The Quebec Voltigeurs in the Canadian militia, 1868–1898). PhD thesis, Université Laval, 1970.

Greenhous, Brereton. *The Battle of Amiens, 8–11 August 1918.* Canadian Battle Series #15. Toronto: Canadian War Museum and Balmuir Books, 1995, 38 pp.

Greenhous, Brereton (Ed.). *Guarding the Goldfields: The Story of the Yukon Field Force.* Ottawa: National Museums of Canada, 1987, 222 pp.

Halliday, H.A. *Chronology of Canadian Military Aviation.* Canadian War Museum #6. Ottawa: National Museums of Canada, 1975, 168 pp.

Hayes, Geoffrey. *The Development of the Canadian Army Officer Corps, 1939–1945.* PhD thesis, University of Western Ontario, 1987.

Konody, P.G. *Art and War: Canadian War Memorials. A selection of the works executed for the Canadian War Memorials Fund to form a record of Canada's part in the Great War and a memorial to those Canadians who have made the great sacrifice.* London: Colour Ltd., 1919, 16 pp., 48 colour plates, 8 b/w plates.

Labat, Gaston P. *Les Voyageurs canadiens à l'expédition du Soudan, Ou quatre-vingt-dix jours avec les crocodiles* (Canadian Voyageurs on the Sudan expedition, Or ninety days with the crocodiles). Quebec: Printer to the *Canadien* and the *Événement* (I.J. Demers & Frère), 1886, 215 pp.

Lamontagne, Léopold. *Les Archives régimentaires des Fusiliers du Saint-Laurent.* Rimouski, QC: n.p., 1943, 246 pp.

Lapointe, Major A.J. *Souvenirs d'un soldat du Québec: 22e Bataillon, 1917–18 (4e édition)* (Recollections of a Quebec soldier: The 22nd Battalion, 1917–18 [4th ed.]). Drummondville, QC: Castor, 1944, 259 pp.

Lavoie, Lieutenant Joseph-A. *Le Régiment de Montmagny 1869 à 1931.* Quebec: n.p., n.d.

Lord Dundonald: Les Motifs de sa révocation (Lord Dundonald: The reasons for his recall). N.p., n.d., 16 pp.

Maloney, Sean M. *War Without Battles: Canada's NATO Brigade in Germany, 1951–1993.* Kanata, ON: 4 CMBG History Book Association, 1997, 546 pp.

Marquis, G.-E. *Les Fortifications de Québec: Un centenaire, 1823–1923.* Quebec: Telegraph Printing Company, 1923, 32 pp.

Marquis, G.-E. *Le Régiment de Lévis: Historique et Album* (The Lévis Regiment: History and album). Lévis, QC: n.p., 1952, 294 pp.

Martigny, Paul de. *L'Envers de la guerre* (The wrong side of war). Ottawa: Lévrier, 1946, 2 vols., 187 and 185 pp.

McIntosh, Teresa. *Other Images of Wars: Canadian Women War Artists of the First and Second World War.* MA thesis, Carleton University, 1990.

Melville, Thomas Richard. *Canada and Sea Power: Canadian Naval Thought and Policy, 1860–1910.* PhD thesis, Duke University, 1981.

Miller, Carman. *Painting the Map Red: Canada and the South African War, 1899–1902.* Montreal and Kingston: Canadian War Museum and McGill-Queen's University Press, 1993, 540 pp.

Miville-Deschênes, Charles. *Souvenirs de guerre* (Recollections of war). Quebec: n.p., 1946, 129 pp.

Morton, Desmond. *A Military History of Canada.* Edmonton: Hurtig, 1990, 311 pp.

Morton, Desmond. *When Your Number's Up: The Canadian Soldier in the First World War.* Toronto: Random House, 1992, 354 pp.

Morton, Desmond, and Granatstein, J.L. *Victory 1945: Canadians from War to Peace.* Toronto: HarperCollins, 1995, 256 pp.

Mulvaney, Charles Pelham. *History of the North-West Rebellion of 1885. Comprising a full and impartial account of the origin and progress of the war, of the various engagements with the Indians and half-breeds, of the heroic deeds performed by officers and men, and of touching scenes in the field, the camp and the cabins; including a history of the Indian tribes of North Western Canada, their numbers, modes of living, habits, customs, religious rites and ceremonies, with thrilling narratives of captures, imprisonment, massacres, and hair-breadth escapes of white settlers, etc.* Toronto: A.H. Hovey, 1885, 424 pp.

Nuttall, Leslie. *Canadianization and the No. 6 Bomber Group RCAF.* PhD thesis, University of Calgary, 1985.

Ouimet, Alphonse. *La Vérité sur la question métisse: Biographie et récit de Gabriel Dumont sur les événements de 1885* (The truth about the Métis question: Gabriel Dumont's biography and account of the events of 1885). Montreal: B.A.T. de Montigny, 1889, 308 pp.

Pariseau, Jean. *French Canadians and Bilingualism in the Canadian Armed Forces. Vol. I: 1763–1969: Fear of a Parallel Army,* with Serge Bernier. Ottawa: Canadian Government Publishing Centre, 1988, 468 pp.

Pariseau, Jean. *Le maintien de l'ordre au Canada: Perspective historique* (Maintaining order in Canada: A historical perspective), Research Notes #9, Papers in Strategic Studies. St Jean, QC: Collège militaire royal de Saint-Jean, 1994, 25 pp.

Pelletier, Jean-Guy. "La presse Canadianne-française et la guerre des Boers" (The French-Canadian press and the Boer War), in *Recherches sociographiques, 4*(3), 1963, 337–347.

Pelletier, Oscar C. *Mémoires, souvenirs de famille et récits* (Memoirs, family recollections and stories). Quebec: n.p., 1940, 396 pp.

Rawling, William. *Surviving Trench Warfare: Technology and the Canadian Corps, 1914–1918.* Toronto: University of Toronto Press, 1992, 325 pp.

Robertson, Peter. *Irréductible vérité/Relentless Verity: Les Photographes militaires canadiens depuis 1885/Canadian Military Photographers since 1885.* Quebec: Presses de l'Université Laval/Public Archives of Canada, 1973, 234 pp.

Roy, Pierre-Georges. *La Famille Panet* (The Panet family). Lévis, QC: Laflamme, 1906, 212 pp.

Sarty, R. *The Maritime Defence of Canada.* Toronto: Canadian Institute of Strategic Studies, 1996, 223 pp.

Sarty, R. *Silent Sentry: A Military and Political History of Canadian Coast Defence, 1860–1945.* PhD thesis, University of Toronto, 1982.

Schull, Joseph. *Far Distant Ships: An Official Account of Canadian Naval Operations in World War II.* Toronto: Stoddart, 1987, 515 pp.

Sévigny, Pierre. *Face à l'ennemi* (Facing the enemy). Montreal: Beauchemin, 1946, 177 pp.

Sir Adolphe Caron, C.C.M.G., ministre de la Milice et ses détracteurs ou huit années d'administration militaire (Sir Adolphe Caron, C.C.M.G., Minister of Militia, and his detractors, or eight years of military administration). Montreal: Gebhardt-Berthiaume, 1888, 34 pp.

Smith, Goldwin. *Devant le tribunal de l'histoire: Un plaidoyer en faveur des Canadiens qui ont condamné la guerre sud-africaine.* Montreal: Beauchemin, 1903, 61 pp. Translation by Henri Bourassa of Smith's *At the Bar of History.*

Stacey, Charles Perry. *The Canadian Army, 1939–1945: An Official Historical Summary.* Ottawa: King's Printer, 1948, 345 pp.

Tooley, R. *The Carleton and York Regiments in the Second World War.* PhD thesis, University of New Brunswick, 1984.

Vallières, Raymond. *La Trésorerie royale militaire Canadienne* (The Royal Canadian Army Pay Corps). Quebec: École supérieure de Commerce, 1951.

Verreault, Georges. *Journal d'un prisonnier de guerre au Japon 1941–1945* (Journal of a prisoner of war in Japan, 1941–1945). Sillery, QC: Septentrion, 1993, 315 pp.

Williams, Jeffery. *First in the Field: Gault of the Patricias.* London: Leo Cooper, 1995, 278 pp.

INDEX*

* Page numbers in italic type indicate illustrations.